Transnational Migration and Lifelong Learning

Economic globalisation, modern transportation, and advanced communication technologies have greatly enhanced the mobility of people across national boundaries. The resulting demographic, social, and cultural changes create new opportunities for development as well as new challenges for lifelong learning.

Transnational Migration and Lifelong Learning examines the changing nature of lifelong learning in the current age of transnational migration. The book brings together international scholars from a range of countries in a dialogue about the relationship between work, learning, mobility, knowledge, and citizenship in the context of globalisation and migration. It covers a wide range of topics, including: global perspectives and analyses of migration; the impact of migration on lifelong learning; processes of exclusion and inclusion in lifelong learning; the tension between mobility, knowledge, and recognition; and transnationalism, learning communities, and citizenship.

This book is based on a special issue of the *International Journal of Lifelong Education*.

Shibao Guo is associate professor in the Faculty of Education at the University of Calgary, Canada. He is an affiliated researcher with the Prairie Metropolis Centre of Excellence for Research on Immigration, Integration, and Diversity (MPC). His research interests include citizenship and immigration, lifelong learning, social justice and equity in education, and comparative and international education. His recent works have appeared in the *Journal of International Migration and Integration*, *Canadian Journal for the Study of Adult Education*, *Canadian Journal of Higher Education*, *Convergence*, and *Frontiers of Education in China*. He was the co-president of the Canadian Association for the Study of Adult Education (2009-2011) and is currently an executive member of the Canadian Ethnic Studies Association.

Transnational Migration and Lifelong Learning
Global Issues and Perspectives

**Edited by
Shibao Guo**

LONDON AND NEW YORK

First published 2013
by Routledge
2 Park Square, Milton Park, Abingdon, Oxon, OX14 4RN

Simultaneously published in the USA and Canada
by Routledge
711 Third Avenue, New York, NY 10017

First issued in paperback 2017

Routledge is an imprint of the Taylor & Francis Group, an informa business

Chapters 1-7 and 9-10 © 2013 Taylor & Francis

Chapter 8 *"Beyond deficit paradigms: exploring informal learning of immigrant parents"* © 2011 Canadian Association for the Study of Adult Education

This book is a reproduction of the *International Journal of Lifelong Learning*, volume 29, issue 2 (2010). The Publisher requests to those authors who may be citing this book to state, also, the bibliographical details of the special issue on which the book was based.

All rights reserved. No part of this book may be reprinted or reproduced or utilised in any form or by any electronic, mechanical, or other means, now known or hereafter invented, including photocopying and recording, or in any information storage or retrieval system, without permission in writing from the publishers.

Trademark notice: Product or corporate names may be trademarks or registered trademarks, and are used only for identification and explanation without intent to infringe.

British Library Cataloguing in Publication Data
A catalogue record for this book is available from the British Library

Typeset in Baskerville
by Taylor & Francis Books

Publisher's Note
The publisher would like to make readers aware that the chapters in this book may be referred to as articles as they are identical to the articles published in the special issue. The publisher accepts responsibility for any inconsistencies that may have arisen in the course of preparing this volume for print.

ISBN 13: 978-1-138-10942-1 (pbk)
ISBN 13: 978-0-415-69859-7 (hbk)

Contents

Notes on Contributors   vii

1. Introduction
   Shibao Guo   1

2. Lifelong learning in the age of transnational migration: emerging trends and challenges
   Shibao Guo   6

3. Lifelong learning as ideological practice: an analysis from the perspective of immigrant women in Canada
   Roxana Ng and Hongxia Shan   22

4. Moving across borders: immigrant women's encounters with globalization, the knowledge economy and lifelong learning
   Tara Gibb and Evelyn Hamdon   38

5. Mobility of knowledge as a recognition challenge: experiences from Sweden
   Per Andersson and Andreas Fejes   54

6. Transnational migration, social capital, and lifelong learning in the USA
   Mary V. Alfred   72

7. Learning through social spaces: migrant women and lifelong learning in post-colonial London
   Sue Jackson   89

8. Beyond deficit paradigms: exploring informal learning of immigrant parents
   Yan Guo   106

9. A changed context of lifelong learning under the influence of migration: South Korea
   Jin-Hee Kim   124

10. Conclusion: toward transnational lifelong learning for recognitive justice and inclusive citizenship
    Shibao Guo   142

Index   146

Notes on Contributors

Mary Alfred is associate professor of adult education and associate dean of faculty affairs in the College of Education and Human Development at Texas A&M University. Her research interests include learning and development among women of the African diaspora, socio-cultural contexts of migration, welfare reform and economic disparities among low-income women, and issues of equity and social justice in higher education and in the workplace. Her most recent book (edited with Carmela Nanton) is *Social Capital and Women's Support Systems: Networking, learning, and surviving*, (San Francisco: Jossey-Bass, 2009). Other recent work has appeared in *Adult Education Quarterly* and *International Journal of Training and Development*.

Per Andersson is associate professor in education in the Department of Behavioural Sciences and Learning, Linköping University, Sweden. His main research interest is educational assessment, particularly recognition of prior learning. He has published (with co-editor Judy Harris) the book *Re-theorising the Recognition of Prior Learning* (Leicester: NIACE), and his recent work appeared in *Adult Education Quarterly, Asia-Pacific Journal of Teacher Education, International Journal of Lifelong Education, Journal of Education Policy*, and *Vocations and Learning: Studies in Vocational and Professional Education*.

Andreas Fejes is associate professor in education in the Department of Behavioural Sciences and Learning, Linköping University, Sweden. His research explores lifelong learning, workplace learning, recognition of prior learning and adult education, in particular drawing on poststructuralist theory. He recently published (with co-editor Katherine Nicoll) the book *Foucault and Lifelong Learning: Governing the subject* (London: Routledge), and his articles have appeared in *Journal of Education Policy, Educational Philosophy and Theory, Journal of Advanced Nursing, British Journal of Sociology of Education, International Journal of Lifelong Education, Studies in the Education of Adults, Teaching in Higher Education*, and *Vocations and Learning: Studies in Vocational and Professional Education*. Fejes is the editor of the *European Journal for Research on the Education and Learning of Adults* (RELA) and he is the secretary of the European Society for Research on the Education of Adults (ESREA).

Tara Gibb is a PhD student at the University of British Columbia. Her research interests include educational policy and issues related to migration and language education.

Shibao Guo is associate professor in the Faculty of Education, University of Calgary, Canada. He is an affiliated researcher with the Prairie Metropolis Centre of Excellence for Research on Immigration, Integration, and Diversity (MPC). His research interests include citizenship and immigration, lifelong learning, social justice and equity in education, and comparative and international education. His recent works have appeared in the *Journal of International Migration and Integration, Canadian Journal for the Study of Adult Education, Canadian Journal of Higher Education, Convergence,* and *Frontiers of Education in China.* He was the co-president of the Canadian Association for the Study of Adult Education (2009-2011) and is currently an executive member of the Canadian Ethnic Studies Association.

Yan Guo is associate professor in the Faculty of Education at the University of Calgary, Canada. Her research interests include English as an Additional Language (EAL) education, immigrant parent knowledge, intercultural communication, second language acquisition, language identity and policy. Her recent works appeared in *Multicultural Education, Language and Education, Intercultural Education, Diaspora, Indigenous, and Minority Education, Journal of Educational Thought, School Community Journal, Convergence, Encounters on Education, TESL Canada Journal,* and *Canadian Journal of University Continuing Education.*

Evelyn Hamdon is a PhD student at the University of Alberta. Her research interests include issues of race and racialization in adult community-based education and post-secondary educational settings.

Sue Jackson is professor of lifelong learning and gender and director of Birkbeck Institute for Lifelong Learning at Birkbeck, University of London. She is currently working on two books, both to be published in 2010: *Innovations in Lifelong Learning: Critical perspectives on diversity, participation and vocational learning,* to be published by Routledge; and *Gendered Choices: Learning, work, identities in lifelong learning,* to be published by Springer Academic Press.

Jin-Hee Kim is a research fellow at the Korean Educational Development Institute in the Republic of Korea. Born and raised in Korea, she received her PhD from the University of Surrey. She is an Endeavour Award Scholar at the University of Technology, Sydney in Australia. She also has academic affiliation with the University of Free State in South Africa. Over the years she has developed academic interests and expertise in global migration, multicultural education, lifelong learning theory, citizenship education, and international education development.

Roxana Ng teaches in the adult education and community development program at OISE, University of Toronto. She has been working with immigrant women in Canada since the mid-1970s and has published widely on this topic. Among her publications are *The Politics of Community Services* (1988, 1996) and *Exploring the Globalized Regime of Ruling from the Standpoint of Immigrant Garment Workers* (2006).

Hongxia Shan is assistant professor in the Department of Educational Studies, University of British Columbia. She specialises in professional learning, emotional work, and immigrant studies. Her research interests also include globalisation; community development; prior learning assessment and recognition; and integrated gender, race and class analysis. Her work brings together sociocultural perspectives of learning, institutional ethnography, and strong sensitivity to the materiality of our learning and working life. She has published in the *Journal of Workplace Learning, International Journal of Lifelong Education, Canadian Journal for the Study of Adult Education, Qualitative Studies,* and *Health Promotion International.*

Introduction

SHIBAO GUO

University of Calgary, Canada

Migration is a topic of great and enduring interest because almost every country is involved in this process as a source, transit or destination country, or indeed all three simultaneously. Economic globalisation and modern transportation technologies have greatly enhanced the mobility of people across national boundaries. In many countries, migration has been adopted as a strategy to compete for the most talented, skilful and resourceful, and to ameliorate the effects of aging populations and labour shortages. It is estimated that about 200 million people live outside their countries of birth (Castles and Miller 2009). Furthermore, migration accounts for at least 40% of total population growth in most countries whose population is still growing (OECD Annual Report 2008).

Migrants' motives and patterns of movement are complex. The fact that they enter through diverse channels leads us to label them as temporary workers, permanent immigrants, international students and asylum seekers. Generally speaking however, migration can be attributed to 'push' and 'pull' factors (Guo 2005). The former are events or features that drive people away from their home countries, such as overpopulation, poverty, natural disasters, war, political and religious persecution and human rights abuses. The latter are events or features that attract people to a destination country, including economic opportunities, a higher standard of living, social and political stability, free and accessible social services, a clean environment and a favourable educational system. While some migrate voluntarily, many are forced to leave their home countries. Because resources are not equally distributed across the globe, transnational migration tends to move one way: from less developed nations to advanced industrial countries. Some of the salient features of today's transnational migration trends in OECD countries include:

(i) migration of both permanent and temporary immigrants continues to increase;
(ii) migrants from eastern Europe and Asia are still dominant;
(iii) there is an increase in the migration of highly skilled workers;
(iv) there are increasing inflows of international students; and
(v) immigrants continue to be over-represented among the unemployed (OECD 2007).

It is evident that migration has changed the demographics and socio-cultural fabric of receiving societies in which we live. It has also had profound implications for lifelong learning. However, there is little research and analysis of the relationship between transnational migration and lifelong learning. We are left to grapple with many important questions, such as: What is the impact of transnational migration on lifelong learning? What are the challenges and opportunities for lifelong learning? How can lifelong learning best facilitate migrants' adaptation in a new society? How are transnational communities and lifelong learning networks being formed through the process of migration and adaptation? How should states and communities work together to develop more coordinated lifelong learning policies and practices in assisting migrants with their adaptation? What is the relationship between migration, identity and lifelong learning? How do notions of gender shape the learning experiences of migrants?

It is therefore the purpose of this book to examine the changing nature of lifelong learning in the age of transnational migration. It also provides an opportunity to rethink the relationships between work, learning, knowledge, mobility and citizenship in the context of globalisation and migration.

This book brings together scholars from five different countries in a dialogue about transnational migration and lifelong learning in the contexts of Canada, Sweden, the United States, the United Kingdom and South Korea. Shibao Guo, the book editor, opens the discussion with an analysis of current issues and debates about globalisation, transnational migration and lifelong learning. He argues that globalisation and migration are inextricably intertwined. Where migration is a response to globalisation, globalisation accelerates migration. One of the new world disorders created by globalisation is mass migration, which provides a flexible workforce to be deployed at the discretion of global capital. As a result of increasing migration, many countries are becoming increasingly ethno-culturally diverse. In the process of adapting to new societies, many migrants encounter a number of barriers, including lack of access to social services and lifelong learning programmes, unemployment and underemployment, devaluation and denigration of their prior learning and work experience, poor economic performance and downward social mobility. Unfortunately, Guo argues, lifelong learning has failed to integrate cultural difference and diversity into educational environments. On the contrary, it has become a vehicle for assimilating immigrants into the dominant norms and values of the host society.

In Chapter 3, Ng and Shan examine how lifelong learning as ideological practice shapes the way in which Chinese immigrant women in Toronto see and understand social reality and organise their job-seeking activities accordingly. In treating lifelong learning as 'ideological practice', the authors draw our attention to how ideas, once they become hegemonic, organise and shape our lives, work and learning. In applying this framework to the lifelong learning discourse, Ng and Shan analyse how professional Chinese immigrant women navigate the gendered and ethnically segregated labour market in Canada. To this end, the authors conducted interviews with 21 immigrant women who indicated that they had completed at least one university degree and worked in their fields of training at the time of immigration. After immigration, most of them were unable to find work commensurate with their professional qualifications and experiences. To return to the Canadian labour market, they constantly had to acquire Canadian credentials, knowledge and skills. This analysis displays how lifelong learning as an ideological frame is naturalised and becomes a mechanism of neo-liberal control to produce ideal workers and learners for the knowledge-based economy. Ng and Shan also provide a nuanced analysis that demonstrates how lifelong learning intersects with other processes, such as credentialism, gendered and racialised construction of Chinese women, and aged, gendered familial relations in perpetuating social and labour market hierarchy, and inequality along lines of gender, race and class.

With the next chapter, Gibb and Hamdon continue with the examination of immigrant women's experience in Canada. The authors locate their study in two immigrant service organisations that self-identify as feminist organisations advocating for the collective rights of immigrant women in Canada. Drawing on interviews with 21 immigrant women, including staff, volunteers and immigrant learners, the authors explore the lived experience of immigrant women seeking recognition of their qualifications, skills and professional experience. Their analysis demonstrates how women in these organisations leverage their collective knowledge to navigate and resist state institutions' responses to global knowledge economy discourses that filter into their daily practices and interactions as they assist their clients in gaining meaningful employment. The authors argue that while globalisation effectively destroys some borders, it also creates new ones. As such, the borders placed around credentialised knowledge render immigrant women's knowledge invalid and deficient and thus become a form of symbolic or cultural injustice. To address this injustice, Gibb and Hamdon suggest the redistribution of recognition that emphasises a critical recognition orientation rather than a liberal one, social change rather than individual change, and the principles of the right over the good.

Andersson and Fejes' contribution explores tensions between mobility, knowledge and recognition in the context of Sweden. Unlike the previous two pieces – which focus on immigrants' experience – this article addresses the situation of asylum seekers and refugees. Historically, Sweden is an important source country for emigration to North America. In recent decades, Sweden has had a relatively open policy towards refugees, and a large number of them have settled permanently in the country. In their resettlement process, many have encountered difficulties in finding jobs and have found that their earnings are much lower than those of native-born Swedish or immigrants from Nordic or Western European countries. The authors attribute these problems to the devaluation and denigration of refugees' foreign credentials and prior work experience. Based on analysis of policy documents, Andersson and Fejes outline two major challenges concerning the recognition process. One challenge concerns the mismatch of context in the mobility of situated knowledge across national boundaries. The second relates to how power operates to exclude and marginalise refugees in the process of assessing their prior knowledge and work experiences. Andersson and Fejes argue that recognition of prior learning has become an instrument of sorting, classifying and excluding. The authors also discuss implications for lifelong learning policies and practices.

In Chapter 6, Alfred examines the intersection of immigration, transnational identities, social capital and lifelong learning in the United States. At the outset of the article, Alfred highlights the change in demographics as a result of increasing immigration. She also outlines differences between early immigrants and their contemporary counterparts. In traditional theories of immigration, early arrivals were portrayed as individuals who were ruptured from their home country to take on permanent residency in the USA with little intention of returning home. Transnational perspectives of immigration reject this view and acknowledge the bicultural identities of contemporary immigrants. Instead of permanent displacement and assimilation, Alfred argues, recent arrivals go through a process of 'acculturation' where they hold on to elements of the home culture while they learn to acquire the values, mores and life ways of the new culture that they find to be fitting. This view of immigrants as transnational nomads has important implications for planning and delivery of educational programmes that speak to the diversity of today's immigrant population. In particular, Alfred contends, social capital and lifelong learning are interconnected because the knowledge, skills and behaviours acquired through social capital networks become funds for future learning. Alfred's analysis broadens our view of learning to one that goes beyond formal, institutional learning to include learning that takes place in networks and communities.

In the next chapter, Jackson takes up some of the themes discussed by Alfred. She provides us with an account of informal learning through social spaces in post-colonial London. The author first describes changes in London as a result of migration. It is estimated that more than 40% of migrants to the UK live in London, accounting for 26% of London's total population. As a result, London has the highest proportion of foreign-born population per head of population in the UK. In post-colonial London, Jackson argues, the histories and experiences of colonialism continue to impact on the colonised and the colonisers by constructing different and diverse identities that are gendered, racialised, classed and sexualised. Drawing on in-depth interviews with South-Asian women, Jackson identifies one method that migrant women can use to resist post-colonial constructions of difference and identities: engaging in informal and non-formal learning through social spaces. Although not formally recognised as sites of learning, Jackson argues that social spaces enable migrant women to network with each other to affirm identities, develop relational capital and an enhanced sense of belonging.

In Chapter 8, Yan Guo continues the discussion of immigrants' experience of informal learning. Based on individual interviews with 38 parents from 15 countries, she explores how immigrant parents construct and mobilise their knowledge through informal learning in support of their children's education. She challenges the deficit views of immigrant parents and their involvement in their children's education and provides a refreshing perspective that helps us better understand the knowledge of immigrant parents which is often unrecognised by teachers and school administrators. Her study reveals that many immigrant parents learned the meaning of parental involvement primarily through trial and error. They learned Canadian curricula by using the Internet, passed on their first-language knowledge, and instilled the best values of both Canadian and country-of-origin cultures. Moving beyond deficit models of immigrant parental involvement, her study demonstrates how immigrant parents learned to advocate on behalf of their children in combating discrimination and racism. The results of this study illustrate the significance of informal learning by immigrant parents which was adopted as a way of coping with various barriers that immigrants faced in support of their children's education in a different cultural environment.

In the next chapter, Kim explores the themes of non-formal and informal learning through social spaces in South Korea. Drawing on a qualitative case study with the Migrant Workers' Centre in Seoul, Kim portrays a specific regional context of lifelong learning in the age of transnational migration. Like other contributors in this special issue, Kim first outlines changes in social configuration in South Korea under the influence of migration. Since the early 1990s, Kim argues, Korea has become a regional hub of migrant workers in East Asia. It attracts large numbers of economically motivated migrant workers from developing nations for employment in '3D' jobs – difficult, dirty, and dangerous. As a result, Korea is gradually transforming into a multicultural and multiracial society, which creates significant learning opportunities for the whole nation as well as newcomers. The author examines how people reconstruct their lifelong learning trajectory by engaging in social interactions with people from different cultural backgrounds. Kim argues that migrants' transnational migratory experience and local people's reactions converge through social engagements in a multicultural learning setting. She also points out that participation in social activities with different cultural agencies promotes cross-cultural dialogue, understanding and participation between migrant workers and local people. Kim's analysis demonstrates that social interactions are important sites for educating people about cultural diversity and for learning to live together in a multicultural setting.

In the conclusion chapter, Shibao Guo proposes *transnational lifelong learning for recognitive justice and inclusive citizenship* as a promising alternative to distributive and retributive approaches to lifelong learning. Guo argues that distributive social justice in lifelong learning treats lifelong learners with the 'sameness' approach, negating the histories, backgrounds and experiences of diverse cultural groups. Such an approach represents an assimilationist ideal that views cultural differences as deficits and immigrants' knowledge inferior. The fatal flaw of the retributive justice, Guo continues, lies in the logic of markets that dictates the selection of immigrants and provision of lifelong learning programmes which privilege those from advantaged social and economic status and who also represent dominant cultural norms. Informed by recognitive justice, the proposed new framework questions the claim that a universality of citizenship transcends cultural difference and particularity. It suggests 'pluralist citizenship' as an alternative form of citizenship that recognises transnational flows of migration and concomitant diasporic allegiances and affiliations. In rejecting the deficit model of lifelong learning, Guo argues, *transnational lifelong learning* acknowledges and affirms cultural difference and diversity as positive and desirable assets. This framework seeks to revitalize the potential of lifelong learning as a critical and emancipatory practice and build inclusive and socially just lifelong learning.

The preceding chapters represent our collective efforts to attempt to explore the changing face of lifelong learning in the age of transnational migration. As a group, we examine the changing demographics as a result of migration in a global context, its concomitant cultural diversity and implications for lifelong learning. The rich national contexts provided across all seven articles enrich our understanding about the magnitude and complexities of migration. Emerging from this examination is a broadened perspective about migration that has shifted from its uni-directional past to its transnational present and future. All contributing authors express a number of concerns about the exclusion and marginalisation of migrants in the process of adapting to a new society. We call on lifelong educators to create inclusive educational environments in embracing today's migrant population.

I wish to thank all authors for their outstanding contributions. I would also like to express my gratitude to Professor Peter Jarvis for his support throughout the whole process. I am also grateful to Emily Ross at Routledge for her help and support.

Shibao Guo
Editor
University of Calgary, Canada

References

CASTLES, S. and MILLER, M. (2009) The Age of Migration: International population movements in the modern world (New York: The Guilford Press).

GUO, S. (2005) Immigration and adult education. In L.M. ENGLISH (ed.) International Encyclopedia of Adult Education (New York: Palgrave Macmillan), pp. 302–304.

ORGANISATION FOR ECONOMIC CO-OPERATION AND DEVELOPMENT [OECD] (2007) International Migration Outlook (Paris: Organisation for Economic Co-Operation and Development).

OECD (2008) International Migration Outlook (Paris: Organisation for Economic Co-Operation and Development).

Lifelong learning in the age of transnational migration: emerging trends and challenges

SHIBAO GUO

University of Calgary, Canada

> This article examines emerging trends and challenges in transnational migration and lifelong learning. It reveals that globalisation and migration are inextricably intertwined. Where migration is a response to globalisation, globalisation accelerates migration. One of the new world disorders created by globalisation is mass migration, which provides a flexible workforce to be deployed at the discretion of global capital. As a result of increasing migration, many countries are becoming increasingly ethnoculturally diverse. In the process of adapting to new societies, many migrants encounter a number of barriers, including lack of access to social services and lifelong learning programmes, unemployment and underemployment, devaluation and denigration of their prior learning and work experience, poor economic performance and downward social mobility. Unfortunately, lifelong learning has failed to integrate cultural difference and diversity into educational environments. Rather than facilitating immigrants' adaptation, lifelong learning has become a vehicle for assimilating immigrants into the dominant norms and values of the host society.

Introduction

Despite the claim that *lifelong learning* is, like ideas about democracy or equality, a normative and value-laden concept, there is growing unease around the concept. The current criticism focuses on how lifelong learning has been co-opted by the market state to serve its interests. As a handmaiden of the market and a universal toolkit adaptable to all circumstances and problems (Griffin 1999, Crowther 2004), lifelong learning has become a guiding principle for policy initiatives ranging from national economic competitiveness to social cohesion and personal fulfilment (Livingstone 2002). Today, responsibility for learning has been shifted solely to the individual, thus undermining a more general sense of welfare and deflecting attention from the impoverishment of the democratic public sphere. People have been repositioned as objects of policy to be worked upon in order to ensure their compliance with the brave new world of flexible capitalism (Crowther 2004). As Jarvis (2008) notes, lifelong learning has come to be associated with learning throughout the *work life*. Accordingly, the learning society has come to emphasise a narrow conception of scientific rationality and *work-life learning* to the exclusion of both a comprehensive understanding of lifelong learning and a focus on the breadth of human experience and knowledge. As a consequence, Jarvis continues, democratic processes are being stifled and active citizenship shunted to the margins. Feminist scholars such as Gouthro (2007) and Burke and Jackson

(2007) argue that current discourses in lifelong learning are frequently delineated by masculine and competitive values that are reflective of a shift in emphasis from cooperation and shared development to concerns around the impact of the global marketplace. It seems evident that the radical potential of lifelong learning in strengthening civil society and democratic citizenship remains unfulfilled. Indeed, it has been hijacked by a neo-liberal economic agenda. As Rogers (2006) notes, lifelong learning has lost its radical, educative dimension and has become profoundly conformist. The dominant discourse of lifelong learning is now concerned with technologies of power and new mechanisms of self-surveillance deployed to forge a compliant and adaptable workforce suited to the era of flexible capitalism (Crowther 2004, Edwards 2008, Nicoll and Fejes 2008).

What is missing from this animated discussion is recognition of the challenges facing lifelong learning in the context of transnational migration. It is estimated that about 3% of the world's population—about 200 million people—live outside their countries of birth (Castles and Miller 2009). As a result of increasing migration, many countries are becoming increasingly ethno-culturally diverse. When migrant learners and their families move to a new country, they bring their values, language, culture and educational backgrounds to the host society, adding to and enriching these new educational environments (Guo and Jamal, 2011). Without a doubt, profound demographic, social and cultural changes brought about through migration have created new opportunities for development as well as new challenges for lifelong learning.

This article explores the emerging trends and challenges in transnational migration and lifelong learning. The discussion that follows is organised into four parts. It begins with a review of the ways in which processes of globalisation fuel migration. Next, it analyses the scope and trends of transnational migration. It then moves on to an examination of recent research on migration that focuses on notions of transnationalism and diaspora. Fourth, these theories and concepts frame a review of empirical work on migrants' adaptation and lifelong learning experiences as well as the challenges facing them.

Globalisation and the new world disorder

Transnational migration is fuelled in the present context by conditions brought about by processes of globalisation. Globalisation and migration, then, are inextricably intertwined. Where migration is a response to globalisation, globalisation accelerates migration. Therefore, it is important to first examine the phenomenon of globalisation, in particular its role in creating a 'new world disorder' (Anderson 2002).

Globalisation is an essentially contested concept that incites controversy (McGrew 2007, Robertson and White 2007). According to McGrew, polarisation of views about globalisation within the academy revolve around questions of the reality and significance of contemporary globalisation, as well as its supposed revolutionary implications for the classical paradigm of the human sciences. In the public sphere, McGrew argues, globalisation elicits sharply divergent responses and fuels radically different political projects from the 'globaphobia' of the extreme right to the 'globaphilia' of neo-liberals. It is not surprising then, that there is no agreed definition. This lack of consensus in the academic and public worlds is mirrored in the transnational sphere, with much deviation regarding ideas about globalisation from one civilisational/national context to another (Robertson and White 2007). Attempts at definition focus on the following dimensions: speed and time, processes and flows, space, and increasing integration and interconnection (Ritzer 2007). Careful negotiation of these aspects leads Ritzer to a definition of globalisation as 'an accelerating set of processes involving flows that encompass ever-greater numbers of the world's spaces and that lead to increasing integration and interconnectivity among those spaces'.[1]

The genesis of contemporary globalisation can be traced to the early 1970s and the development of sophisticated information technology, economic competition from Japan, the demise of the Bretton Woods Agreement and the oil crisis (Jarvis 2007). According to Robertson and White (2007), globalisation comprises four major dimensions: the economic, the social, the political and the cultural. Added to this list is Castells' (2008) notion of network society supported by information technology which has transformed relationships of production, power and experience. Players involved include nation states, transnational corporations, international governmental organisations (IGOs), international non-governmental organisations (INGOs) and individuals (Thomas 2007). Among these, the first two are 'the most powerful global players' and form the juggernaut of globalisation (Thomas 2007: 87). For their part, IGOs, such as the World Bank and the International Monetary Fund, are the ones that set global policies and provide incentive structures for states and other actors. Secondary in influence but nonetheless vital to globalisation, INGOs are not-for-profit organisations established and run by activist groups that represent the 'crucibles and institutional instruments of most serious efforts to globalise from below' (Appadurai 2002: 282). Well-known actors amongst these are Amnesty International and Greenpeace. These groups play an important intervention role, voicing opposition to political and environmental destruction and injustice, as well as intervening in the proceedings of international courts. Finally, discussions of globalisation often exclude the individual from the realm of global change. According to Thomas (2007), under contemporary globalisation, individuals are, more so than in the past, authorised to discover problems and to take actions to solve them. The multiple players involved in globalisation reveal the complexity of global contexts.

The globalisation process consists of a global substructure, a technological economic core, exercising a centralised power over the world's nation-states through transnational corporations (Jarvis 2007). The core has the power to advertise its products globally and to generate a huge market for its products. For Jarvis, the powerful core is protected by the political and military might of the United States and through the institutions over which it exercises hegemonic control (e.g., World Bank, IMF). Through political, military and institutional might, the substructure exercises power over the superstructure, including the international, national, local and individual. In discussing its outcomes, Jarvis maintains that globalisation has led to an increasing degree of 'standardisation', 'McDonaldisation' and 'Americanisation'. To be more specific, through investment, the transnational corporations exercise power economically and politically without regard to national boundaries, a consequence of which is an ever-greater degree of standardisation between countries in the superstructure. The McDonaldisation model has created mass production, mass selling and mass consumption. However, Jarvis argues, it is technology that provides the means by which this is achieved. By generating and providing the necessary knowledge for the production of consumer commodities, the substructure controls both the knowledge and capital for an increasingly unfettered market economy. Inseparable from the knowledge and capital is the superpower—the US political and military state. As a consequence, the processes of globalisation and Americanisation are coconstitutive: in the cultural sphere, globalisation *is* Americanisation, the production of a consumer culture that is 'commodifying cultural phenomena and colonising language and thereby generating a culture which people learn to treat as objective reality' (Jarvis 2007: 59). It is in this context that the discourse of lifelong learning has emerged.

One of the most contentious issues in the field of globalisation studies today pertains to the significance of the nation-state in the era of globalisation (Ritzer 2007). Bruff (2005) summarises this debate into a 'three waves' analysis. The first wave literature, characterised by a state constraint perspective, maintains that the state is severely restricted in what it can do as a result of unprecedented changes caused by globalisation in the establishment of global markets, prices and production. The state has been pushed into a marketised corner, attracting, facilitating and supporting capital. The second wave, according to Bruff, argues that the change has not been overwhelming, and that the state's capacity to autonomously adapt to new circumstances is still considerable. It stresses the unexceptional characteristics of the present era of 'globalisation' while also pointing to state capacity in exercising controls over both capital and labour.

The first wave is criticised by Bruff as overly structuralist, deterministic and narrowly focused, while the second wave neglects the extra-state factors that have pride of place in the social world. Bruff argues that the third wave represents an important step forward. It seeks to move beyond the empirical focus of the previous two by asking how 'globalisation' is perceived and acted upon across space and time. It problematises not just the impact of globalisation, but the term 'globalisation' itself. It posits that globalisation is deeply political, contested, contingent and complex. It focuses on how agents interpret and act upon their circumstances. As Ritzer (2007) points out, what matters most from this perspective are those constructions and not globalisation *per se*. Another important message this perspective conveys is that we should not reify globalisation because it is 'not a thing, not an "it"' (Robertson and White 2007: 64). Robertson and White go on to state that recognising its conceptual status and understanding the global nature of the interest in, the discourse about and the analysis of globalisation are more important than viewing it as an ontological matter.

In the current literature on globalisation, the neglect of the social dimension is 'rather glaring', particularly with regard to questions of social inequality, power and the global–local relationship (Robertson and White 2007: 58). It is evident that globalisation from above favours open markets, free trade, deregulation and privatisation, all of which work for the benefit of wealthy nations and, moreover, the economic elite of these nations. Some scholars do draw attention to the ways in which markets and deregulation produce greater wealth at the price of increased inequality (Appadurai 2002). There is evidence suggesting that we are experiencing widening gaps between the 'haves' and the 'have-nots' in global society, devastating environmental problems, declining civic participation and community and increasing mistrust and alienation among citizenries (Welch 2001). Global capitalism, it seems, has created a global society that is unequal and unjust (Jarvis 2007). Another aspect that deserves our attention is the implications of globalisation for education. As Welch (2001) points out, globalisation is having substantial effects on education, as manifested in the homogenisation, commodification and marketisation of higher education. Furthermore, globalisation creates 'a fragmented and uneven distribution of just those resources for learning, teaching, and cultural criticism' that are most vital for the formation of democratic research communities (Appadurai 2002: 273). Unfortunately, the dominant discourse on educational globalisation focuses on 'educational restructuring', 'educational institutionalism' and 'educational multilateralism', and fails to propose alternatives to the neoliberal order (Chan-Tiberghien 2004). In response, Chan-Tiberghien proposes a new programme of global education justice that links global citizenship, education and transnational social movements.

The integration of the world economy has required the mobility of people across national boundaries as 'global nomads' (Jordan and Düvell 2003). Conceived thus, migration is less about a choice of work than 'a requirement of, a response to and a resistance against, global institutional transformations and the integration of the world economy' (Jordan and Duvell 2003: 63). According to Anderson (2002), one of the new world disorders created by globalisation is mass migration. Migration has become integral to the creation and maintenance of a globally flexible workforce to be deployed at the discretion of the host country. Hence, the following section maps the landscape of transnational migration, including its scope, magnitude and trends.

Mapping transnational migration

Migration is a broad term used to describe the movement of populations from one place to another. Another term that is often used interchangeably with migration is *immigration*, which refers to the movement of people from one country to another on a permanent basis.1 This said, many hold that it is no longer important whether the initial intention of movement is temporary or permanent relocation; many migrants eventually settle down (Castles and Miller 2009). Castles and Miller maintain that movement takes many forms depending on, among other factors, whether the moving subject is a manual worker, highly qualified specialist, entrepreneur or refugee, or if the impetus for migration is the reunion of past-migrants with family. I will use Canada as an example to illustrate. In Canada, immigrants are admitted under four major categories: the skilled worker class, the business class, the family class and refugees. Skilled workers are admitted under a point system using prescribed selection criteria based on education, occupation, language skills and work experience. Skilled workers and business immigrants are also referred to as economic immigrants. The second category seeks to attract experienced business people who are expected to invest in or establish businesses in the host societies. Canada has three classes of business immigrants—investors, entrepreneurs and self-employed persons—each with separate eligibility criteria. Family class immigration reunites close family members of an adult resident or citizen of the host countries, such as children, parents, a spouse or common-law partner. Refugee protection is usually offered to those who fear returning to their country of nationality or habitual residence because of war, or due to fear of persecution, torture or cruel and unusual treatment or punishment. In Canada, a business program was created in the late 1980s to favour an entrepreneurial class of immigrants who would invest in the country's economic development. Since the mid-1990s, immigrant selection practices in Canada have continued to favour economic immigrants over family-class immigrants and refugees. As a result, as of the late 1990s, this class of immigrants has accounted for more than half of all admissions (Li 2003).

Jordan and Düvell (2003) maintain that there are four views on migration, namely the nationalist, globalist, federalist and ethical perspectives. Nationalists advocate from a conviction that strong national sovereignty makes nation states still the most viable systems for security, membership and migration. From this perspective, migration is viewed as a threat because 'it can overwhelm collective infrastructures, lay waste environments and destroy cultures, [and provoke] provoking civil disorders' (Jordan and Düvell 2003: 1). From the globalist perspective, there is a need for more effective international governance. On this view, global economic integration demands a stronger role for international organisations, such as the International Organisation for Migration, in managing movements of population. Globalists favour free trade rather than free movement of people, according to Jordan and Düvell, because they seldom challenge national governments in relation to their role as a restrictor of immigration. Free movement is a key principle for federalists. Like globalisation itself, federalism sees national boundaries as potential barriers to efficiency. It tends to promote mobility across borders and oppose migration restrictions. However, one major paradox in the federalist position, Jordan and Düvell argue, is that economic membership takes no account of citizenship or nationality. Alleviation of this gap is the entry point for various ethical perspectives that concern themselves with new vulnerabilities and needs for new social protections that have resulted from accelerated globalisation and migration. For Jordan and Düvell, ethical critiques focus on victims of globalism and nationalism in their evaluations of management systems.

At present, however, it is not clear exactly how many transnational migrants there are. In order to draw some conclusions on the magnitude of contemporary transnational migration, it is useful to look at the Organisation for Economic Co-operation and Development's (OECD) comprehensive annual report on recent developments in migration in its member countries. According to recent OECD annual reports (OECD 2007, 2008), net migration from outside the OECD to OECD countries is steadily rising. In terms of permanent migration, from an average of 790,000 persons per year between 1956 and 1976, 1.24 million per year between 1977 and 1990, and 2.65 million per year from 1991 to 2003, numbers in 2006 reached four million. Temporary migration is also increasing, but at a slower pace than permanent-type migration, sitting at 2.5 million in 2006. Within the European Economic Area, where free-movement migration is proportionally important, there is little hard evidence on the scale of the unauthorised migration generally believed to be going on. However, asylum seeking in OECD countries declined for the fourth consecutive year in 2006. Overall, international students increased by about 50% from 2000 to 2005, with the United States and the United Kingdom each showing an increase of 120,000 students. It is important to note that 57% of immigrant inflows in Europe were of European origin while movements from Asia to OECD countries outside of Europe accounted for almost 50% of total flows to that area. In terms of source countries, the top 20 countries of origin accounted for fully 60% of all inflows in 2006, with China (10.7%), Poland (5.3%) and Romania (4.6%) at the top of the list. As a result of transnational migration, the foreign-born population of OECD countries reached 12% of the total population in 2006, with Australia leading at 22.2%, followed by Canada at 19.8% (Statistics Canada 2007). In addition, the OECD (2008) also reports that depending on the country of destination and the period of time considered, 20% to 50% of immigrants leave the host country within five years after their arrival, either to return home or to move to a third country. According to the same report, their decision to move again derives from four major reasons, including failure to integrate in the host country, individuals' preferences for their home country, achievement of a savings objective or the opening of employment opportunities in the home country (OECD 2008).

With the exception of Australia, immigrants across all categories, including high-qualified immigrants, earn less than native-born individuals in OECD countries. In the United States, for example, immigrants earn about 20% less than native-born Americans. According to the OECD Annual Report (2008), immigrants from non-OECD countries are at a particular disadvantage because the labour market tends to strongly value host country credentials and experience and to devalue those from non-OECD countries. The same report also reveals that immigrants tend to be overrepresented in manual labour, service and manufacturing jobs, and greatly underrepresented among office workers.

Castles and Miller (2009) identify six trends in contemporary migration. The first is the 'globalisation of migration': increasing numbers of countries are affected by migratory movements with entrants from a broad spectrum of economic, social and cultural backgrounds. The 'acceleration of migration' shows that the international movements of people are growing in volume in all regions. The third trend, the 'differentiation of migration', indicates that more countries have diversified their intake of immigrants to include a whole range of types. The 'feminisation of migration', the fourth trend identified by Castles and Miller, demonstrates that, particularly since the 1960s, women play a significant role in all regions and in most types of migration. The growing 'politicisation of migration' suggests that domestic politics, bilateral and regional relationships and national security policies of states are increasingly affected by international migration. The last of these trends is the 'proliferation of migration transition' that occurs when traditional lands of emigration become lands of transit for both migration and immigration. Taken together, these trends highlight the links between migratory flows and economic, political and cultural change in the context of globalisation.

The above discussion attempts to map the landscape of transnational migration. Owing to divergence in national contexts as well as differences between and within migrant groups, it is difficult to capture its complexities. Nonetheless, it is hoped that the above analysis provides a glimpse of the magnitude, scope and trends of transnational migration in the context of globalisation, as well as some sense of the proliferation in perspectives on these processes. It is evident that migration has been adopted by many countries as a strategy to compete for the most talented, skilful and resourceful and to ameliorate the negative effects of population aging and labour shortages. The above examination also shows that the circulatory and transnational nature of contemporary international migration represents a significant shift from its uni-directional past. It is safe to say that the boundary between traditional migrant sending and migrant receiving countries is now blurring.

Transnationalism, diaspora and migration

To fully understand the phenomenon of transnational migration, it is necessary to examine the concept of 'transnationalism'. In fact, the condition of transnationalism is not new. Precursors of contemporary immigrant transnationalism can be traced back several centuries (Portes et al. 1999). Early examples of such migrations, however, tended to be unidirectional. Although the flow of returnees to their home countries was not unheard of, such movements lacked the 'regularity, routine involvement, and critical mass characterising contemporary examples of transnationalism' (Portes et al. 1999: 225). Advanced communication and transportation technologies have made possible the emergence and proliferation of transnationalism. According to Kivisto (2001), those most responsible for popularising and expanding the use of the transnational perspective are Alejandro Portes and his associates.

Portes et al. (1999) propose three criteria for identifying a transnational phenomenon: first, the process involves a significant proportion of persons in the relevant universe; second, the activities of interest possess certain stability and resilience over time; and third, the content of these activities is not captured by some pre-existing concept. When analysing transnationalism, individuals and their support networks are regarded as the proper units of analysis. According to Portes *et al.*, a study that begins with the history and activities of individuals is 'the most efficient way of learning about the institutional underpinnings of transnationalism and its structural effects' (220). A useful distinction is made between transnationalism 'from above' and 'from below', movements that are initiated, on the one hand, by powerful states and corporations and on the other, by grass-roots immigrants and their home-country counterparts. Unlike early transnationalism, which was often limited to the movement of elites, contemporary grass-roots transnational activities commonly develop in reaction to the negative effects of government policies or in response to the condition of dependent capitalism foisted on weaker countries. In such cases, transnational movement serves to circumvent the permanent subordination of immigrants and their families. At the grass-roots level, Portes (1999) points out elsewhere, transnationalism offers an economic alternative to immigrants' low-wage dead-end employment situations, gives them political voice and allows them to reaffirm their own self-worth.

Portes *et al.* (1999) organise transnational activities into three types: economic, political and socio-cultural. The main goals of each type are different. Specifically, transnational economic entrepreneurs are interested in mobilising their contacts across borders in search of suppliers, capital and markets; transnational political activities designate the actions of those who aim to achieve political power and influence in the sending or receiving countries; and socio-cultural transnationalism orients its actors towards the reinforcement of a national identity abroad or the collective enjoyment of cultural events and goods. In commenting on the fear that transnational activities slow the process of assimilation in immigrant host nations, Portes (1999) maintains that transnational activities can actually facilitate successful adaptation by providing opportunities for economic mobility and for a vital and purposeful group life. He also points out that the overall effect of transnational activities on sending countries is positive in both economic and political terms. While both migrant remittances and business investments promote economic growth, political activism is more likely to line up with the forces of change in promoting democracy and reducing corruption and violation of human rights at home.

In assessing these works, Kivisto (2001) contends that Portes offers a sustained articulation of what transnationalism entails, why it is unique, and what its implications are for ethnic communities over time. However, he also points out that Portes' unit of analysis excludes communities and more overarching structural units such as governments. In commenting on three types of transnationalism, Kivisto argues that labour and professional immigrants have been displaced from Portes' definition of economic transnationalism in favour of mobile capitalist entrepreneurs. Regarding his political transnationalism, Portes' emphasis on party officials, governmental functionaries, or community leaders excludes community activists, thus violating his stated intention of keeping transnationalism from below analytically distinct from transnationalism from above. Lastly, with respect to the category of socio-cultural transnationalism, his emphasis on the collective enjoyment of cultural events and goods tends to preserve immigrants' nostalgic 'symbolic ethnicity'.

Another relevant concept closely associated with transnationalism is 'diaspora'. In the age of globalisation, a globalised economy permits greater connectivity and creates new opportunities for the emergence of diasporic communities. Unidirectional 'migration to' is now being 'replaced by asynchronous, transversal, oscillating flows that involve visiting, studying, seasonal work, temporary contracts, tourism and sojourning, rather than whole-family migration, permanent settlement and the adaptation of exclusive citizenship' (Cohen 2008: 123). Early notions of diaspora portray the phenomenon as catastrophic—a traumatic dispersal of victimised groups from a homeland and the salience of that homeland in the collective memory of a forcibly dispersed group (Cohen 2008). Jews, a religio-ethno-cultural grouping far more diverse than is typically recognised in public discourse, are often seen as the prototypical diaspora. The concept of diaspora, however, allows for recognition of unity in the face of the historical effects as well as memories of alienation, displacement, exile, and, of course, extermination. The association of victimhood and diaspora also applies to other groups such as Africans, Armenians, Irish and Palestinians. More recently, the concept has been extended to include labour, trade, imperial and cultural diasporas (Cohen 2008). Grounded in forms of physical dispersal, Butler's (2001) typology groups diasporas into six categories: captivity, state-eradication exile, forced and voluntary exile, emigration, migration and imperial diaspora. This more relaxed definition of diaspora allows for its broad application to many kinds of dispersals and the communities that emerge as a result.

In delineating what makes a diaspora, Van Hear (1998) suggests three minimal criteria, including dispersal from a homeland, an enduring presence abroad and some kind of exchange between or among the spatially separated populations comprising the diaspora. For Safran (1991) and Cohen (2008), however, diasporas should satisfy more precise criteria. Each thus proposes an extended list of criteria. Since the two authors' criteria share many similarities, Cohen's list is presented here as it is most recent and more inclusive. Cohen (2008) describes nine common features of diasporas, including dispersal from an original homeland, the expansion from a homeland in search of work or pursuit of trade or colonial activities, a collective memory and myth about the homeland, an idealisation of the real or imagined ancestral home, a return movement or intermittent visits, a strong ethnic group consciousness, a troubled relationship with host societies, a sense of solidarity with co-ethnic members in other countries, and the possibility of a distinctive creative, enriching life in host countries. Three core elements can be extracted as constitutive of diasporas: dispersion in space, a psychological orientation to the homeland, and identity boundary maintenance (Brubaker 2005).

Of these, dispersal represents an important resource when it is claimed and optimised by the homeland of a diaspora and its subjects (Ma Mung 2004). Diasporic connections can lead to profound changes at points of origin in many areas including agriculture, trade, business, poverty reduction and peace-making (Cohen 2008). Furthermore, Cohen argues, diasporas perform a vital social role in bridging the gap between the individual and society, the local and the global and the cosmopolitan and the particular. As such, many sending countries step up their efforts to strengthen ties with their overseas citizenries through proactive initiatives (Ho 2008). These include emphasising that migrants are an asset to the country of origin, establishing state agencies to promote the formation of migrant associations, developing collaborative projects in the homeland with groups of transmigrants, disseminating the work of nationalist artists, writers and musicians, and extending dual citizenship to overseas nationals (Ho 2008). These actions, suggests Ho, nurture an extra-territorial form of national identity.

The concepts of diaspora and transnationalism are helpful in pointing out new paths to the analysis of the complexities of transnational migration. The two concepts share a number of similarities but also have some differences. According to Satzewick and Liodakis (2007), the two have had similar careers in recent years, each becoming popular in scholarly circles at about the same time. Second, each was presented as an alternative to conceptually ill-equipped traditional studies of immigration and ethnic relations. Proponents of both concepts argue that diaspora and transnationalism put analysts in a better position to capture:

the importance of real and imagined places of origin in immigrant and ethnic groups lives and identities as well as the complex interactions between 'here' and 'there' for individuals, families, and communities that have moved abroad. (Satzewick and Liodakis 2007: 208)

Despite having in common popularity and analytical concerns, the two concepts differ in important ways. Satzewick and Liodakis further point out one of these differences—the extent to which they have permeated popular consciousness and wider public discourse. While the popular reach of diaspora has reached outside of an immigrant or ethnic nexus, transnationalism has generally not gone beyond the scholarly community and entered immigrant and ethnic community organisations. At the same time, the concept of diaspora has been more sharply criticised than its counterpart, perhaps because of its popular uptake. For example, Butler (2001) warns of the risk of moving towards essentialising 'diaspora' as an ethnic label rather than a framework of analysis. Cohen (2008) also illustrates social constructionist critiques of diaspora that focus on the fixed origins of the concept.

Immigrant adaptation and lifelong learning

Up to this point, this article has discussed the phenomenon of globalisation and the ways in which it fuels migration. It has made an attempt to map the complexities of transnational migration in a global context. It also analysed the concepts of transnationalism and diaspora that provide theoretical underpinning for transnational migration. Now it is time to examine the experience of immigrants' adaptation and lifelong learning in their host society.

In delineating lifelong learning, Jarvis (2006) argues that humanity remains an unfinished project that requires all human beings unceasingly to continue learning throughout their lives. In this view, learning is intrinsic to living, being and becoming lie at the heart of our thinking about learning and learning is the driving force of social change. According to Delors (1996), learning comprises four dimensions: learning to know, learning to do, learning to be and learning to live together. For immigrants, the move to a new country means that they need assistance with language, employment, housing, daycare, education, health, counselling, legal and social services. They experience tremendous changes and disjunctural situations that provide an impetus to substantial learning. In this context, learning to live together becomes the most important dimension of lifelong learning for immigrants. It is part of the being, living and becoming of which Jarvis speaks.

Unfortunately, the right conditions and opportunities for learning are often absent from immigrants' living and adapting to a new life. Research shows that one of the major barriers facing immigrants' adaptation is lack of access to social services (Bergin 1988, Leung 2000, Nguyen 1991, Reitz 1995). Reitz (1995) reviewed nearly 400 publications from Australia, Britain, Canada and the USA on aspects of ethnoracial access, utilisation and delivery of social services. He concluded that recent immigrants very often experience low rates of utilisation of many important social and health services, despite evidence of significant need and the fact that immigrants contribute more to the economy through taxation than they use in services. Low utilisation can be attributed to a number of barriers, including language difficulties, lack of information about services, cultural patterns of help seeking, lack of cultural sensitivity by service providers, financial barriers and lack of service availability. Unfortunately, since the publication of Reitz's work, little has changed. Nearly 15 years later, a study conducted by Canadian scholars identified similar challenges to those reported by Reitz (Stewart *et al.* 2008). While many commentators view barriers to social services for immigrants as cultural and linguistic issues, the persistence of racial inequality in immigrant settlement and adaptation can also be attributed to existing ideologies of 'democratic racism' and 'universalism' (Henry *et al.* 2006). Despite the fact that people in most immigrant-receiving countries are committed to democratic principles such as justice, equality and fairness, the same people often respond negatively towards efforts that aim to ameliorate the low status of minority groups. This state of value contradiction represents an ideological context of 'democratic racism' (Henry *et al.* 2006). Democratic racism prevents governments from effecting change in the existing social, economic and political order, and from supporting policies and practices to improve the conditions of immigrants. Often, ameliorative policies are perceived to be in conflict with and a threat to liberal democracy. Indeed, Henry *et al.* assert that failure to provide immigrants with services that are 'racially sensitive, culturally appropriate and linguistically accessible' can be attributed to liberal universalism, which assumes that people are all the same and therefore require similar modes of service and intervention (Henry *et al.* 2006: 223). Where some mainstream agencies have attempted to provide more accessible and equitable services by introducing a multicultural organisational model, changes are often 'cosmetic' rather than substantive, because 'the needs and interest of minorities are dealt with on an *ad hoc* basis rather than being integrated into the structure, policies, programs and practices of the organisation' (Henry et al. 2006: 191). As an alternative, ethno-racial organisations have taken responsibility for providing more effective, responsive and equitable services to minority communities (Weinfeld 2000, Guo 2008).

Learning through work is another important dimension of lifelong learning (Fenwick 2003). Unfortunately, immigrants are deprived of this opportunity due to lack of access to the labour market. Despite the fact that they bring significant human capital resources to the host countries, research shows that unemployment and underemployment are major barriers facing immigrants. Taking Canada—a country where immigrants are supposedly welcome—as an example, the last census of Canada reveals that between 2001 and 2006, 1.1 million new immigrants arrived (Statistics Canada 2008a). Canada's population has been aging over the same period, meaning that immigrants supplied one-fifth (21.2%) of Canada's total labour force by 2006. However, census data also show that recent immigrants continued to have lower employment rates (67%) and higher unemployment rates than the Canadian-born—this despite the fact that Canada led Group of Seven (G7) nations in creating jobs at an annual average rate of 1.7% (Statistics Canada 2008a). Furthermore, the earnings gap between recent immigrants and the Canadian-born has widened significantly over the past quarter century (Statistics Canada 2008b). In 1980, recent immigrant men who had some employment income earned 85 cents for each dollar received by Canadian-born men. By 2005, this figure had dropped to 63 cents. The situation for immigrant women was even worse. The corresponding numbers for that group were 85 cents and 56 cents respectively. The fact that this decline is set against the backdrop of a much more rapid increase in educational attainment amongst recent immigrant earners when compared to that of their Canadian-born counterparts merely drives home Henry *et al.*'s point about democratic racism. Statistics Canada (2008c) reports that among immigrants to Canada between 2001 and 2006, over half (51%) had a university degree, twice the proportion of degree holders among the Canadian-born population (20%). It is worth noting that among recent immigrants aged 25 to 64, many held doctoral (49%) and masters (40%) degrees.

The employment situation in Europe is no better, particularly among youth and second-generation immigrants. In Germany, for example, the unemployment rate for immigrants reached 22.5% in 2004, twice the national average. For immigrant youth under the age of 35, figures are alarmingly high, with 41% chronically unemployed (Drever and Hoffmeister 2008). In a study that looked at the structural integration of second-generation Turkish migrants in six European countries (Austria, Belgium, France, Germany, the Netherlands and Sweden), Crul and Vermeulen (2003) conducted a cross-national comparison of the immigrant experience in terms of educational attainment and transition from school to work. The study shows that the Turkish population of Europe is about four million, 60% of whom reside in Germany. It also reveals that labour migration formed the vast majority of the Turkish entrants to Europe and peaked during the early 1970s. By the 1990s, the children of the earlier generation had reached the age of labour market entry. The study found that, across all six nations, second-generation Turkish young people experience tremendous challenges in their integration processes. High numbers of school dropouts and high unemployment rates are of particular note. In France, for example, almost half left high school without a diploma (Simon 2003). In Germany and Sweden, unemployment rates for second-generation Turks were twice as high as the national average (Westin 2003, Worbs 2003). In Austria and Germany, the apprenticeship system was useful to securing labour market positions. Still, many of these were unskilled or semiskilled jobs (Herzog-Punzenberger 2003, Worbs 2003). What seems clear is that the lives of this second generation of Turkish immigrants represent a reproduction of the experience and prospects of the first generation (Simon 2003). Second-class citizenship and limited social mobility may be their lot in life. Simon warns of the serious risk of forming a Turkish underclass. The cross-nation comparisons identified racial discrimination as a common contributing factor to the marginalisation of second generation Turks in Europe. As Westin (2003) explains, migrants from Turkey are a stigmatised group who are 'consistently conceived as ethnically distant, as the Other' (993). 'In everyday xenophobic discourse', he continues, 'the label "Turk" is used to denote most non-European and Southern European migrants' (993).

Another challenge closely associated with lifelong learning is the devaluation and denigration of immigrants' prior learning and work experience. In Australia, where recruitment addresses specific skills gaps and labour market shortages, skilled migrants, particularly those from culturally and linguistically diverse backgrounds, face an ironic situation in which those whose skills are most needed encounter special difficulties in gaining access to these professions (Wagner and Childs 2006). As Wagner and Childs observe, immigrant optometrists become taxi drivers, social workers become hospital cleaners, teachers become clerical assistants and environmental engineers stack supermarket shelves. Unfortunately, this experience is not unique to Australia. Italy's 'brain gain' has become 'brain waste' (Brandi 2001). Brandi reports that more than 40% of Rome's skilled migrants, particularly these from Africa, Asia and Latin America, work in low-skill jobs.

Another country that has been successful in attracting well-educated migrants is Canada. Despite the fact that skilled immigrants bring significant human capital resources to Canada, a number of studies demonstrate that highly educated immigrant professionals experience deskilling and devaluation of their prior learning and work experience after immigrating to Canada (Mojab 1999, Ng 1999, Krahn *et al.* 2000, Guo and DeVoretz 2006). In a Vancouver-based study with immigrants from the People's Republic of China, Guo and DeVoretz found that most recent Chinese immigrants came to Canada with post-secondary education (72.5%). However, they could not find jobs in their original professions because their Chinese qualifications and work experiences were not recognised. Their lack of access to professional occupations resulted in downward social mobility to the extent that some lived in poverty. Highly educated refugees also encounter similar barriers in Canada (Krahn *et al.* 2000). The situation for immigrant women is even worse. Many feminist scholars argue that in the labour force, the category of 'immigrant women' has served to commodify these women to employers, reinforcing their class position in providing cheap docile labour to the state in exploitive conditions, a process often permeated with racism and sexism (Mojab 1999, Ng 1999).

The lack of access to professional occupations for which current immigrants have prior learning and work experience leads to unemployment and underemployment, poor economic performance and downward social mobility. In tracing its root causes, Guo (2009) attributed the devaluation phenomenon to the following contributing factors. First and foremost, epistemological misperceptions of difference and knowledge can be blamed. The deficit model of difference leads to conflation of 'difference' and 'deficiency' as well as a belief that the knowledge of immigrant professionals, particularly those from Third World countries, is incompatible and inferior and, hence invalid. Knowledge has been racialised and materialised on the basis of ethnic and national origins. Furthermore, our commitment to an objectivist ontology and liberal universalism exacerbates the complexity of this process. Objectivists believe that if something exists, it can be measured. By adopting a set of 'value-free' criteria, it is argued that knowledge can be measured without accounting the social, political, historical and cultural context within which it is produced. In a similar vein, by applying a 'one-size-fits-all' criterion to measure immigrants' credentials and experience, liberal universalism denies immigrants opportunities to be successful in a new society. The claimed neutral assessment and measuring usually disguises itself under the cloak of professional standards, quality and excellence without questioning whose standard is put in place and whose interests it represents. As such, prior learning assessment and recognition (PLAR) procedures are deployed as technologies of power and a system of governing in discounting and devaluating immigrants' prior learning and work experience, reducing lifelong learning to a system of exclusion and a mode of social control (Andersson and Guo 2009).

Conclusion

It seems evident from the above discussion that lifelong learning is at a crossroads. As a result of globalisation and associated processes of transnational migration, many countries are becoming increasingly ethno-culturally diverse. Profound demographic, social and cultural changes are creating new opportunities for development as well as new challenges for lifelong learning. Unfortunately, lifelong learning has failed to respond positively to these challenges. On the contrary, it is implicated in the denial of opportunities for immigrants to learn by failing to improve their access to social services and the labour market. By treating difference as deficit and deficiency, lifelong learning denigrates and devalues immigrants' prior learning and work experience. As a result, many immigrants suffer from poor economic performance and downward social mobility. It is apparent that lifelong learning fails to integrate cultural difference and diversity into educational environment. Rather than facilitating immigrants' adaptation, it has become a serious barrier and a gatekeeper, and by extension, a means of social control and subordination. Through processes of deskilling and re-skilling, lifelong learning acts as a vehicle to colonising immigrants into the dominant norms and values of the host society. The seriousness of the issue requires us to consider a paradigm shift in recognising and accepting differences as valid and valuable expressions of the human experience. In the concluding chapter, the framework of *transnational lifelong learning for recognitive justice and inclusive citizenship* (transnational lifelong learning [TLL or TL²] for short) will be explored.

Note

1 Another important piece of the migration puzzle is internal migration. Although migration is often used to describe the movement of populations between nation-states, it is important to note that the term is also used to describe movements of population within nation states (Solinger 2008). It is claimed that China has the largest internal migration in human history.

References

ANDERSON, B. (2002) The new world disorder. In J. VINCENT (ed.) *The Anthropology of Politics: A reader in ethnography, theory, and critique* (Malden, MA: Blackwell Publishers), pp. 261–270.
ANDERSSON, P. and GUO, S. (2009) Governing through non/recognition: The missing 'R' in the PLAR for immigrant professionals in Canada and Sweden. *International Journal of Lifelong Education*, **28,** 423–437.
APPADURAI, A. (2002) Grassroots globalisation and the research imagination. In J. VINCENT (ed.) *The Anthropology of Politics: A reader in ethnography, theory, and critique* (Malden, MA: Blackwell Publishers), pp. 271–284.
BERGIN, B. (1988) *Equality is the Issue: A study of minority ethnic group access to health and social services in Ottawa-Carleton* (Ottawa: Social Planning Council of Ottawa-Carleton).
BRANDI, M.C. (2001) Skilled immigrants in Rome. *International Migration*, **39,** 101–116.
BRUBAKER, R. (2005) The 'diaspora' diaspora. *Ethnic and Racial Studies*, **28,** 1–19.
BRUFF, I. (2005) Making sense of the globalisation debate when engaging in political economy analysis. *British Journal of Politics and International Relations*, **7,** 261–280.
BURKE, P.J. and JACKSON, S. (2007) *Reconceptualising Lifelong Learning: Feminist interventions* (London: Routledge).
BUTLER, K.D. (2001) Defining diaspora, refining a discourse. *Diaspora: A Journal of Transnational Studies*, **10,** 189–219.
CASTELLS, M. (2008) A new society. In S. SEIDMAN and J. ALEXANDER (eds.) *The New Social Theory Reader* (London: Routledge), pp. 315–324.
CASTLES, S. and MILLER, M. (2009) *The Age of Migration: International population movements in the modern world* (New York: The Guilford Press).
CHAN-TIBERGHIEN, J. (2004) Towards a 'global educational justice' research paradigm: cognitive justice, decolonizing methodologies and critical pedagogy. *Globalisation, Societies and Education*, **2,** 191–213.
COHEN, R. (2008) *Global Diaspora: An introduction* (London and New York: Routledge).
CROWTHER, J. (2004) 'In and against' lifelong learning: Flexibility and the corrosion of character. *International Journal of Lifelong Education*, **24,** 125–136.
CRUL, M. and VERMEULEN, H. (2003) The second generation in Europe. *International Migration Review*, **37,** 965–986.
DELORS, J. (1996) *Learning: The treasure within* (Paris: UNESCO).
DREVER, A. and HOFFMEISTER, O. (2008) Immigrants and social networks in a job-scarce environment: The case of Germany. *International Migration Review*, **42,** 425–448.
EDWARDS, R. (2008) Actively seeking subjects. In A. FEJES and K. NICOLL (eds.) *Foucault and Lifelong Learning: Governing the subject* (Routledge: London), pp. 21–33.
FENWICK, T. (2003) *Learning Through Experience: Troubling assumptions and intersecting questions* (Florida: Krieger).

GOUTHRO, P. (2007) Active and inclusive citizenship for women: Democratic considerations for fostering lifelong education. *International Journal of Lifelong Education*, **26**, 143–154.

GRIFFIN, C. (1999) Lifelong learning and welfare reform. *International Journal of Lifelong Education*, **18**, 431–452.

GUO, S. (2008) The promotion of minority group rights as the protection of individual rights and freedoms for immigrants: A Canadian case study. *Interchange*, **39**, 259–275.

GUO, S., (2009) Difference, deficiency, and devaluation: Tracing the roots of non-recognition of foreign credentials for immigrant professionals in Canada. *Canadian Journal for the Study of Adult Education*, **22**, 37–52.

GUO, S. and DEVORETZ, D. (2006) Chinese immigrants in Vancouver: Quo vadis? *Journal of International Migration and Integration*, **7**, 425–447.

GUO, S. and JAMAL, Z. (2011) Toward inclusive education: Embracing cultural diversity in lifelong learning. In S. JACKSON (ed.) *Innovations in Lifelong Learning: International perspectives on diversity, participation and vocational learning* (London: Routledge), pp. 15-33.

HENRY, F., TATOR, C., MATTIS, W. and REES, T. (2006) *The Colour of Democracy: Racism in Canadian society* (Toronto: Thompson Nelson).

HERZOG-PUNZENBERGER, B. (2003) Ethnic segmentation in school and labor market—40 year legacy of Austrian guestworker policy. *International Migration Review*, **37**, 1120–1144.

HO, E. (2008) 'Flexible citizenship' or familial ties that bind? Singaporean transmigrants in London. *International Migration*, **46**, 145–175.

JARVIS, P. (2006) *Towards a Comprehensive Theory of Human Learning* (Routledge: London and New York).

JARVIS, P. (2007) *Globalisation, Lifelong Learning and the Learning Society: Sociological Perspectives* (Routledge: London and New York).

JARVIS, P. (2008) *Democracy, Lifelong Learning and the Learning Society* (Routledge: London and New York).

JORDAN, B. and DÜVELL, F. (2003) *Migration: The boundaries of equality and justice* (Cambridge: Polity).

KIVISTO, P. (2001) Theorizing transnational immigration: A critical review of current efforts. *Ethnic and Racial Studies*, **24**, 549–577.

KRAHN, H., DERWING, T., MULDER, M. and WILKINSON, L. (2000) Educated and underemployed: Refugee integration into the Canadian labour market. *Journal of International Migration and Integration*, **1**, 59–84.

LEUNG, H.H. (2000) *Settlement Services for the Chinese Canadians in Toronto: The challenges toward an integrated planning* (Toronto: Ontario Administration of Settlement and Integration Services).

LI, P.S. (2003), *Destination Canada: Immigration debates and issues* (Don Mills: Oxford University Press).

LIVINGSTONE, D.W. (2002) *The Changing Nature of Work and Lifelong Learning in the New Economy: National and case study perspectives*. WALL Working Paper No. 1. Toronto.

MA MUNG, E. (2004) Dispersal as a resource. *Diaspora: A Journal of Transnational Studies*, **13**, 211–225.

MCGREW, A. (2007) Globalisation in hard times: Contention in the academy and beyond. In G. RITZER (Ed.) *The Blackwell Companion to Globalisation* (Malden, MA: Blackwell Publishing), pp. 29–53.

MOJAB, S. (1999) De-skilling immigrant women. *Canadian Woman Studies*, **19**, 123–128.

NG, R., (1999) Homeworking: Dream realized or freedom constrained? The globalized reality of immigrant garment workers. *Canadian Woman Studies*, **19**, 10–114.

NGUYEN, T.C. (1991) *Report on the Vietnamese Community in the City of York* (York: York Community Services).

NICOLL, K. and FEJES, A. (2008) Mobilizing Foucault in studies of lifelong learning. In A. FEJES and K. NICOLL (eds.) *Foucault and Lifelong Learning: Governing the Subject* (Routledge: London), pp. 1–18.

ORGANISATION FOR ECONOMIC CO-OPERATION AND DEVELOPMENT [OECD] (2007) *International Migration Outlook* (Paris: Organisation for Economic Co-Operation and Development).

OECD (2008) *International Migration Outlook* (Paris: Organisation for Economic Co-Operation and Development).
PORTES, A. (1999), Conclusion: Towards a new world—the origin and effects of transnational activities. *Ethnic and Racial Studies*, **22,** 463–477.
PORTES, A., GUARNIZO, L.E. and LANDOLT, P. (1999), The study of transnationalism: pitfalls and promise of an emergent research field. *Ethnic and Racial Studies*, **22,** 217–237.
REITZ, J.G. (1995) A review of the literature on aspects of ethno–racial access, utilization and delivery of social services (online) http://ceris.metropolis.net/VirtualLibrary/other/reitz1/reitz1.html (accessed 4 July, 2009).
RITZER, G. (2007) Introduction. In G. RITZER (ed.) *The Blackwell Companion to Globalisation* (Malden, MA: Blackwell Publishing), pp. 1–13.
ROBERTSON, R. and WHITE, K.E. (2007) What is globalisation? In G. RITZER (ed.) *The Blackwell Companion to Globalisation* (Malden, MA: Blackwell Publishing), pp. 54–66.
ROGERS, A. (2006) Escaping the slums or changing the slums? Lifelong learning and social transformation. *International Journal of Lifelong Education*, **25,** 125–137.
SAFRAN, W. (1991) Diasporas in modern societies: myths of homeland and return. *Diaspora: A Journal of Transnational Studies*, **1,** 83–99.
SATZEWICK, V. and LIODAKIS, N. (2007) *Race and Ethnicity in Canada: A critical introduction* (Don Mills, ON: Oxford University Press).
SIMON, P. (2003) France and the unknown second generation: Preliminary results on social mobility. *International Migration Review*, **37,** 1091–1119.
SOLINGER, D., (2008) The political implications of China's social future: Complacency, scorn, and the forlorn. In L. CHENG (ed.), *China's Changing Political Landscape: Prospects for democracy* (Washington, D.C.: Brookings Institution Press), pp. 251–266.
STATISTICS CANADA (2007) *Immigration in Canada: A portrait of the foreign-born population, 2006* (Ottawa: Statistics Canada).
STATISTICS CANADA (2008a) *Canada's Changing Labour Force, 2006 Census* (Ottawa: Statistics Canada).
STATISTICS CANADA (2008b) *Earnings and Incomes of Canadians Over the Past Quarter Century, 2006 Census* (Ottawa: Statistics Canada).
STATISTICS CANADA (2008c) *Educational Portrait of Canada, 2006 Census* (Ottawa: Statistics Canada).
STEWART, M., ANDERSON, J., BEISER, M., MWAKARIMBA, E., NEUFELD, A., SIMICH, L. and SPITZER, D. (2008) Multicultural meanings of social support among immigrants and refugees. *International Migration*, **46,** 123–159.
THOMAS, G. (2007) Globalisation: The major players. In G. RITZER (ed.) *The Blackwell Companion to Globalisation* (Malden, MA: Blackwell Publishing), pp. 84–102.
VAN HEAR, N. (1998) *New Diasporas: The mass exodus, dispersal and regrouping of migrant communities* (Seattle: University of Washington Press).
WAGNER, R. and CHILDS, M. (2006) Exclusionary narratives as barriers to the recognition of qualifications, skills and experience—a case of skilled migrants in Australia. *Studies in Continuing Education*, **28,** 49–62.
WEINFELD, M. (2000) The integration of Jewish immigrants in Montreal: Models and dilemmas of ethnic match. In D.J. ELAZAR and M. WEINFELD (eds.) *Still Moving: Recent Jewish migration in corporative perspective* (New Jersey: Transaction), pp. 285–98.
WELCH, A.R. (2001) Globalisation, post-modernity and the state: comparative education facing the third millennium. *Comparative Education*, **37,** 475–492.
WESTIN, C. (2003) Young people of migrant origin in Sweden. *International Migration Review*, **37,** 987–1010.
WORBS, S. (2003) The second generation in Germany: Between school and labor market. *International Migration Review*, **37,** 1011–1038.

Lifelong learning as ideological practice: an analysis from the perspective of immigrant women in Canada

ROXANA NG[a] and HONGXIA SHAN[b]
[a]Ontario Institute for Studies in Education, University of Toronto; [b]University of British Columbia, Canada

Critiques of lifelong learning have focused on the neo-liberal underpinning of state policy, where individuals are expected to take responsibility for meeting the needs of changing labour market conditions in the post-Fordist economy. We treat lifelong learning as an 'ideological frame' that (re)shapes how people see and understand social reality, and organise their job seeking activities accordingly. Our argument is supported with data from two studies that examine how professional immigrant women from China navigate the Canadian labour market from their perspectives. Specifically, we identify how lifelong learning as a discursive frame intersects with credentialism, the gendered and racialised construction of Chinese women, age and gendered familial relations to channel professional immigrant women into a labour market segmented along gender, ethnic and racial lines. We end with the policy implications of our discussion.

The discourse of lifelong learning

Since the late 1990s, lifelong learning has been adopted as state policy in many countries in the economic North, such as Canada (Hake 1999). In its recent policy document, *Knowledge Matters: Skills and learning for Canadians,* the Canadian government makes it clear that 'to remain competitive and keep up with the accelerating pace of technological change, Canada must continuously renew and upgrade the skills of its workforce' (Human Resources Development Canada [HRDC] 2002). Implicitly, lifelong learning is endorsed with the neo-liberal conviction that it will enable individuals to keep up with the economic and technological changes of globalisation and enable Canada as a nation state to remain competitive.

One manifestation of the lifelong learning policy in Canada is the state's investment in immigrant training and education (HRDC 2002), and the recognition that immigrants have played a major role in the demographic and economic growth in Canada. The federal government has long provided English training and labour market orientation for immigrants. In the province of Ontario, the Ministry of Citizenship and Education is funding 'bridging programs' to provide newcomers with education and skill assessment, skills training, workplace experience, assistance in licence or certification examination, language training and individual learning plans (Ontario Ministry of Citizenship and Immigration 2007a). In February 2007, the Ministry in Ontario announced an additional $29 million investment to expand programs province-wide for skilled newcomers (Ontario Ministry of Citizenship and Immigration 2007b).

While lifelong learning, as it is adopted in state policies, is invariably linked to individual up-skilling in the post-Fordist, post-industrial knowledge-based economy (Amin 1994), researchers and educators see in it a much broader purpose. When the UNESCO educational report *Learning to Be* was published in 1973, it advocated that educational and training facilities should be made accessible to all for humanistic reasons. Recent publications at UNESCO, such as the Hamburg *Declaration for Action* (1997) and the *Dakar Framework for Action* (2000), provide a vision of learning that centres issues such as citizenship and social justice for equity-seeking groups. Furthermore, the social and democratic dimension of learning has been the focus of many critical scholars (e.g. Foley 1999, Allman 2000, Grace 2002, Gouthro 2007). However, this social agenda is often rendered secondary to economic imperative in state policy and practice. It is sidelined in state allocation of training and education funding (see Stephen 2000, Mojab and Gorman 2001). When Boshier examined the New Zealand's economic reform during the 1980 and 1990s, which Canada took as a model, he observed:

> Lifelong learning tends to render invisible any obligation to address social conditions. It is nested in an ideology of vocationalism. Learning is for acquiring skills alleged to enable the learner to work harder, faster and smarter and thus enables their employer to better compete in the global economy. (2001: 368)

Critics also note the neo-liberal underpinning of the dominant lifelong learning discourse: individuals are expected to take responsibility for learning (Butler 2000) and to become entrepreneurs who can recognise opportunities, marshal resources and make appropriate investment to achieve various goals (Reimers-Hild *et al.* 2005, Olssen 2006). Meanwhile, provision for training and education is increasingly open to marketisation and privatisation so that it dovetails the needs of the market (Boshier 2001, Gouthro 2002).

Ironically, amidst the popular call for people to engage in lifelong learning, there are gaps between the number of qualified workers and the number of jobs that actually make use of workers' higher qualifications (Livingstone 1999a, b). That is, while the state emphasises improving the 'quality' of workers or the supply side of the labour market, it downplays the reality of the demand side or the availability of good jobs (Cruikshank 2001, 2002). For example, drawing on the data from the CPRN-Ekos changing employment relationships survey of 2500 employees and self-employed, Lowe (2000) found that 23% of workers felt overqualified for their jobs, and one in five workers with post-secondary credentials were in jobs requiring only a high school diploma.

Thus, many critics have come to see the lifelong learning discourse as a mechanism of neo-liberal control (Olssen 2006) or a 'technique of governance' in a knowledge-based economy to produce certain kinds of learners/workers (e.g. Edwards 2002, 2003, Fejes 2005). In the European Union, for example, lifelong learning is used as a way of integrating vastly different educational frameworks amongst its member states. It has not only rearranged the field of learning, making informal and non-formal learning legitimate learning events, thereby giving rise to the development of 'credential regimes'. It has also functioned as a 'subjectivation' (Tuschling and Engemann 2006). Individuals are expected to develop the motivation and ability to make use of various kinds of opportunities to learn. Using discourse analysis, some critics unravel the way in which current lifelong learning policies play a key role in producing new subjects for the post-industrial economy (e.g. Edwards 2002, Fejes 2005, Ailwood 2008). In particular, the discourse of lifelong learning is used as the political rationale to reform the relations between governments and citizens. Individuals are treated as a homogenous unit who can maximise their life chances through training while minimising costs to the state and to employers.

While these critiques are useful in pointing out lifelong learning as a hegemonic discourse, they focus on the deployment of this discourse in the policy arena. This paper asks the question: how do individuals orient themselves to this discourse when they participate in the labour market? We examine this question using data from two studies that focus on the way in which professional immigrant women from China navigate the Canadian labour market. After Smith (1990) and Ng (1995), we treat lifelong learning as an 'ideological frame'; once it becomes hegemonic, it (re)shapes how people see and understand social reality, and organize their job seeking activities accordingly. This conceptualisation enables us to see how the discourse of lifelong learning is taken up, activated and operates in people's everyday lives.

Lifelong learning as ideological practice

The term 'ideological frame' was used by Ng (1995) in her textual analysis of multiculturalism as Canadian state policy. Her analysis interrogates multiculturalism as a 'natural' phenomenon in Canada and draws attention to its constructed character. She argues that the term multiculturalism was first used by Pierre Trudeau, then Prime Minister of Canada, in 1971 to shift state policy and practice from Anglo-conformity as a way of meeting the challenges posed by a nation marked by social tension culminating from the historical conflicts between English Canada and Quebec, the aboriginal peoples and immigrants. Multiculturalism within a bilingual framework gave the Canadian state a new way of managing national unity by restructuring existing programs and services under a new framework. Once in place, this frame comes to shape not only state officials', but also the general population's perception of social reality. The term 'ideological frame', as Ng uses it, does not simply refer to a bias or a set of beliefs.

It identifies ideologies as processes that are produced and constructed through human activities. They are ways in which capitalist societies are ruled and governed (see Marx and Engels 1970, Gramsci 1971). Once an ideological frame is in place, it renders the very work process that produced it invisible and the idea that it references as common sense. That is, the idea(s) contained within the ideological frame become normalized; they become taken for granted as 'that's how it is' or 'that's how it should be' (Ng 1995: 36).

This notion of ideology in turn comes from Dorothy Smith, a Canadian feminist theorist (Smith 1990). Smith's concept of ideology, which she refers to as 'ideological practice', is extrapolated from Marx's analysis of political economy. She makes an analogy between how commodities created for exchange render invisible the concrete process of production. Sociologically, she points out that knowledge made into abstract concepts and categories 'hides' social relations that need to be explored and explicated. Here is how Smith explains her treatment of ideology:

> Marx views concepts and categories as expressions of social relations and hence as opening up a universe for exploration that is 'present' in them but not explicated. The problem of what we are calling *ideological practices* is that they confine us to the conceptual level, suppressing the presence and workings of the underlying relations they express. Thus Marx criticizes the bourgeois economists for treating as fact what has to be explained. Terms such as *division of labor, exchange,* and *competition* are the primitives of their theories. Such terms express social relations organizing the actual activities of people, but the social relations themselves are presupposed without being explored or analyzed. Ideological theories conceal the presence and workings of these relations. What I am calling ideological practices or procedures are the methods of reasoning that effect that concealment. (Smith 1990: 37)

According to Smith, abstract ideas and concepts are not necessarily ideological. They become ideological only when they are used in ways that naturalise and objectify social reality and that mask human actions (Smith 1987). The term 'ideological practice', therefore, draws attention to how ideas, once they become hegemonic, organise and shape our work and lives. Furthermore, in contemporary societies, ideological practices are mediated by discourses. Smith goes beyond Foucault's notion of discourse as conversation mediated by texts, and interrogates how actual people take up a particular discourse, as well as how it works with other related discourses to coordinate the activities of people who may otherwise be unconnected to one another (Smith 1999: 158).

Seen in this light, we can see that the discourse of lifelong learning has taken on an ideological character. In their examination and critique of lifelong learning from an adult education perspective, Mojab and Gorman (2001) postulate that this concept grew out of the political and economic upheaval of the 1990s resulting from drastic restructuring of the global capitalist system. These made extraordinary demands on education in general and adult education in particular. It necessitated the reorganization of adult education into a training/learning enterprise that was more responsive to the requirements of the market. Other studies that analyse the genealogy, practices and/or policy discourse of lifelong learning in different countries also indicate how this discourse has become a way of governance aimed at producing ideal learners and workers for the post-industrial knowledge-based economy.

This paper takes as its starting point lifelong learning as a hegemonic discourse promoted by the state, by employers and by educational institutions. By arguing that it has become an ideological practice, we focus on how this discourse, together with other discourses, has seeped into the everyday world so that it is taken up automatically, without question, by the general population in search of jobs. Specifically, we argue that lifelong learning has become a taken-for-granted way in which professional Chinese immigrant women organize their labour market behaviour while obscuring the social and power relations that (re)produce market segmentation and social inequality.

Context of our studies

Historically, Canada depends on immigrants for its economic and demographic growth. In the 1960s, Canada significantly changed its immigration policy from one that privileged white males from European countries to a point system based on labour market needs. That is, under the point system, immigrants are assessed for their skills and qualifications and not on the basis of gender, race and ethnicity. This led to changes in the demographic composition of immigrants. In recent years, in particular, the number of immigrants from Asia has increased dramatically. China, which signed an immigration agreement with Canada in 1995, became the top source country of immigration in 1998.

Despite Canada's preference for skilled immigrants minimally with university degrees and professional experience (Iredale 2001), most skilled immigrants end up in jobs far from commensurate with their previous educational backgrounds and work experience (see Basran and Zong 1998, JobStart and Skills for Change 2001). Statistical studies have shown that the employment earnings of recent immigrants have declined compared to that of their counterparts before the 1970s, and that there is a correlation between the scale of this decline and the changing composition of recent immigrants (e.g. Baker and Benjamin 1994, Frenette and Morrisette 2003, Moore and Pacey 2003). Based on a 2006 labour force survey in Canada, Lewkowicz (2008) shows that the weekly wage of recent immigrants of core working age (between 25 and 54) who are in the country 5 to 10 years is just under 20% less than their Canadian counterparts. The differential is over 30% for recent immigrants and Canadian-born of the core working age in Toronto, the top designation city for immigrants (Toronto Training Board 2009). Although in general it takes about 10 years for immigrants to achieve relative wage parity with Canadians born in Ontario and Canada as a whole, this is not the case for Toronto (Lewkowicz 2008). Other researchers have shown that immigrants, particularly immigrant women, including those from China, are channelled into gendered and racialized sectors of the labour market, which is most evident in Toronto as the Canadian city with the largest immigrant population (see Man 2004, Mirchandani et al. 2008).

It is against this backdrop that we have initiated two studies since 2005 to explore how professional Chinese immigrant women navigate the gendered and ethnically segregated labour market in Toronto—Chinese being one of the largest immigrant groups in Canada and the second largest immigrant group in Toronto (Toronto Training Board 2009). It is also one of the groups that do not fare well in Canada (Wang and Lo 2008). The first study began in 2005,[1] and led to another study that included professional women from India.[2] Interviewees were identified through word of mouth, email networks of professional immigrants and organisations serving new immigrants in the city of Toronto, where the majority of immigrants reside.

We interviewed 10 Chinese women in the first study and 11 women in the second study. Both studies made use of life-history-style interviews as the primary data collection tool so as to give women ample space to recollect their immigration and job search experience. We asked the women to describe their occupations, as well as their expectations and knowledge of the Canadian labour market prior to immigration, and traced their stories navigating the Canadian labour market. We invited them to contextualize their stories in relation to social and economic conditions in which their experience was situated. The interviews were between two and three hours; we also asked for permission to conduct a second interview if necessary at the end. In the first study, in which women were asked to choose their language of preference, all but one interview was conducted in Chinese. As much as possible, in the second study, with the exception of one interview, all were conducted in English. We transcribed all interviews verbatim in the language of the interviews. In the first study, the transcripts were not translated in English unless we wanted to quote from them, since all the researchers could read Chinese. In the second study, the sole Chinese interview was translated into English because non-Chinese researchers are part of the team.

Analytically, we relied on the institutional ethnography (IE) approach developed by Smith (1987, 2005), which begins from and takes up the standpoint of people's daily experiences, in this case women's labour market experiences. Our analysis is not restricted to the women's narratives, however; it aims to situate and understand their experiences in the larger context of society. Thus, we locate women's job-search activities in a labour market segregated by gender, ethnicity, race and other axes of differentiation. We pay particular attention to how their narratives were shaped by the conditions, such as the taken-for-granted assumption of Canadian qualifications and work experience, existing in the larger society prior to their entry into it. In this way, we are able to see how the notion of lifelong learning became part of the discourse that women took up and internalized when they looked for paid employment. This approach enabled us to see how ideologies and other pre-existing conditions become operative in people's experience. While we did not utilize resistance as an analytical category, our focus on *how* women navigate the labour market enabled us to document the dialectics of structure and agency as they look for employment and move around labour market barriers.

All the 21 Chinese immigrant women came to Canada after 1998 as skilled professional immigrants. All had at least one university degree at the time of immigration. The majority of them were under 40 years old at the time of the interviews. Most were married with at least one child. In terms of occupations prior to immigration, seven were trained in engineering, six in English literature, three in commerce, two in medical sciences, two in law and one in library information. In China, most of them worked in their fields of training although some shifted to other occupations in preparation for immigration. For example, one woman trained in engineering, two in English literature and one in law entered the commercial and sales fields at different stages of their careers. After immigration, all the women interviewees experienced tremendous difficulty locating a job in their fields of training and/or practice. Only two women found jobs relevant to their fields within six months of landing. Many, especially initially, took low-end service or manufacturing jobs, working at call centres and factories—a far cry from their training and prior work experience. At the time of the interviews, a few of them were still in labour-intensive service or manufacturing work. While some women did not prepare for what they might encounter in Canada, many, especially in the second study, did research the labour market situation in Canada prior to immigration and expected a short period of adjustment. However, many were surprised by the actual difficulties encountered and the length of time it took to regain a foothold in the host society. Many were also disheartened by their inability to re-enter their former professional fields.

Changing occupational trajectories

In both studies, we find that Chinese immigrants often resort to Canadian training and education in order to optimise their labour market outcomes (Ng *et al.* 2006, Shan 2009a). Although the term 'lifelong learning' never appeared in the interviews, the idea of having to acquire credentials, knowledge and skills that underpin the lifelong learning discourse was evident as women tried to insert themselves into the Canadian labour market. Among the 21 interviewees, 16 attended at least one occupation-specific training program in colleges, universities, community centres and for-profit organizations to acquire Canadian credentials. Two were planning to go back to school. One was preparing to write exams to re-qualify as a medical doctor (she became a lab technician in a medical school after immigration), and one was taking English as a second language (ESL) classes full-time as she was getting ready to return to China given her and her husband's dismal job prospects. Only one woman managed to switch from being an English teacher to being a superintendent of an apartment building without any training.

Among the 16 women who took further training, 11 found jobs in their new areas of training, two failed to get into their new fields of training, one studied finance but ended up in community services through the advice of an employment counsellor, and one, who was in a Master's program, went on to study for her doctorate. Upon closer examination, two interesting phenomena emerged. First, only two of the women stayed somewhat close to their previous careers—one worked in higher education and the other as a customs broker. All the other women had to change their career paths, many from traditionally male-dominated fields (such as engineering) to jobs that are female-dominated, such as community and settlement services and early childhood education, which are increasingly occupied by women of colour and immigrant women. Second, regardless of the sector into which they have inserted themselves, many found that they were in lower echelon positions; some failed to find full-time employment and worked on a part-time or contract basis. Many found that they were over-qualified for the positions they occupied. While some of the women, having acquired additional training and qualification, managed to shift from labour-intensive services and manufacturing jobs, they were in sectors that are deeply gendered and racialised. This picture is consistent with the changing structure of the post-industrial labour market characterised by the rapid increase of part-time, contingent work (Vosko 2000). In Toronto, as elsewhere, the impact of labour market restructuring and the most recent global economic crisis has resulted in even more precarious employment and an overall drop in family income (Toronto Training Board 2009).

Below, we explore women's re-training and re-education decisions and trajectories. We display how, as an ideological frame, the notion of lifelong learning is naturalized and how this frame, now thoroughly embedded in different settings and sites (such as immigrant services), works in concert with other ideological and materials relations to perpetuate social and labour market hierarchy along lines of gender, race and class. Specifically, we are identifying three sets of processes—credentialism, gendered and racialised construction of Chinese women, and age, gendered familial relations—that intersect with lifelong learning to shape the career and job (re)orientation of professional immigrant women in our studies. In order to distinguish these studies, in this paper we are identifying them by letters and number. Thus, we use A and B to refer to the two studies. The interviewees are identified by number in terms of the sequence of the interviews.

Credentialism

Reviewing the women's stories, it is clear that their (re)training decisions were shaped, not by a singular circumstance or experience, but by a complex set of social processes and practices. Central to their decision is what Shan (2009a) has identified as a 'credential and certificate regime' that privileges Western, especially North American, qualifications and credentials and that devalues foreign credentials, especially those from non-Western countries (see Reitz 2003, Guo and Andersson 2006). This regime is promoted aggressively by Canadian employers, educational institutions and professional organisations. Thus, once in Canada, immigrants are compelled to 'Canadianise' their education and training in order to regain a foothold in the labour market.

Within this credential and certificate regime, those who hold jobs in the regulated professions[4] in Canada are affected the most. Upon landing, immigrants are stripped of the right to practise in the regulated professions such as medicine and engineering until they satisfy the credential requirements in Canada and are recertified by professional bodies. Here is an example: A1 was a senior doctor in China. She immigrated to Canada with her husband, who was engaged in graduate study. At the time of the interview, she was about to follow her husband back to China and to take care of her elderly parents. She was resigned but bitter about her inability to practise medicine in Canada:

> When you immigrate, you are asked to sign something, to put a signature on a form. For example, if you are a doctor [you are asked to declare that] you are not to practise if you do not go through training and get licensed.... Some people willingly give up [their profession].

To exert control over the professions, many professional associations have developed strict measures for the recertification of foreign trained individuals. In addition, we found that many immigrants are left to their own devices to acquire the requisite credentials, and to take expensive and time-consuming exams for recertification. Although government-sponsored programs are available for basic language training, many immigrants deem these classes too elementary for them to function in professional environments. Currently, the few bridging and mentoring programs available to facilitate the re-entry of foreign trained professionals are inadequate to address fully the redeployment of these professionals. More seriously, they serve to reinforce existing recertification processes rather than truly to recognise the value of foreign credentials. In our two studies, seven out of the nine women in the regulated professions changed their careers because of the lengthy and costly process of recertification.

Women's decision to change their employment trajectories is accomplished, in part, through a market rationale underpinning the lifelong learning discourse. When selecting an appropriate training program, women tried to align themselves with current labour market needs, which they identified via the internet (such as government or employers' websites) or by word of mouth. In this process, employers' requirements and what they consider valued skills play a significant role in shaping women's 'choice'. For instance, B7 was a university teacher and consultant in China. She came to Canada as an international student in education and obtained her landed immigrant status while studying. When she was writing her Master's thesis, she identified settlement services as a field for immigrant women and decided to join this sector. To prepare herself for a position in this sector, she attended a training program where she would obtain a lifelong coaching certificate—a desirable credential requested by many employers in their job advertisements. She said:

> [So I went to the YMCA], it's only a [one]-week training programme, it's called lifelong coaching certificate. One of the colleges [has] that as well but you have to spend a semester in getting that. And then some of the agencies, like—or, um, some—church, um, community services, they require that. So I went there and I got it, you know. It's $600 something. [In that college] it's very expensive. And then you only spend a week, five, four days [at the YMCA]. And then I was a student so they give me half price [laughs], you know, so $300 something.

Like B7, B5 also made what may be considered 'rational' decisions about her career advancement. A computer network engineer in China and in Canada until she got pregnant, B5 made a point of acquiring certificates related to her field of computer sciences. She wrote a number of tests to obtain certificates of different levels in computer languages and programs (such as C ++, Cisco network, Novell network, Unix administration). What made these certificates appealing is that they were associated with salary returns. For instance, B5 said if she got the highest-level certificate in Cisco route operation, '$100,000 yearly salary is no problem'. Indeed, many certificate training programs specified certain salary returns for certificate holders. These certificates were expensive; B5 reported that some cost US$250 per exam. After obtaining these certificates, however, B5 did not proceed to find paid employment, as she had to attend to the needs of her expanding family. Subsequently, she took tax return courses delivered by a large tax return company. Eventually she was given a seasonal job as a tax specialist in the company where she was trained.

The dismissal and devaluation of immigrants' credentials prior to immigration is so prevalent that it has become a fact that many immigrants accept unquestioningly. B2 began her career in China as a university teacher and transitioned to the rank of manager in the marketing department of a company. However, in Canada, she first worked in a call centre and then as a clerk in a maintenance company. Upon being dismissed suddenly, she decided to go back to school to obtain Canadian credentials. Her account in the following excerpt indicates how immigrants need to operate within the credential regime:

> All of a sudden I got laid off. I remember it was before Christmas. I was very unhappy, I [felt] a little bit depressed I remember. And then I decided I would take some local education. I [felt although] I have a Master's degree from China, the degree was just not recognised, yeah so. And also the pay [was] not good. You cannot, that is not enough to support a whole family at that time. So I decided I will go back to school.

The non-recognition of foreign education and credentials clearly indicates the power dynamic operating in the immigration process and how people from non-Western societies are devalued in a society organised by a racial and ethnic hierarchy originating from Canada's colonial past. It is also clear that neither the credential regime nor the lifelong learning discourse operate on their own to disadvantage the immigrant women in our studies. However, when they intersect in people's everyday lives they produce powerful effects, the result of which is the re-inscription of inequality on the basis of ethnicity and race.

The gendered and racialised construction of Chinese women

The seemingly neutral training programs are deeply implicated in (re)producing and maintaining the gendered and racialised segregation of the Canadian labour market. As we mentioned above, few of the immigrant women in our studies who participated in training and learning opportunities in Canada re-entered their former professions. Instead, they were channelled into low-paid occupations, such as settlement services, childcare and counter helps, that rely on a feminised and racialised workforce. What can be seen in the following discussion is how the gender and racialised reality of the labour market becomes the context in which people make decisions about the types of training and further education they should take up in their attempt to secure employment.

Embarking on further training and education meant that the women in our studies had to balance and rebalance their personal and professional preferences with what they perceived to be the reality of the labour market. We found that the gendered and racialised construction of 'suitable' employment for Chinese women significantly shaped their selection process and eventually their occupational choice. B2's decision-making process presents an excellent illustration: B2 came from a background in marketing. She had had a couple of jobs in sales and marketing with large foreign companies before immigration. She had wanted to stay close to her background in marketing when she explored training options initially. However, she gave up that idea fairly quickly based on conversations with friends:

> When I was working at [those] two jobs, I had taken at one time a marketing course. That was because I worked in the marketing field before.... But one of my friends, she has been here at that time [for] five, six years. One day, she said, 'why did you take [marketing]...you cannot get any jobs even if you finish education. The marketing field is mainly dominated by local white people'—something like that. I think although I like this field very much, maybe it is not a good choice.

To avoid competition with white Canadians, B2 started considering accounting because 'a lot of Chinese women learn accounting'. She tried out one accounting course, and realised she disliked dealing with numbers so much that she needed to explore other options. At one point, she considered nursing:

> I was still not sure actually which program to take. And because most of the people around [me] either [took] accounting or took nursing. One of my friends from Shanghai took nursing. Actually it's [the wife of one of my husband's colleagues]. [The colleague] said, 'Oh you should take nursing. Yeah, my wife is going to take nursing courses.' I even discussed, debated with my husband [about] that and he said, 'No, it's not a good choice for you. Always you should use your language [refers to English], that is your strength.'

Eventually B2 decided to study for settlement services:

> I took [a] social service worker program. I remember [in the] first week, first couple of days I was in Toronto I actually went to one of the, I should say just one time, immigrant agenc[ies]. And there I met I should say a[n] immigrant counsellor there. And she is a Chinese, she can of course speak English well. She came from Guangdong but she was not born there. She was born in another city of China so she can speak Mandarin, Cantonese and English, all three languages well. And I was kind of impressed by her. I just visit[ed] her once, I never met her again. But I still have an impression, a very strong impression about her. So I'm just thinking maybe it's a good choice. I can learn, take some education and later become something like her.

Note here that while B2 realised that she needed to gain new credentials through further training, thereby orienting herself, intentionally or otherwise, to the lifelong learning discursive frame, the decision of what type of training in which she should engage was not straightforward. To decide, she needed to and indeed did take into account sectors where she was most likely to be employed (i.e. the structure of the labour market), personal preferences and strengths, as well as family circumstances. In excerpts from the interview quoted above, we see how she reshaped her personal preferences in relation to where she thought she would have a better chance in getting a job. Her exploration and decision were informed by the discourse around 'jobs for the Chinese', which in turn is shaped by gender, race and class as interwoven social relations in Canadian society (see Ng 1993, 1998). She decided that it was not realistic to try to gain entry into marketing, which was dominated by white people. The sectors where other Chinese immigrants were employed became the scope of her exploration (Shan 2009b). Inspired by a Chinese Canadian employment counsellor, she felt she should focus on the settlement services sector, which employs a good percentage of women and racialised minorities (Lee, 1999)—a decision that departed from her work experience in China.

Similarly, A2 was informed by the discourse of jobs most suited for the Chinese or minority women. While B2 was successful in locating a job in her new field, A2 was not. A2 was an engineer in China. She learned from the internet that engineering is a regulated profession and decided to drop engineering altogether. She also learned from the internet that, due to the perceived language deficiency of Chinese immigrants, the women had a better chance with accounting and men had a better chance with computer science. On this basis, she enrolled in an accounting program shortly after landing. Unfortunately, two years later, she could only find a part-time job as a bakery clerk in a grocery store.

Age and gendered familial relations

The employment trajectories of professional Chinese immigrant women are also circumscribed by age and familial relations, including the financial circumstance of the household. This is illustrated by A1's immigration experience. At the time of immigration, this woman, who was in her fifties at the time of the interview, was the head of a department in a leading hospital in Beijing. She came to be with her husband, who was undertaking graduate study. She felt it was her duty as a wife to accompany her husband, and felt regret in leaving her high-powered position as a medical doctor. Unfortunately, she was unable to find work commensurate with her qualifications and experience in Canada, and worked for a number of years in a small business repackaging artifacts imported from China. When it came time for her to follow her husband back to China, she realised that she had gained nothing and had lost much from her stay in Canada. To make up for lost time, she decided to stop working and study English in a college as a full-time student. She felt that if she had learned English earlier, when she first immigrated, she might be able to practise medicine in Canada. Here is what she said:

> It is undeniable that I am very good in my field of practice.... I wanted to practise my profession. However, it was impossible.... My language is a huge barrier.... I think in order to integrate...you have to get the language barrier cleared.... After I [joined the English program], probably as I was improving my English, I got to know more about the society. I think when I first came I should have started schooling. At that time, I was still young, still energetic. I may have entered my field of practice very quickly. I may feel better now.

In this case, gendered familial ideology and age were amongst the dynamics shaping A1's job opportunities and her decision to study.

Although B3's experience was very different from that of A1, we found similar dynamics at play. A translator in China, B3 worked in telemarketing in Canada. At the time of the interview, she was considering going back to school. She said:

> My husband got a job. He is a programmer but he worked in that job for six months. That's a contract job. And then I [am] just sort of weighing you know if he got a permanent offer and maybe I don't have that much pressure, I can study. And now he's permanent so I'm thinking maybe it's good time for me to study. I'm thinking about [a program of] less than two years. If there is like accelerated program like one year or something 'cause I like studying but just—at my age it's not my first priority. I always think I can work first and if I can do some on-the-job learning. And I believe I do that very fast. So maybe [when] I have a job, I [can] use my spare time to take some courses.

Again, while most of the women in our studies firmly believed in the necessity and utility of lifelong learning, age, time and money entered into women's decisions and choices of training. The age discourse is evident in both of studies. Younger immigrants in the 1930s were more likely to invest in longer-term training and education, whereas the older women opted for short-term training plans.

Financial consideration played a prominent role in women's decisions regarding the type and duration of training they would engage in. This goes beyond money and is closely tied to gender relations within the family. While gender dynamic varied from family to family, and some of the women felt totally equal to their husbands in the family unit, the finances in most immigrant households could only support one member participating in training courses or in formal education at any one time. The decision as to who should engage in training or education was thus a household, rather than individual, decision. In the case of A1, she had to work to sustain the household when her husband was undergoing full-time graduate training. When she was working, she could only attend free English training classes provided by the government, which were not helpful to her career. It was not until her husband found a stable job in China that she could finally begin to study English full time. In the case of A7, a paediatrician who worked as a lab technician in Canada, she and her husband, also a medical doctor, decided to put their resources toward his recertification first. Although she wanted to practise medicine in Canada eventually, she decided to put her plan on hold. Meanwhile, she also took the bulk of the responsibility for housework and childcare to enable her husband to study for his exams. Thus, gender ideology, age and financial relations within the family all intersect with the ideology of lifelong learning, shaping the decision-making processes of professional immigrants as they orient themselves toward a labour market organised along gender, ethnic and racial lines.

Conclusion

To reiterate, critics of lifelong learning as state policy suggest that this discourse has become a new technology of governance serving to redefine the relationship between the state and the individual. The onus in neo-liberal globalisation is to require individuals to take responsibility to keep up with economic and social change. The power of lifelong learning as an ideological and discursive frame, we argue, is precisely its ability to render continual (re)education as an individualistic, natural and neutral phenomenon. This frame shifts attention away from the structure and nature of a post-Fordist and post-industrial economy (in the current era of globalisation), which is characterised by a progressively flexible, non-permanent and disposable work force (Vosko 2000, Panitch and Leys 2000).

By focusing on the experiences of workers themselves, in this case professional Chinese immigrant women in Canada, we show how individuals take up this discursive frame in fitting themselves into a segmented labour market. We further display how this frame intersects with other ideological and material practices to organise, reproduce and maintain gender and racial inequalities both in the labour market and in the society. In Canada, these processes are superimposed on a colonial legacy that downgrades education, training and credentials from non-Western societies, thereby re-inscribing and exacerbating existing inequalities based on age, gender and race. We draw attention to the fact that once in place, ideological practices are no longer simply imposed from above. As we show in the stories of 21 professional women, people participate actively in the perpetuation of these inequalities in order to find employment and support the household. Meanwhile, the active pursuit of learning opportunities by the women in our studies indicates precisely their resilience in a society that systematically devalues their social and economic worth.

Our discussion has obvious implications for state policies. First and foremost, in agreement with the demands of advocacy groups such as the Ontario Network for Access to Professions and Trade and the Policy Roundtable Mobilizing Professions and Trades (PROMPT), we argue that the proper evaluation, acknowledgement and recognition of foreign credentials and work experience will go a long way in addressing existing inequalities in education and employment relations. This requires state initiative and negotiations between/among state departments, professional bodies and employers. More seriously, efforts are needed to interrogate and rectify the structure of the labour market, which is not sustainable as evidenced by the financial melt-down and massive global economic collapse unfolding in front of our eyes since the latter part of 2008. Ultimately, the logical extension of our discussion for intellectuals and policymakers requires an examination of how to reframe the notion of lifelong learning for the collective good, rather than narrowly for jobs and profit.

Acknowledgements

We gratefully acknowledge the anonymous reviewers' helpful comments, Willa Lichun Liu's and Tara La Rose's research assistance, and Dr. Shibao Guo's encouragement in bringing this paper to fruition.

Notes

1. This study, entitled *Learning to be good citizens: Informal learning and the labour market experiences of professional Chinese immigrant women*, was funded by the Toronto Metropolis Centre of Excellence for Research on Immigration and Settlement (CERIS) between 2005 and 2006. The research team included R. Ng (principal researcher), G. Man (co-researcher), two doctoral candidates as research assistants (H. Shan and W. Liu) and a community researcher (L. Peng) with a community partner, the Chinese Canadian National Council Toronto Chapter.
2. The second study, entitled *Professional immigrant women navigating the Canadian labour market: A study in adult learning*, is funded by SSHRC (#410-2006-1437) from 2006 to 2010. Team members are R. Ng (principal researcher), T. Das Gupta, G. Man, K. Mirchandani (co-researchers) and a team of doctoral students as research assistants. This paper only focuses on the experience of the Chinese women.
3. By law, professionals in regulated professions have to be certified by the regulatory bodies in their respective professions in order to practise and/or use their professional designations.

References

AILWOOD, J. (2008) Learning or earning in the 'smart state' changing tactics for governing early childhood. *Childhood*, **15**(4), 535–551.
ALLMAN, P. (2000) *Revolutionary Social Transformation: Democratic Hopes, Political Possibilities and Critical Education* (London: Bergin & Garvey).
AMIN, A. (ed) (1994) *Post-Fordism* (London: Blackwell).
BAKER, M., and BENJAMIN, D. (1994) The performance of immigrants in the Canadian labour market. *Journal of Labor Economics*, **12,** 369–405.
BASRAN, G.S., and ZONG, L. (1998) Devaluation of foreign credentials as perceived by visible minority professional immigrants. *Canadian Ethnic Studies*, **30**(3), 7–23.

BOSHIER, R. (2001) Lifelong learning as bungy jumping: In New Zealand what goes down doesn't always come up. *International Journal of Lifelong Education*, **20**(5), 361–377.
BUTLER, E. (2001) The power of discourse. Work-related learning in the 'learning age. In CERVERO, R.M., WILSON, A.L., and associates (eds.), *Power in Practice. Adult Education and the struggle for Knowledge and Power in Society* (San Francisco & Oxford: Jossey-Bass), pp. 60–82.
CRUIKSHANK, J. (2001) Lifelong learning in the new economy: A great leap backwards. *Canadian Journal of University Contributing Education*, **27**(2), 61–78.
CRUIKSHANK, J. (2002) Lifelong learning or re-training for life: Scapegoating the worker. *Studies in the Education of Adults*, **34**(2), 54–59.
EDWARDS, R. (2002) Mobilizing lifelong learning: Governmetality in educational practices. *Journal of Education Policy*, **17**(3), 353–365.
EDWARDS, R. (2003) Ordering subjects: Actor-networks and intellectual technologies in lifelong learning. *Studies in the Education of Adults*, **35**(1), 55–67.
FEJES, A. (2005) New wine in old skins: Changing patterns in the governing of the adult learner in Sweden. *International Journal of Lifelong Education*, **24**(1), 71–86.
FOLEY, G. (1999) *Learning in Social Action: A contribution to understanding informal education* (New York: Zed).
FRENETTE, M. and MORRISETTE, R. (2003) Will they ever converge? Earnings of immigrant and Canadian born workers over the last two decades. *Analytical Studies Research Paper Series*. No. 215, Ottawa, Statistics Canada.
GOUTHRO, P. (2002) Education for sale: at what cost? Lifelong learning and the market place. *International Journal of Lifelong Education*, **21**(4), 334–346.
GOUTHRO, P.A. (2007) Active and inclusive citizenship for women: Democratic considerations for fostering lifelong education. *International Journal of Lifelong Education*. **26**(2), 143–154.
GRACE, A. (2002) Lifelong learning: International perspectives on policy and practice. In S. MOJAB and W. MCQUEEN (eds), *Adult Education and the Contested Terrain of Public Policy* (Toronto: the Canadian Association for the Study of Adult Education), pp. 128–133.
GRAMSCI, A. (1971) *Selections from the Prison Notebooks of Antonio Gramsci* (New York: International Publishers).
GUO, S. and ANDERSON, P. (2006) The politics of difference: Non/recognition of foreign credentials and prior work experience for immigrant professionals and Canada and Sweden. In P. ANDERSON, and J. HARRIS, (eds.) *Re-theorising the Recognition of Prior Learning* (Leiscester, UK: NIACE), pp. 183–203.
HAKE, B. (1999) Lifelong learning in late modernity: The challenges to society, organizations and individuals. *Adult Education Quarterly*, **49**(2), 79–90.
HUMAN RESOURCES DEVELOPMENT CANADA [HRDC] (2002) *Knowledge Matters: Skills and learning for Canadians* (Quebec: Hull).
IREDALE, R. (2001) The migration of professionals: Theories and typologies. *International Migration*, **39**(5), 7–26.
JOBSTART AND SKILLS FOR CHANGE (2001) *Access for Foreign-trained IT Professionals: An Exploration of Systemic Barriers to Employment* (online) www.skillsforchange.org (accessed 22 February, 2005).
LEE, J. (1999) Immigrant women workers in the immigrant settlement sector. *Canadian Woman Studies*, **19**(3), 97–103.
LEWKOWICZ, P. (2008) Institutional innovation for better skilled immigrant labour market integration: A study of the Toronto region immigrant employment council (TRIEC). Master's thesis. Kingston: Queen's University.
LIVINGSTONE, D.W. (1999a) Lifelong learning and underemployment in the knowledge society: A North American perspective. *Comparative Education*, **35**(2), 163–187.
LIVINGSTONE, D.W. (1999b), *The Education–Jobs Gap: Underemployment or Economic Democracy* (Toronto, ON: Garamond Press).
LOWE, G. (2000) The quality of work: why it matters for workers and employers (online) www.cprn.com (accessed 4 February 2009).
MAN, G. (2004) Gender, work and migration: Deskilling Chinese immigrant women in Canada. *Women=s Studies International Forum*, **27**(2), 135–148.
MARX, K. and ENGELS, F. (1970) *The Germain Ideology. Part I* (New York: International Publishers).
MIRCHANDANI, K., NG, R., COLOMO-MOYA, N., MAITRA, S., RAWLINGS, T., SHAN, H., SIDDIQUI, K., and SLADE, B., (2008) The paradox of training and learning in a culture of contingency. In LIVINGSTONE, D.W., MIRCHANDANI, K., and SAWCHUK, P.H. (eds.) *The Future of Lifelong Learning and Work* (Rotterdam: Sense Publishers), pp. 171–184.
MOJAB, S., and GORMAN, R. (2001) The struggle over lifelong learning: A Marxist-feminist analysis. Proceedings of the Adult Education Research Conference (Michigan State University in East Lansing, Michigan, 1 June).
MOORE, E.G. and PACEY, M.A. (2003) Changing income inequality and immigration in Canada, 1980–1995. *Canadian Public Policy*, **29**(1), 33–52.
NG, R. (1993) Racism, sexism, and nation building in Canada. In C. MCCARTHY and W. CRICHLOW (eds.) *Race, Identity and Representation in Education* (New York: Routledge), pp. 50–59.

NG, R. (1995) Multiculturalism as ideology: A textual analysis. In M.L. CAMPBELL, and A. MANICOM (eds.) *Knowledge, Experience, and Ruling Relations: Studies in the social organization of knowledge* (Toronto: University of Toronto Press), pp. 35–48.

NG., R. (1998) Work restructuring and recolonizing third world women: An example from the garment industry. *Canadian Woman Studies*, 18(1), 21–25.

NG, R. (2000) Restructuring gender, race and class relations: The case of garment workers and labour adjustment. In S. NEYSMITH (ed.) *Restructuring Caring: Labour, discourse, state practice, and everyday life* (Toronto: Oxford University Press), pp. 226–245.

NG, R., MAN, G., SHAN, H., and LIU, L. (2006) *Learning to be Good Citizens: Informal learning and the labour market experiences of professional Chinese immigrant women*. Final report for the Centre of Excellence on Research on Immigration and Settlement. Available online at: http://ceris.metropolis.net/Virtual%20 Library/RFPReports/Ng2005.pdf (accessed 12 January 2008).

OLSSEN, M. (2006) Understanding the mechanisms of neoliberal control: Lifelong learning, flexibility and knowledge capitalism. *International Journal of Lifelong Education*, 25(3), 213–230.

ONTARIO MINISTRY OF CITIZENSHIP AND IMMIGRATION (2007a) *About Ontario's Bridge Training Programs*. Available online at: http://www.citizenship.gov.on.ca/english/working/experience/ (accessed 1 January 2009).

ONTARIO MINISTRY OF CITIZENSHIP AND IMMIGRATION (2007b) *McGuinty Government Announces $29 Million Investment to Expand Programs Province-wide for Skilled Newcomers*. Available online at: http://www.citizenship.gov.on.ca/english/news/2007/n20070201.shtml (accessed 26 February 2010).

PANITCH, L. and LEYS, C. (eds.) (2000) *Working Classes, Global Realities—Socialist Register 2001* (London: The Merlin Press).

REIMERS-HILD, C., KING, J.W., FOSTER, J.E., FRITZ, S.M., WALLER, S.S., and WHEELER, D.W. (2005) A framework for the entrepreneurial learner of the 21st century. *Online Journal of Distance Learning Administration*, 8(2). Available online at: http://www.westga.edu/~distance/ojdla/summer82/hild 82.htm (accessed 15 January 2009).

REITZ, J.G. (2003) Immigration and Canadian nation-building in the transition to a knowledge economy. In W.A. CORNELIUS, P.L. MARTIN, J.F. HOLLIFIELD, and T. TSUDA (eds.) *Controlling Immigration: A global perspective*, 2nd Edition (Stanford CA: Stanford University Press), pp. 79–133.

SHAN, H. (2009a) Shaping the re-training and re-education experiences of immigrant women: The credential and certificate regime in Canada. *International Journal of Lifelong Education*, 28(3), 353–369.

SHAN, H. (2009b) Practices on the periphery: Chinese immigrant women negotiating occupational niches in Canada. *Canadian Journal for the Study of Adult Education*, 21(2).

SMITH, D.E. (1987) *The Everyday World as Problematic: A Feminist Sociology* (Toronto: University of Toronto Press).

SMITH, D.E. (1990) The ideological practice of sociology. In D.E. SMITH (ed.) *The Conceptual Practices of Power: A feminist sociology of knowledge* (Toronto: Toronto University of Toronto Press), pp. 31–57.

SMITH, D.E. (1999) The standard North American family SNAF as an ideological code. In D.E. SMITH (ed.) *Writing the Social: Critique, Theory, and Investigations* (Toronto: University of Toronto Press), pp. 157–171.

SMITH, D.E. (2005) *Institutional Ethnography: A sociology for people* (Lanham & New York: Altamira Press).

STEPHEN, J. (2000) *Access Diminished: A report on women's training and employment services in Ontario* (Toronto, Ontario: ACTEW).

TORONTO TRAINING BOARD (2009) *TOP (Trends, Opportunities, Priorities) Report, January 2009* (Toronto, Ontario: Author).

TUSCHLING, A. and ENGEMANN, C. (2006) From education to lifelong learning: the emerging regime of learning in the European Union. *Education Philosophy and Theory*, 38(4), 451–469.

UNESCO (1997) *Hamburg Declaration for Action: The Agenda for the Future*. Available online at: http://www.unesco.org /education/uie/confintea/pdf/con5eng.pdf (accessed 2 January 2009).

UNESCO (2000) *The Dakar Framework for Action, Education for all: Meeting our Collective Commitments*. Available online at: http://unesdoc.unesco.org/images/0012/001211/121147e.pdf (accessed 2 January 2009).

VOSKO, L. (2000) *Temporary Work: The gendered rise of precarious employment relationship* (Toronto: University of Toronto Press).

WANG, S. and LO, L. (2005) Chinese immigrants in Canada: their changing composition and economic performance. *International Migration*, 43(3), 35–71.

Moving across borders: immigrant women's encounters with globalization, the knowledge economy and lifelong learning

TARA GIBB[a] and EVELYN HAMDON[b]
[a]University of British Columbia, Canada; [b]University of Alberta, Canada

The (un)reality of open/porous borders is starkly represented/manifested in the experiences of immigrant women in lifelong learning contexts. While globalization effectively destroys some borders, it simultaneously creates new ones. State institutions respond to global reconfigurations of borders at local levels by establishing policies that exclude women from working in their fields unless they participate in re-education programs. At the same time the global competition among states within the discourses of the knowledge economy for attracting 'the best and the brightest' entice women to leave (or the effects of Western imperialism force them to flee) their homes with the promise of economic wellbeing or physical safety. Within this environment, lifelong learning can (dangerously) serve to privilege some forms of learning, knowledge and citizenship while devaluing others. This paper draws on research conducted between 2004 and 2006 in two immigrant service organizations. We explore possibilities for developing policies and practices that redress symbolic and cultural injustices with respect to immigrant women in Canada.

Globalization is a complex and widely contested term because of the multiple meanings attached to it (Robertson 2006). Current globalization discourses suggest that people and knowledge are able to flow freely between and among nation states (Forstorp 2008). However, while there is some agreement that globalization effectively erodes some forms of bordering, as Brodie (2004) and Mojab (2006) point out, globalization also creates new types of borders and exacerbates old ones. For example, globalization has contributed to an increase in economic competitiveness resulting in the privileging of some skills and credentials.

In an extensive review of the literature on globalization, global citizenship and education, Shultz and Jorgenson (2008) note that those whose credentials and professional experience are obtained in the West are able to move more freely across borders, compared to those who are educated and trained in what is considered to be the global South and East. This form of differentiating creates a divide that we consider in this paper to constitute a form of bordering. While some forms of (credentialed) knowledge enable the initial crossing of national borders, after migration migrants encounter new borders that require the holder of less 'valuable' education and training to redress their 'deficiencies' through particular prescribed forms of (re)training and (re)accreditation in order to (re)gain employment in their field. In this context, education and re-education has become commodified as a means through which immigrants pay to gain access to desirable professional and skilled labour jobs.

Within this context, lifelong learning is being constituted as one means of facilitating the global movement of people, knowledge and skills through very particular types of re-training programs. According to Crowther (2004: 127), 'the poverty of the dominant discourse of lifelong learning is not primarily its narrow vocationalism but its hidden agenda of creating malleable, disconnected, transient, disciplined workers and citizens'. Crowther (2004: 130) traces the shift in emphasis from lifelong education to lifelong learning and suggests that the shift is meant to buttress the neo-liberal form of globalization by shifting the responsibility for learning to individuals, undermining welfare, disguising the reduction of the democratic public sphere and working on people as objects of policy to ensure their compliance with the brave new world of flexible capitalism. This examination of 'flexibility' surfaces a complex set of educational and employment (credentialing) structures, which, although ostensibly extra-national, privilege those from within existing and privileged national and classist structures.

In Canada, immigrant service organizations (ISOs) participate in systems of lifelong learning by assisting newcomers in navigating the national employment terrain that requires them to retrain for their professions. Administrators of ISOs, and the women who access their services, are knowledgeable about the problematic intersection of employment and immigration policies, yet their dependence on state funding often places them in a position of maintaining the status quo in which they become subject to state control (Ng 1996). Despite this, until recently, ISOs not only provided settlement services for new immigrants, but administrators and staff also acted as advocates for individual women and for the collective rights of immigrant women in Canada (Fenwick et al. 2006). Recent changes to federal funding structures, however, restrict the amount of advocacy work not-for-profit organizations can engage in without losing their funding further, subjecting them to compliance in maintaining inequitable relations.

Given this state of affairs, this article revisits data from a previous study to consider Nancy Fraser's (1995, 2001) work on the redistribution of recognition in order to understand how ISOs, immigrant women and their allies might continue to build alliances for advocacy. Fraser's work is useful due to its focus on reclaiming identity issues from the realm of identity politics, with its focus on individual remediation and individual acts of morality and recasting issues of sexism, racism, and sexuality as forms of symbolic or cultural injustice that require redress through a redistribution of recognition. By using Fraser, we are able to shift the analysis of this issue from the bodies of immigrant women to the political and economic structures and discourses (including educational discourses).

The struggles administrators of the ISOs and their clients face as they comply with and resist current approaches to educational programmes for women are examined. We proceed with this exploration by providing background information about the initial study and the methods employed therein. Following is a discussion of the global knowledge economy, migration and lifelong learning to situate the experiences the women encounter as immigrants, learners, and knowledge workers. Next, consideration is given to Fraser's ideas in relation to the women's stories. We engage Fraser's ideas to politicize the issue of credentialing and re-credentialing and to draw attention to the politics of 'serving immigrants'. Finally, we suggest ways that ISOs might begin to expand their analysis of the problems their clients face from one of individual remediation and solitary struggles for program funding to programs of political education to highlight structural injustices, including symbolic injustice.

Background and method

History of the organizations

Immigrant service organizations (ISOs) are vital for their work in facilitating transitions to Canadian life for new immigrants. They often serve as a bridge by providing orientation to social and cultural information, formal programs for language education and employment preparation, as well as facilitating access to other social services such as health care (Guo 2006a). This is certainly true of the ISOs within which the larger study took place (and from which the data for this article are taken). For the purposes of this article, we revisited the data from two ISOs whose mandates have a particular focus on serving immigrant women. Both were established in the early 1980s as a result of research conducted by the local university that concluded that settlement support for immigrant women in the local area was lacking. From that research, these two not-for-profit agencies were established for the express purpose of assisting immigrant women with settlement and family life-related concerns. At present, their services include computer classes, employment counselling, language education, and workshops on women's legal rights within Canada. Based upon their self-identification as feminist organizations, both agencies viewed themselves as advocates for individual women and for the collective rights of immigrant women in Canada.

The original study

The original research questions guiding the study were: What are the formal and informal learning processes that occur in immigrant service organizations? And how might these learning processes be used to teach immigrant workers essential skills for employment?[1] To answer these questions, four graduate researchers and their faculty mentors spent a year in four immigrant service organizations (ISOs) in western Canada observing classes, social spaces, administrative meetings and formal functions. For each of the four sites, a case study was developed that enabled the researchers to focus on the complexity and particularity of a single case in order to understand an activity, its context, and its significance (Stake 1995). While the original research questions have been discussed by other members of the research team (Guo 2006a, 2006b) for this paper we revisited the data by asking how the staff and students understand the re-credentialing issue and how they respond both intellectually and practically to it. We present the women's voices within the context of theoretical frameworks that we find helpful in understanding how ISOs, immigrant women and their allies might continue to build structures of advocacy (such as those which the organizations in this study are endeavouring to do).

In the two sites from which data for this article have been drawn, we interviewed 21 women in total including staff, volunteers and immigrant students. Twelve were current or former clients or learners, five were staff members and two were members of the board (one from each ISO). Of course, their respective positions and relationships with the organizations are so much more complex. Some of the volunteers were former students, some of the staff had been both students and volunteers and of course all but one of those we interviewed are immigrant women. All interviews were audio-taped and fully transcribed. Those we interviewed were provided the transcriptions for validation, amendment and for their final approval to have their data included in the final study. Of those we interviewed, only one participant chose to withdraw her interview stating that she was not happy with the quality of her answers. In addition, we reviewed key organizational documents, such as mission and vision statements, websites, proceedings from conferences and symposia the organizations hosted, and program documents. We were also provided with many opportunities to participate in or observe formal learning sessions (e.g., computer classes and job readiness classes), to attend informal and social functions, to socialize with the learners, clients and staff in their lunch space, and to attend meetings and public events. We chose to keep our recording practices, in these contexts, very subtle, taking notes or recording recollections after the event.

Revisiting the data

The original analysis focused on developing an understanding of the informal educational issues that the women learners and administrators faced. Comparison of the two case studies through researcher journals and critically reflective dialogues among the researchers yielded the writing of two earlier articles (Fenwick *et al.* 2006, Gibb *et al.* 2008), guided by feminist postcolonial theories of multiple oppressions through situational analysis (Alexander and Mohanty 1997, Mohanty 2003). Nonetheless, we were still left pondering the ways in which the women in these organizations leverage their collective knowledge to navigate, critique and resist state institutions' responses to global knowledge economy discourses that filter into their daily practices and interactions as they assist their clients in gaining meaningful employment. Thus we revisit the original data, now guided by the work of Fraser, to consider the possibilities for ISOs for developing policies and practices that redress symbolic and cultural injustice. We accomplished this through a re-examination of the narratives of the women interviewed and re-coding the data for evidence of political analysis and critique of the re-credentialing process, including English language training. In particular we draw upon the reflections of the executive director of ISO#2, the individual experiences of women accessing services at the ISOs and our observation of a group of women taking a class together, as they endeavour to make sense of apparently nonsensical policy, credentialing and language requirements mandated by the state and by their respective professional organizations.

Migrating in the new economy

The knowledge economy is a key aspect of globalization, and in developed countries it has been constituted as an essential theoretical ingredient for developing policy in order to secure the economic and social well being of the post-industrial nation state (Forstorp 2008, Organisation for Economic Development and Cooperation [OECD] 1996). Under the rhetoric of the knowledge economy, nations that can efficiently produce and disseminate knowledge widely will benefit the most economically, most notably those countries in the West (Forstorp 2008). Increasingly, however, regions beyond Western Europe and North America are also being subjected to 'the Western hegemony of knowledge and meanings of "knowledge economy"' (Farrell and Fenwick 2007: 6). According to the logic of the knowledge economy, sustaining an economy where knowledge is the key resource requires a highly skilled labour force capable of adapting to rapid changes in information and communication technologies (ICT). Farrell (2006), however, explains that notions of what constitutes knowledge and skill are socially constructed by particular groups to reinforce occupational inclusion and exclusion. What is less well understood is the way gender stratification occurs in the knowledge economy (Kofman 2004). Kofman (2004) argues that women and men travel differently through national systems of immigration, particularly in an unevenly globalized economy. Systems of migration generate forms of stratification in countries of origin and destination, and most of the literature on gendered systems of stratification has been focused on the less skilled (Kofman 2004). Building on Kofman's survey of the literature, our analysis explores the experiences of professional women who migrate, paradoxically situated as they are as necessary knowledge workers whose credentialed knowledge often goes unrecognized.

In a similar vein to other OECD countries, aspects of knowledge economy discourses have influenced Canadian federal policy formation, particularly in the areas of employment, training and immigration. From 1967, immigration policy in Canada has been designed through the implementation of a point system to privilege potential immigrants based on levels of education in conjunction with other criteria such as proficiency in either the English or French language (Reitz 2001). The assumption of immigration policy is that Canada will require large amounts of highly skilled labour to compete in the global knowledge economy. In Canada, well-educated immigrants are seen as essential for securing the economic future of the country such that the Ministry of Human Resources and Skills Development Canada (2004) predicted that by 2011 immigrants will account for 70% of labour force growth. Yet, despite the high levels of education many immigrants to Canada possess, Reitz (2001) explains that their economic success has been declining steadily since the 1990s compared to that of Canadian-born citizens. Reitz's (2001) analysis indicates that within the knowledge economy, workers' knowledge is valued differently despite the alleged demand for a more highly skilled work force. In a review of the literature on skilled female migrants, Kofman (2004) concluded that perceptions of skill are often gendered, and knowledge is valued differently based on which sector of the economy women participate in. Official policy rarely acknowledges women's contributions to the labour market and when it is acknowledged, it is often framed as supplementary to household income (Kofman 2004).

Even though high levels of education are an advantage under the current immigration system, women are often subject to a cycle of re-education, re-training and re-credentialing. Continuous learning through formal and non-formal education is seen as paramount to participation in the knowledge economy. In competition with other immigrant-receiving nations, Canada attempts to attract the most highly skilled people from countries such as China and India, yet the job vacancies needing to be filled are in production and service sectors and do not require high levels of knowledge generation (Schugurensky 2007). Nonetheless, newcomers to Canada are expected to—and in large numbers do—participate in this continuous cycle of learning and skill upgrading. Schugurensky (2007) notes that the learning society as human capital for economic development is the prevalent theme in lifelong learning in North America. Newcomers are actively recruited by the federal government for their technical and professional knowledge in order to build Canada's knowledge economy, yet after arrival, their credentialed knowledge no longer carries the same value that it did prior to migration. Additional education is often deemed necessary for entry into one's profession.

In the global knowledge economy, recognition of knowledge is a significant issue (Farrell and Fenwick 2007). It is significant because it begs questions such as whose knowledge is recognized and whose knowledge is absent in the global economy (Robertson 2006). For the women interviewed in this study, their professional knowledge is represented through credentials such as diplomas and degrees. Initially, these symbolic representations of their knowledge provided them with entry into Canada. After they arrive, however, these same representations of knowledge are scrutinized under cultural systems of credential recognition that in many cases attempt to invalidate their knowledge, and therefore their access to employment in their professions.

Seeking a redistribution of recognition and justice

Administrators of ISOs, and the women who access their services, are knowledgeable about the problematic intersection of immigration and employment policies, yet their survival as organizations is dependent on their ability to subscribe to liberal policies. The tenuous nature of their existence often places them in a contradictory existence of activism and adaptation. Despite this incongruous state, ISOs have the potential to play a role in supporting immigrant women's critiques and resistance to the practices that invalidate their education and skill in the global knowledge economy. While the women we interviewed at both sites had high levels of education that assisted in their initial efforts to immigrate to Canada, after they arrived finding work in their professions proved difficult.

In site #1, five out of seven of the women we interviewed were unable to find work in their professions. Three of the women had given up hope of re-entering their professions (nursing, teaching and administration) and were biding their time taking computer classes and volunteering while they were trying to decide what direction they should take with their education and professional future. One of the women was working as a teacher's aide and taking courses to upgrade her credentials, even though she already possessed two advanced degrees in the field of education. Her hope was to re-qualify as an elementary school teacher in Canada. The fifth woman had obtained an administrative position in an immigrant settlement organization but was hoping to return to an academic position as a researcher or lecturer.

In site #2, two out of 13 women were able to return to their professions without retraining, nine had not returned to their field or had given up on doing so. Of these nine, three had abandoned their first professions and had or were contemplating entering the human service field (immigrant settlement) while the other six were still hopeful that with re-training and further education they would be able to, eventually, return to their first professions.

The reflections of Nadia, Xin and students in an employment readiness class at ISO #2 provide important entry points into the lived experience of immigrant women seeking recognition for their own, or their clients' education, skills and experience. Nadia's perspective is that of an ISO executive director whose role includes advocacy/political work and individual mentoring and support. Xin's story challenges the assumption that lifelong learning is a mediating force at the border and suggests that it constitutes another type of bordering and a form of symbolic or cultural injustice. This section concludes with the recollections of one of the researchers who observed a group of students over the course of eight hours as they used informal spaces within a structured learning environment to interrogate the intent and effects of their mandatory English language classes. While these stories are not new, the reading of them through the work of Fraser (1995, 2001) invites the reader to re-direct his or her gaze from the bodies of immigrants to the body of policies and practices (relating to globalization, immigration, settlement, lifelong learning and the knowledge economy) that create unjust societies in which people such as Nadia, Xin and others are struggling to survive.

Recognition and participatory parity

Nadia

Nadia was the executive director (at the time of the study) of ISO#2 and is a self-described immigrant woman. She came to Canada in the 1970s with a degree in journalism but found herself working as a data entry clerk in the federal civil service. Now, some 30 years later, she heads up an ISO run by and for immigrant women whose life trajectories, in many ways, parallel her own. For Nadia, her work at the ISO is both political and personal. She is a fierce advocate on issues relating to immigration, immigrant women's employment and funding for immigrant issues and organizations and is a mentor to many of the women who pass through the ISO's doors. She once declared that immigrant women need to learn to 'brag' about themselves; to be fearless in promoting their rights and their abilities.

Nadia recounted a story (and there were many other similar stories) about a woman whom she had placed as a volunteer in an organization. Eventually the position in which she was volunteering became a paid position. Nadia recalled the incident and the conversation she had with the supervisor:

> She [the volunteer] was working at that organization for more than four months full time, data entry. When the position came, they advertised the position, she applied, they turned her down. So she came here and she was very upset and I said to her, 'Give me the name of the supervisor.' So I phoned her,

> I said, 'I'm calling about the position you hired' [and the supervisor said] 'Yeah that position has been taken'. I said, 'I know but I forward it to one volunteer—how come she wasn't hired for the job?' 'Oh, she doesn't have Canadian experience.' I said, 'You mean, you mean that she was OK as a volunteer but she's not good as employee?' I said, 'You know what, from now on don't call us if you need volunteers, because our volunteers should be rewarded for their work.' Yeah that's [what] I said. I said to her, 'Didn't we say that volunteering gives work experience and that's why we're a volunteer program?' She said, 'Yeah but she's still missing some skills.' I said to her, 'I'm not going to argue about it but you can't depend on our volunteers any more. I said this is exploitation.'

Exploitation, according to Nadia, is the result of social and institutional structures that systematically exclude racialized Others, and in the particular case of her work, immigrant women from the global East and South. She works collectively, with other executive directors of other ISOs to:

> focus on strategies.... If we focus this commission on racism, access to services, to education and to employment...these are the big barriers facing immigrant and visible minority now. And the, darker the colour is, the more barrier[s] for the people it seems, and it's reality. You see people coming from Europe [and] suddenly you don't feel their accent. You don't see lack of the English or whatever.... When you have people coming let's say from Africa with skills and experience and so on, they're not hired as fast as white people. And it's reality. Always I say, I say even if you're going to take long to improve your English, it pays because you can transfer your skills to Canadian society. But if you are not given the chance to, for the job you'll be wasting your money on English if you're not going to be hired.

Nadia's analysis of current government programs intended to address immigrant employment issues hints at what Fraser describes as 'the claimants' attempts to 'show that current arrangements prevent them from participating on par with others in social life' (2001: 32). In Nadia's estimation, governments, in spite of information forwarded to them by ISOs, continue to spend money on programs that do not work. In her words this spending:

> looks good as report card for government saying. [They are] funding this program but it's not helping visible and immigrant minority women. We need transitional programs where we can benefit from what we are learning and will move us to jobs.

In many respects, Nadia understands issues of immigrant unemployment and underemployment as the absence of recognitional justice, and although she is forced by government funding priorities and restrictions to limit the formal operations of her ISO to the delivery of essential skills-type programming, she nonetheless devotes a significant amount of energy and analysis to interrogating social systems and state policies that in fact perpetuate symbolic injustice. The themes of recognition, absence and the appropriation of knowledge continue with Xin's story.

Symbolic injustice

Xin

Xin is a professionally trained engineer from China. In fact, she has two advanced degrees in engineering. She is qualified to work as both a mechanical engineer and as a computational engineer. She came to Canada with her daughter while her husband remains in China because in his field (human resource management, in which he has a PhD) his lack of English would be even more of a handicap. Their hope was that Xin would get work in her profession that would allow her husband to come and begin the process of learning English and retraining for his field of work.

Xin's story communicates her sense of alienation of her knowledge, acquired through long years of study and work in her profession. In the context of her adopted home, Canada, her university education is extracted for assessment purposes, accorded a value and in the process she is robbed of her professional identity and left wondering if she should give up her professional identity and surrender her claim to the expert knowledge she has worked to obtain. In Fraser's (1995) words, Xin has experienced 'nonrecognition' (71) through the systematic and systemic renunciation of her qualifications because they are Chinese.

In many ways Xin's story reflects that of other so-called foreign-trained engineers and doctors and is one that is well documented in the literature (Mojab 1999, Reitz 2001). She begins by describing her educational background, and it is clear that she is both passionate about her field and proud of her academic accomplishments:

> Yes, yes I study many years. And almost seven years in mechanical engineering. Yes, yes. And I have another, another degree in computational engineering. Mechanical engineering and the computational engineering but according to this, this guy's introduction [in a seminar she attended to help foreign trained engineers learn how to re-enter their profession], to be a registered engineer in [Province] must be very difficult for the foreigner [living in Province]. Because if we don't have a degree [from] Canada, US or France from those country then you have to pass sixteen exams. Yes. Yes. Sixteen exams. Otherwise you have to go back to university or U of [Province]. You have to get a Master's....[I] have two Master [s degrees in engineering].

She continues by explaining the options available to her and her uncertainty about the future:

> [Or] you have to pass so many exams, that you can't prepare. And the, the guy said if you fail in one time then for next time....taking the exam it's very hard because you have a bad record. So if he's suggesting is if you are not prepared very well for this exam, no, don't take. Don't take it. So if I want to be a[n] engineer in Canada I have [to take these exams] so I have no choice. Or go back to university. I check the website of U of [Province]. I don't think they did some researches [that] are better than me. I don't know. Mmm I hate this. Too bad. And some people attending this introduction [on becoming an engineer in Canada with a degree obtained from a foreign university] all complain. No. Not, not his problem. Not say but [he] implied. (Xin laughs

here). I [have] one problem.... Of course English.... Maybe if I don't want to go back to, to university. I may changing my, my goal to be a technician. I find some training courses, city of [name] for example and to be a, a CNC or operator. CNC means computer and I forgot the name. I have some materials. Maybe I will take this course. But I don't want to pursue another degree. What can I do?

This symbolic or cultural injustice is accentuated by the borders being placed around what constitutes legitimate engineering knowledge and the confusion that appears evident in Xin's attempt to decipher where the borders lay:

For example in Germany if get a degree then you are automatic an engineer. If you get a degree engineer, yah, automatically.

QUESTION: Could you use your degree in Germany?
RESPONSE: Yes.
RESPONSE: But in Canada no. In United States you can use a, a German degree. I ask a professor in, in, in Germany before. He said in Germany the German degree is very valuable. But in US you can use our degree, yeah no problem but in Canada, no. Yeah and because French degree but German degree...French ...England, Australia, US, Canada...Oh South Africa. Even Hong Kong. Oh. Those country used to be a, a member of...British [empire].... Bad. (Laughs)...A German degree is valuable.

The borders placed around credentialed knowledge appear almost indecipherable to Xin (and others we spoke with at both ISOs). The rapid dissolution of borders and acceleration of the movement of people seem not to have resulted in plurality or multiplicity but rather a proliferation of monocultures. These monocultures leave the other as absent in most respects. While the immigrant body is here, many must begin the long process of letting go of, bracketing or grieving the denial of their knowledges, professional histories and hard-won skills.

As Xin discovered, engineering degrees do not translate easily from one place to another. And the logic of where and how they are accepted is baffling. Chinese degrees (so she has been told) are accepted in Germany and the United States, but not Canada. She laments that so many other foreign degrees are accepted in Canada, theorizing that some of that recognition resides in old colonial ties. But that is no salve for Xin, a woman with two graduate degrees who is forced to choose between getting a third degree (the subject matter of which she has already mastered) or work as a technician. As long as immigration practices continue to welcome bodies, but not their professional knowledge, and their labour not their credentials, people like Xin will continue to go unrecognized as professionals. However, it is important to note that Xin is aware of and has named the problem. She is not deficient, her knowledge is valuable (to herself and potentially to others in other countries): it is the system, according to Xin, that is deficient and she is going to resist being rendered 'unrecognized' for as long as she can.

Moving from incidental spaces of resistance to intentional resistance: women in an employment readiness class

One day we were observing an employment readiness program in ISO#2. During the first coffee break we noticed three women off to the side talking earnestly with one another. They appeared to be sharing their latest results in one of their English as a second language (ESL) classes. These ESL assessments often determine whether a learner will be able to access employment and professional re-training programs. The women appeared to be disappointed with their scores and used self-deprecating language, perhaps reflecting a sense of having internalized their own inadequacies and using English language proficiency as a benchmark for assessing their own capacity for success. They seemed to accept that the deficiency was with themselves and not the curriculum or testing methods, or indeed the standards set to determine proficiency.

At the lunch break the women continued their conversation and began to compare their teacher's instructional methods and the general structure of the course. During this conversation, there was some dissatisfaction expressed regarding the amount of time allotted for practising English, a lack of which limited their chances for success in the course. By the last coffee break, the women had identified the courses as being too expensive and were suggesting that the system is working against them, setting unnecessarily high standards that consequently led to insufficient marks, and their having to retake courses and therefore incurring extra costs. As professionally trained women (they all had at least one university degree) they felt the instruction was both inadequate to prepare them for working in their fields and in spite of the time and expense involved in taking the courses—they were no closer to practising in the professions for which they had been educated. This exchange among the women reflects Haque and Cray's (2006) critique that language education policies and programs in Canada position learners as submissive and provide instruction that enables obtaining no more than an entry-level occupation.

Perhaps, more than any interview or any other observation opportunity, this affected our understanding of immigrant women's struggles to resist becoming absences within the Canadian cultural and professional landscape. While state policies dictate that their brains and bodies must be retrained and re-educated, and while they do so in order to get jobs and reclaim and retain some of their former professional identities, they simultaneously, from the margins—where things are often much clearer—can see that these policies and practices are about protecting and patrolling the invisible borders of professional and credentialed knowledge. They see that the standards are not universal but rather particular; they see that evaluations are not based so much on 'science' as on politics. That this conversation is not happening in a more concerted way within ISOs is not a reflection on administration and staff, who are protecting their own survival, but is a reflection of globalized knowledge economy discourses intersecting with immigration policy. The conjunction paradoxically positions immigrant women as valuable knowledge workers prior to migration, but in need of remediation post-migration.

Recognitional justice and the new economy

According to Fraser (1995), 'the "struggle for recognition" is fast becoming the paradigmatic form of political conflict in the late twentieth century' and will require both redistributive and recognitional forms of justice (68). We argue that this remains true into the twenty-first century and we situate immigrants' struggles for all kinds of recognition, including the recognition of their credentials, skills and professional experience, to be an indicator of the ongoing nature of this struggle. Nancy Fraser's project to correct the dichotomization of redistribution and recognition has important implications for immigrant education, employment programs and the policies that shape them, and which in turn affect the lived experiences of immigrants themselves. By recasting recognition as an issue of justice, rather than morality, Fraser makes it possible to shift the focus of any correctives from the bodies of immigrants to the structures that determine what counts as knowledge. In other words, her argument facilitates the interrogation of the ideologies, systems and structures that regulate the conversion of symbolic knowledge (e.g. credentials) into a commodity and which, within the current structure, often results in the alienation of immigrants from their knowledge and prevents them from benefitting from it.

Historically economic and cultural wellbeing (distribution and recognition respectively) have been theoretically separate and, according to Fraser (2001), falsely dichotomized. She proposes that the struggle for recognition is a struggle for justice. Rethinking recognition helps point the way forward to address injustices associated with the subordination of particular identities (Fraser 1995), and, we would add, some forms of knowledge. In part, and what is of particular value here, is that she accomplishes this by reframing issues of recognition as a kind of symbolic injustice thus reconciling misrecognition with distributive injustice. While a full discussion of her argument is beyond the scope of this article, what is of crucial importance here is that her argument expands the context of injustice to include 'cultural or symbolic injustice.... rooted in social patterns of representation, interpretation and communication' (71). This implicates both statist policies such as those relating to essential skills for immigrant Canadians and the implementation of those policies through the funding of particular programs and training schemes. We understand Fraser's project to be about the redistribution of recognition—and that recognition in this framework relates to the overcoming of subordination for the purpose of achieving 'reciprocal recognition and status equality' (Fraser 2001: 24).

The non-recognition of immigrant women's (and men's) education and experience is illustrative, we claim, of one manifestation of the redistribution–recognition dilemma. Using Fraser's (1995, 2001) arguments for the redistribution of recognition we have identified four key elements (from her work) that would be necessary (but not necessarily sufficient) in order that retraining, re-credentialing and other lifelong and adult education programs constitute a redistributive justice rather than a perpetuation of current inequities.

The first element is that policies would reflect a critical recognition orientation rather than a liberal one. Policy documents and related text in the policy field ought to reflect the use of signs and symbols (written and visual text) that are non-essentializing (including language that might inculcate or communicate a sense that racialized others or cultural Others are better served through their separation from the main polity). So, for example, the category 'immigrant' would cease being used to denote a category of people that are presumed to bring with them to Canada a series of deficiencies, including educational or knowledge-based deficiencies.

Second, the policy would reflect a focus on social change rather than individual change. In terms of ISOs, federal funding policies would cease privileging programs aimed at redressing learning deficits and would allow for guaranteed base funding for organizations enabling them to resume an advocacy role. As Scott (2003) notes, current funding climates in fact serve to limit the advocacy role of grassroots organizations such as ISOs:

> When organizations must cobble together projects and partners to survive, being seen as an outspoken advocate on behalf of one's client group can be regarded as too risky, despite the justice of the cause. You do not want to have your name in the media when your next funding submission comes up for approval. Advocacy organizations have been effectively marginalized over the past 10 years. (5)

Third, culture (including Canadian culture) is redefined as fluid and emergent, so the protection of static norms would be devalued or absent. Within such a paradigm it is recognized that there is no fixed Canadian identity into which immigrants must assimilate; rather it is presumed that cultures (which includes bodies of knowledge) proliferate, influence one another and sometimes result in hybrid cultural expressions that are neither wholly of one culture or another. We found Susan Robertson's (2006) use of the terms *absences* and monoculture (drawing upon the work of Boaventura de Sousa Santos) useful for operationalizing this element. Absences are *present* when a monoculture exists. Monocultures privilege one form of knowledge, culture, productivity, time and difference (in a hierarchical or binary relationship with a subordinate form) over another or others. The privileging of monocultures entails creating absences such as the absence of knowledges, identities and notions of what counts as productivity. Therefore, policies and practices relating to immigrant workers and professionals cease to focus exclusively on eradicating the possibility of the multiple by making space for Canadian professionals to learn from so-called foreign trained professionals.

Finally, normatively policies would reflect the principles of the right over the good; that is, they would seek to include the promotion of recognition as a matter of justice and would identify the lack of it as injustice. This final element has particular salience for immigrants, knowledge and the invalidation of their knowledge at various borders. We propose that this element in particular (using Fraser's work) could make a significant contribution to critiques of prior learning assessment and the (non)recognition of credentials and post-secondary education acquired outside of Canada. The struggle for equality would not reside wholly in providing immigrant Canadians with access to remedial education and training, but would expand to challenge and change our notions of what constitutes valid knowledge, skills and education.

Conclusion

Even though it is questionable as to whether Canada's economy demonstrates the characteristics deemed necessary to be a participant in the global knowledge economy, the discourses of globalization and the knowledge economy have influenced immigration and lifelong learning policy (Schugurensky 2007). Therefore, despite the constructed and problematic aspects of the knowledge economy, the discourses do have material effects (Kenway *et al.* 2007). Through the narratives of women learning in ISOs, we have attempted to show that the symbolic representation of knowledge through credentials establishes a type of border. Globalization and knowledge economy discourses suggest that knowledge is able to flow freely across national borders. However, when the immigrant women we interviewed crossed the Canadian border they found, paradoxically, that their bodies as 'knowledge workers' were admitted while their credentialed and professional knowledge was invalidated. Their degrees and professional experiences, which are symbolic representations of their knowledge, have not been recognized, resulting in what Nancy Fraser calls 'recognitional injustice'.

Lifelong learning discourses, in combination with this symbolic injustice, have given rise to an educational industry in Canada that is focused on re-dressing the knowledge 'deficits' of professionally trained and university-educated immigrant women. For the most part, this has not resulted in justice or equity for the women who participated in this study, but rather has cost them time, their dignity and self-esteem and their professions. Justice is not solely about the redistribution of economic wealth but requires expanding to include other forms of redistribution, such as the redistribution of recognition. Acknowledging the existence of symbolic injustice offers a lens for considering the ways in which immigration and adult education policies devalue credentialed knowledge of immigrant women and limit establishing a system of participatory parity.

Administrators of ISOs, and the women who access their services, are knowledgeable about the problematic intersection of immigration and employment policies, yet their survival as organizations and as newly migrated Canadians is dependent on their ability to subscribe to liberal policies. The tenuous nature of their existence necessitates their acting both as activists and as implementers of problematic state policies. Despite this incongruous state, ISOs have the potential to play a role in supporting immigrant women's critiques and resistance to the practices that invalidate their education and skill in the global knowledge economy. To facilitate this shift from implementers to innovators will, in part, require the lifting of restrictive policies that currently limit their ability to address injustice. In addition, ISOs and their allies will require a theoretical framework that will allow for the development of policies whose primary focus is a just and equitable distribution of work through a similarly just recognition of knowledges. Fraser's focus on recognition opens up spaces of possibility for developing policies and practices that recognize the women as knowledgeable citizens and participants in the economy.

Acknowledgements

The study from which the data are drawn is entitled *The effectiveness of formal and informal processes of learning essential skills: A study of immigrant service organizations*, funded by the Social Sciences and Humanities Research Council of Canada (Campbell *et al.* 2006). The principal investigator was Dr Shibao Guo, University of Calgary. Co-investigators were Dr Katy Campbell, University of Alberta, Dr Tara Fenwick, University of Alberta, currently with the University of British Columbia, and Dr Yan Guo, University of Calgary. We wish to acknowledge their support.

Note

1. Understanding essential skills: essential skills are the skills needed for work, learning and life. They provide the foundation for learning all other skills and enable people to evolve with their jobs and

adapt to workplace change. Through extensive research, the Government of Canada and other national and international agencies have identified and validated nine essential skills. These skills are used in nearly every occupation and throughout daily life in different ways and at different levels of complexity. The nine essential skills identified by HRDC are: reading text, document use, numeracy, writing, oral communication, working with others, continuous learning, thinking skills and computer skills. See also HRSDC 2004.

References

ALEXANDER, M.J. and MOHANTY, C.T. (1997) *Feminist Genealogies, Colonial Legacies, Democratic Futures* (New York: Routledge).
BRODIE, J. (2004) Introduction: Globalization and citizenship beyond the national state. *Citizenship Studies* **8**, 323–332.
CAMPBELL, K., FENWICK, T., GIBB, T., GUO, S., GUO, Y., HAMDON, E. and JAMAL, Z. (2006) Formal and informal processes of learning essential skills: A study of immigrant service organizations. Proceedings of the Essential Skills Workshop: Looking back, moving forward (Montreal, QC: Université du Québec à Montréal), pp. 31–39.
CROWTHER, J. (2004) 'In and against' lifelong learning: Flexibility and the corrosion of character. *International Journal of Lifelong Education*, **23**, 125–136.
FARRELL, L. (2006) *Making Knowledge Common: Literacy & knowledge at work* (New York: Peter Lang).
FARRELL, L. and FENWICK, T. (2007) Introduction. In L. FARRELL and T. FENWICK (eds.) *World Yearbook of Education 2007: Educating the global workforce: knowledge, knowledge work and knowledge workers* (New York: Routledge), pp. 1–10.
FENWICK, T., CAMPBELL, K., GIBB, T., HAMDON, E. and JAMAL, Z. (2006) Tangled nets and gentle nettles: Negotiating research questions with immigrant service organisations. Proceedings of The Standing Conference on University Teaching and Research in the Education of Adults (SCUTREA) (Leeds: UK), pp. 105–111.
FORSTORP, P.-A. (2008) Who's colonizing who? The knowledge society thesis and the global challenges in higher education. *Studies in Philosophy and Education*, **27**, 227–236.
FRASER, N. (1995) From redistribution to recognition? Dilemmas of justice in a postsocialist age. *New Left Review*, **212**, 68–93.
FRASER. N. (2001) Recognition without ethics? *Theory, Culture & Society*, **18**, 21–42.
GIBB, T., HAMDON, E. and JAMAL, Z. (2008) Re/claiming agency: learning, liminality and immigrant service organizations. *Journal of Contemporary Issues in Education*, **3**, 4–16.
GUO, S. (2006a) Adult education for social change: The role of a grassroots organization in Canada. *Convergence*, **39**, 107–122.
GUO. S. (2006b) Mapping the iceberg of informal learning: Exploring the experience of Chinese volunteers in Vancouver. Proceedings of the 25th Canadian Association for the Study of Adult Education (CASAE) Conference (Toronto: CDN), pp. 108–113.
HAQUE, E. and CRAY, E. (2006) Putting them in their place: Language policies and newcomers to Canada. In N. AMIN and G.J.S. DEI (eds) *The Poetics of Anti-Racism* (Halifax: CDN: Fernwood), pp. 73–84.
KENWAY, J., BULLEN, E., FAHEY, J. and ROBB, S. (2006) *Haunting the Knowledge Economy* (New York: Routledge).
KOFMAN, E. (2004) Gendered global migrations: Diversity and stratification. *International Feminist Journal of Politics,* **6**, 643–665.
MINISTRY OF HUMAN RESOURCES AND SKILLS DEVELOPMENT CANADA (2004) *Meeting the Challenge: A guide to working with essential skills* (Gatinuau, CDN: Government of Canada HIP-007-03-04).
MOHANTY, C.T. (2003) *Feminism Without Borders: Decolonizing theory, practicing solidarity* (Durham: Duke University Press).
MOJAB, S. (1999) De-skilling immigrant women. *Canadian Women Studies*, **19**, 123–128.
MOJAB, S. (2006) Adult education without borders. In T. FENWICK, T. NESBIT, and B. SPENCER (eds.) *Contexts of Adult Education: Canadian perspectives* (Toronto, ON: Thompson Education), pp. 347–356.
NG, R. (1996) *The Politics of Community Services: Immigrant women, class and state* (Halifax, NS: Fernwood Publishing).
ORGANISATION FOR ECONOMIC CO-OPERATION AND DEVELOPKENT [OECD] (1996) *The Knowledge-Based Economy* (Paris: OECD).
REITZ, J.G. (2001) Immigrant success in the knowledge economy: Institutional change and the immigrant experience in Canada, 1970–1995. *Journal of Social Issues*, **57**, 579–613.
ROBERTSON, S.L. (2006) Absences and imaginings: The production of knowledge on globalisation and education (Bristol: Centre for Globalisation, Education and Societies). Available online at:http://www.bris.ac.uk/education/people/academicStaff/edslr/publications/02slr/(accessed 11 December 2008)

SCHUGURENSKY, D. (2007) The learning society in Canada and the US. In M. KUHN (ed.) *New Society Models for a New Millennium: The learning society in Europe and beyond* (New York: Peter Lang), pp. 295–334.
SCOTT, K. (2003) Funding Matters: The impact of Canada's new funding regime on nonprofit and voluntary organizations (Summary Report). Canadian Council on Social Development. Available online at: http://www.ccsd.ca/pubs/2003/fm/summary-fundingmatters.pdf (accessed 14 June 2009).
SHULTZ, L. and JORGENSON, S. (2007) Citizenship education in post-secondary institutions: A review of the literature. Available online at: http://www.uofaweb.ualberta.ca/uai_globaleducation/pdfs/GCE_lit_ review.pdf (accessed 18 January 2009).
STAKE, R.E. (1995) *The Art of Case Study Research* (Thousand Oaks, CA: Sage Publications).

Mobility of knowledge as a recognition challenge: experiences from Sweden

PER ANDERSSON and ANDREAS FEJES
Linköping University, Sweden

This article focuses on the tensions between mobility, knowledge and recognition, and what the impact of migration could be on lifelong education and society. This is discussed with the case of Sweden as the starting point. The main issue in Sweden concerning migration is the admission of refugees. Sweden has had a relatively open policy concerning refugees in recent decades, and a large number of refugees have also been granted residence permits. Thus, they have not come to Sweden due to a labour shortage, and the demand for their knowledge in the labour market has not been high. Their knowledge is not recognised in terms of employment in vocations where their prior learning could be utilised. This means that Sweden has faced challenges concerning questions of recognition and lifelong education. In this article, we take as our starting point the policy in this area, including policy texts and national initiatives as well as experiences from such initiatives, to discuss the role of lifelong education and recognition of prior learning in a situation where mobility concerns not only migration of people but also of knowledge. We discuss how this knowledge, which has been situated in another national context, can be recognised and included in further lifelong education, and what type of lifelong education or lifelong learning is needed in this situation.

Introduction

The age of transnational migration is characterised by mobility—a mobility that is sometimes voluntary but often more or less imposed upon people. This mobility of people also involves a mobility of knowledge. However, the mobility of knowledge is not unproblematic. If knowledge is understood as being situated in its context, mobility results in a huge challenge concerning the recognition of knowledge, or recognition of prior learning. This article focuses on the tensions between mobility, knowledge and recognition, which are possible consequences of migration, and what the impact of migration could be on lifelong education and society. We will discuss this with the case of Sweden as our starting point.

The main issue concerning migration in Sweden today is the admission of refugees, something that is the result of imposed mobility. Sweden has had a relatively open policy concerning refugees in recent decades, and a large number of refugees have also been granted residence permits. They have not come to Sweden due to a labour shortage, and the demand for their knowledge in the labour market has not been high. Consequently, their knowledge is not necessarily recognised in terms of employment in vocations where their prior learning could be utilised. We have seen how the threshold that faces knowledge originally situated in foreign contexts is higher in vocations/professions without a labour shortage. This means that Sweden has faced challenges concerning questions of recognition and lifelong education. In this article, we will outline the policy initiatives in this area as well as experiences from such initiatives so as to discuss the role of lifelong education and recognition of prior learning in a situation where mobility means not only migration of people but also migration of their situationally contextualised knowledge.

The present article is based on our prior research in the area of recognition of prior learning in Sweden. The aim is to provide an overview of how the problems of mobility, in terms of the recognition challenge, are enacted in this context. The article focuses on the following questions: How has immigration and immigrants' employment developed in Sweden? What policy concerning recognition of immigrants' prior learning has developed in Sweden? What central challenges have emerged in the practice of recognition of prior learning (RPL) for immigrants? The results and discussion concerning these three questions are based on data from and analyses of official statistics, policy documents and field studies (observations and interviews) in different practices of RPL respectively. We have been inspired by Lave and Wenger (1991) and Wenger's (1998) notions of community of practice and situated knowledge in our analysis, although we extend their notions by including more profoundly issues of power and power relations.

Recognition and mobility of knowledge

Our focus is on what is often called recognition of prior learning (RPL), accreditation of prior experiential learning (APEL), prior learning assessment and recognition (PLAR) or in Sweden and some other countries *validation* ('validering' in Swedish) (Andersson and Harris 2006). Policies and practices for recognising prior learning have developed in recent decades around the world. RPL initiatives are often related to mobility in one sense or another. It could be a matter of stimulating mobility in the labour market, particularly in times of structural changes and unemployment, or of widening access to higher education, or of meeting the recognition challenges related to migration, which is the focus of this article.

In RPL, it is not the prior learning *per se* of the candidates that different institutions give recognition for, but rather the results of their prior learning; that is, the formal and/or actual competence/knowledge which institutions assess in different ways, for example, through methods such as interviews, portfolios, formal tests and authentic assessments in workplaces.[1] As indicated above, recognition is mostly related to processes of transfer/mobility of knowledge—in place and/or time. People need to get recognition for what they have learnt before, often in another context, to be able to use their knowledge—in terms of its use value and/or its exchange value—in the new context. It could be a matter of mobility between countries, between workplaces, or from informal to formal learning contexts (from daily/working life to education). A recognition process could employ different methods and have different results. The results could be that the candidates gain admission to education or to working life, get credits/exemptions in study programs, and/or get formal/non-formal documentation of competence—e.g., certificates, CVs, etc. The demands on the assessment in RPL could be more or less strict—from equivalence to similarity compared to the demands on 'valid' knowledge in the 'new' context. That is, if equivalence is required, it is more difficult to give recognition to knowledge developed and situated in another context, while it is easier to give recognition when, instead, similarity is demanded, which means that more variation is accepted.

Mobility is a broad concept that is related to the mobility of people, ideas, knowledge etc. between different contexts and positions, within and between societies. The concept of social mobility includes horizontal as well as vertical transitions of individuals, social objects, values etc. between social positions (Sorokin 1959). Mobility is often discussed as something 'good'. The 'good' mobility of individuals includes voluntary horizontal and ascending vertical mobility. But there is also another side of the coin: mobility could be not only voluntary but also imposed, or in other cases restricted, and vertical mobility could be descending.

Our focus in this article is mainly on mobility in terms of migration, including imposed migration: the mobility of refugees. A central aspect of the recognition challenge is related to precisely this imposed mobility. When mobility is voluntary—horizontal or vertical—and related to a demand in working life, working class immigrants get recognition in terms of admission to working life and employment. But for refugees, there is no outspoken demand for their knowledge, and it is much more difficult for them to get this actual recognition in terms of employment. Further, our results also touch on the aspect of restricted mobility, which could be the case for immigrants in their new country if they do not get recognition for their prior learning and not are accepted in the labour market. Our understanding of mobility in this article is therefore related to the perspective on knowledge and learning as situated, which is presented in the next section.

Theoretical perspective

We want to problematise the recognition challenge related to mobility in terms of a situated perspective on knowledge. According to Lave and Wenger (1991), knowledge has a more or less situated character. If knowledge is situated in a context where it has been developed and used, and its value proven, it is not evident that this very knowledge retains its value and usefulness if it is transferred to a new context. To what extent could knowledge get recognition in a new context, and to what extent is it situated only in the 'old' context? The result could, in somewhat different mobility terms, be the experience of a descending vertical mobility. However, when persons are situated in the community, learning takes place in terms of participation in the community of practice and they move more and more towards the 'centre' of the practice—i.e. their participation will be seen as 'fuller', and they probably experience an 'ascending vertical' mobility. Such a perspective can be helpful when trying to understand some of the problems faced when trying to recognise immigrants' vocational knowledge.

In relation to such ideas, the concept of community of practice is raised by Wenger (1998). He defines three elements of a community of practice. Mutual engagement means the mutual understanding of what it means to belong to a certain community, what the norms and values of that community are and how one interacts. The second element, joint enterprise, means the ability to understand what the community stands for and a feeling of shared responsibility for it. The third element, shared repertoire, contains common resources that could be seen as symbols for the community (cf. Nyström 2009). A newcomer within such a practice gains legitimacy by participation, and she thus moves from the periphery to the centre.

However, such a perspective has been criticised for its lack of a notion of power relations (Contu and Willmott 2003, Köpsén 2008, Nyström 2009): for example, the relation between gender and learning (Tangaard 2006). Billett (2006) argues that 'these kinds of accounts fail to consider how power relations between the personal and social are experienced and enacted including the role of the subject as both an exerciser of power and being subject to it' (Billett 2006: 11). Contu and Willmott (2003) acknowledge that Lave and Wenger have a notion of power incorporated in their learning theory although it is an 'underdeveloped conception of the power-invested situatedness of learning' (Contu and Willmott 2003: 284). Unfortunately, they argue, most popularised versions of such a theory have not followed the route of analysing the power relations more specifically. There is a lack of analysis in which the focus is on what makes specific communities act/think in the way they do. Developing the ideas of Lave and Wenger (1991), they thus argue that one needs to take into account the wider conditions—historical, cultural and social—that make possible a certain way of acting/thinking, and they emphasise the need to incorporate concepts such as contradiction, ideology and conflict into analyses of situated learning.

Fuller et al. (2005) pursue a similar argument and call for more detailed analyses of how power operates within communities of practices as power shapes boundaries that can either limit or make possible participation. They especially point to the need to see newcomers' dispositions as part of shaping a community of practice. Contu and Willmott (2003), Fuller et al. (2005) and Billett (2006) suggest an analytical path where the focus should be on power and power relations and how these operate within communities of practice.

Drawing on the above, our interest is directed at analysing power relations that operate within practices of assessing immigrants' prior knowledge: practices that exclude, even if the ambition is to include. In a situation in which immigrants enter a new community of practice in terms of a country and a new vocational practice, both as newcomers in this specific culturally shaped practice and maybe as 'old timers' in terms of vocational competences within the area where they are being recognised through RPL, interesting questions arise such as: What knowledge counts and what does not count in the process of RPL? In what ways are the immigrants allowed to enter the new practice and what might the barriers against participation be? What are the conditions that make such distinctions possible and what role does ethnicity play in such a practice?

In the next section, we contextualise Sweden as an immigrant country and follow this with an introduction of Swedish RPL policy in general and in relation to immigrants specifically. Three central challenges in RPL practices are then problematised with a specific emphasis on issues of power. Finally, we discuss how immigrants' knowledge, which has been situated in another context (country), can get recognition and be included in further lifelong education, and what type of lifelong education or lifelong learning is needed in this situation.

Sweden as an immigrant country—a contextualisation[2]

How have immigration and immigrants' employment developed in Sweden? In this section, we will introduce Sweden as an immigrant country serving as a contextualisation in relation to which we can understand the policies developed concerning RPL and the challenges posed within such systems.

Sweden is a relatively small country with a population of 9.3 million people (Statistiska centralbyrån 2009a). Migration has played a major part in the economic development of Swedish society as well as in the transformation into what is now an ethno-culturally diverse nation. However, it is a relatively young immigrant country. Today, 14% of the Swedish population were born abroad, compared with 1% in 1940 and 7% in 1970 (Ekberg and Rooth 2000, Statistiska centralbyrån 2009a). The older migration history is characterised mainly by emigration. From the seventeenth century, with a peak in the late nineteenth and early twentieth centuries, the emigration patterns are similar to those of other Western European countries. During the 80-year period from 1851 to 1930, almost 1.2 million Swedes left for North America (Nationalencyklopedin 1991). The total Swedish population in 1930 was about six million, which means that this emigration was very high. Even if there were refugees who came to Sweden during the Second World War, the country remained, at least until the middle of the twentieth century, essentially a mono-cultural country.[3] Since the 1930s, there have been more immigrants than emigrants, but the number of immigrants in the 1930s and early 1940s was low. More extensive immigration started in the late 1940s and in the 1950s (Statistiska centralbyrån 2009b).

At that time, Sweden was a step ahead of many other European countries in terms of conditions for economic development. The Second World War did not have much impact on the country because it was not actively involved. The economy expanded significantly, but there was a lack of qualified labour. There was a discussion about a 'reserve of talent' or a 'reserve of ability' in the population (Härnquist 2003) and how this reserve could be educated and employed. Still, there was an immediate need for competent workers, and as a result of this need, many skilled working-class immigrants came to Sweden at the end of the 1940s and in the 1950s. In addition, a number of refugees came from Eastern European countries: for example, Hungarians fleeing the 1956 uprising. In the 1960s, there were still large numbers of working-class immigrants and refugees from Eastern Europe and Greece (Gustafsson, Hammarstedt and Zheng 2004). The difference in the 1960s was that the immigrants had lower qualifications, as they were needed for less qualified positions in industry (Bevelander 2000). After the 1960s, decreasing labour demand led to a more restrictive immigration policy, and the number of immigrants from outside the Nordic countries declined (Gustafsson, Hammarstedt and Zheng 2004).

Since the mid-1970s, migration to Sweden has shifted from labour immigration to immigration primarily consisting of asylum seekers and refugees. Refugees came mainly from Chile in the 1970s, the Middle East in the 1980s, and the former Yugoslavia and the Middle East in the 1990s (Gustafsson, Hammarstedt and Zheng 2004). These shifts in the origins of immigrants can be seen in the following figures: in 1970, more than 90% of those born abroad came from Europe, and 60% of these from the Nordic countries. By the end of the 1990s, 30% of immigrants were born in the Nordic countries, 35% in other European countries, and 35% in countries outside Europe (Ekberg and Rooth 2000).

The influx of refugees to Sweden in the mid-1980s and early 1990s coincided with the economic crisis in the 1980s. This crisis led to the restructuring of the Swedish economy from an industrial to a post-industrial economy. In this process, immigrants, both new and old, were hit hard. The majority of them were employed in industries, in jobs that required little or no competence, and a lot of these jobs and industries were relocated to developing countries in Eastern Europe and Asia. Consequently, the loss of industrial jobs together with the influx of refugees contributed to a marginalisation and exclusion of immigrants in Swedish society (Andersson and Osman 2008).

As discussed above, mobility of people also means mobility of knowledge or competence. But what competence do the migrants have, and how is it recognised in the new context? We will now see how the problem of recognition is indicated by employment rates, correspondence of employment to formal qualifications, influence of the origin of qualifications and levels of earnings. This is also related to some relevant findings from other contexts outside Sweden.

Employment rates

A comparison of employment rates among all Swedish immigrants aged 16–64, including those who have come as refugees, and a corresponding group of native Swedes shows significant differences in employment rates depending on immigrants' national origins, as well as changes over time. In 1969, the employment rate among immigrants from Finland and Yugoslavia was 120% of that for natives, and the corresponding rate for immigrants from Germany was 103%. That is, the immigrants were mainly working class and were given immediate recognition of their competence in terms of employment. A comparison with the figures for 1999 shows another picture—then, the rate for Finland was 93%, for Germany 89%, and 71% for the former Yugoslavia (Gustafsson *et al.* 2004). Thus, the situation has worsened for working-class immigrants, as illustrated by the decreasing employment rate for immigrants from Finland and Germany. Furthermore, an increasing number of refugees have contributed to a significantly lower employment rate in the (former) Yugoslavian group, compared to the Finnish and German groups. Finally, other immigrants who have come as refugees have problems getting a job: the average employment rate in 1999 among people from Africa and Asia was 62% of that for native Swedes (Gustavsson *et al.* 2004).

To sum up, we can see that the average unemployment in 2003 among 15–64 year old Swedish-born citizens was 4.8% (5.2% for men and 4.4% for women), compared with 11.1% for immigrants (12.7% for men and 9.5% for women) (Gustavsson *et al.* 2004). Further, it seems that the differences between the contexts where immigrants and their knowledge were originally situated and the Swedish context influence the degree of recognition in terms of employment. These varying employment rates depending on contexts of origin have been identified in a number of studies in different countries. For example, Barrett and Duffy (2008) show how better occupational attainments among earlier arrivals in Ireland could be explained by the changing national origins of immigrants rather than by an improved situation in general over time. Renaud and Cayn (2007) analyse employment among immigrants in Québec, and identify problematic differences between groups, where immigrants from Asia, the Middle East, and the Americas outside the USA have significant problems compared to other groups. These problems are sometimes discussed in terms of racism and discrimination, which will be related to somewhat in the following sections. What should be noted here, in the Swedish context with a high number of refugees among immigrants, is that the difference between working class immigrants and refugees seems to be important when it comes to employment rates, and the difference in the immigrant class co-varies with the context of origin.

The role of qualifications

Sweden has a formal system for recognition of foreign academic credentials that will be more fully elaborated on later in this article. If the foreign qualification is recognised as equivalent to a Swedish qualification, an individual is more likely to secure a qualified job. The difference between qualifications recognised as equivalent or non-equivalent is most significant in the health care sector, where a number of professions are regulated and require formal authorisation or certification. Here, 80% of those with an equivalent qualification have a qualified job, compared with only 20% of those with non-equivalent qualifications. In the technical/scientific area, the corresponding figures are 56% and 36%. Further, many working immigrants are employed within the area of their qualification but at a lower level; that is, employers have employees with relevant qualifications that are not being fully utilised or remunerated. This means that there is considerable existing competence that could be recognised and utilised (Berggren and Omarsson 2001). In other words, there is a potential for employing RPL, particularly as these employees are already participating in the community of practice of the workplace, and it should be possible to assess the prior learning that is relevant and valuable in their new work community, which in turn would help them to participate more fully in this practice.

However, if such RPL practices are to be further developed, the potential problem of discrimination between different groups should be taken seriously. We have shown that there are differences in employment rates depending on context of origin. Buzdugan and Halli (2009) identify how the devaluation of foreign education varies and indicates racial discrimination: 'It can be argued that while some white immigrants encounter devaluation of their foreign credentials, visible minority immigrants face a lack of recognition of foreign education' (383).

Earnings

Another indicator of recognition in working life is earnings. In Sweden, the average earnings of immigrants are lower than for those born in Sweden, which reflects both the lower employment rate and the often part-time nature of immigrants' work. In 1999, the average earnings of men born outside Sweden were 61% of those born in the country, and the corresponding figure for women was 69% (Gustafsson *et al.* 2004). Here too, there are big differences depending on country of origin. Immigrants from the Nordic countries, Western Europe and North America, who are mainly working-class immigrants, have slightly lower earnings, but immigrants from countries outside Europe, who are mainly refugees, have much lower earnings. Eastern and Southern Europe are somewhere in between but there are also differences depending on when different groups came to Sweden. For example, in 1999, men from Finland earned 82% of the earnings of Swedish-born men, and women from Finland 101% of Swedish-born women. The corresponding figures for people from the USA were 96% for men and 80% for women; the figures for Hungary were 71% and 87%, for Chile 55% and 68%, for Bosnia 43% and 44%, for Iraq 21% and 16% and for Somalia 16% and 17% (Gustafsson *et al.* 2004). This shows clearly the differences between countries/contexts of origin, arrival times and reasons for migration in terms of position in the labour market. The racial factor is not explicitly present in the Swedish debate on these issues. However, the figures can be compared with the results presented by Nakhaie (2007) who, in the Canadian context, identifies the main income gap between visible-minority and British male immigrants. In addition to these differences, the fact that immigrants who have studied mainly in Sweden earn about the same as native Swedes, and more than those who have studied abroad (leGrande *et al.* 2004) could indicate that a major problem is also the non-recognition of foreign credentials and work experience. This problem will be discussed further on in this article.

Policy and development of RPL in Sweden

The development of immigration has, among other things, resulted in a growing interest in the recognition of foreign vocational competence. The initiatives implemented to respond to this recognition challenge, and to facilitate the inclusion of immigrants in the new community, have included a number of pilot programs for recognition of prior learning (validation). The word *validation* was first mentioned in Swedish adult education policy in 1996 (Ministry of Education 1996). RPL, or validation, was introduced as a tool that could be used to assess and document the knowledge already acquired through prior learning, no matter where this knowledge had been developed. The hope was (and still is) that this will make it possible to use and acknowledge people's knowledge and to shorten their participation in adult education. In the early 2000s, validation was also introduced at the university level, where the focus was on the assessment of 'real [actual] competence' for assessing eligibility for admission and for credit.

It should be noted that the introduction of the term validation did not introduce a totally new idea. Assessment and documentation of prior learning have taken place in many different historical contexts, for example, within the guilds or the church during the sixteenth and seventeenth centuries in Sweden (Fejes and Andersson 2007). The discussion concerning the 'reserve of talent/ability' in the 1950s and the introduction of new measures to recognise different backgrounds and broaden access to higher education in the 1970s are also examples of how the idea has earlier turned up in policy and practice (Andersson and Fejes 2005). However, with the introduction of the concept of *validation*, a stronger emphasis was placed on developing processes where the individual's knowledge, no matter where it had been acquired, was acknowledged. The problems that might arise in such processes, however, as we can see from a situated learning perspective, are not reflected upon in policy.

RPL at upper secondary level

As a consequence of the introduction of validation in education policy, the government introduced and funded a pilot project aimed at developing methods for and systems of recognition of prior learning especially focused on the upper secondary level (Ministry of Education 1998, 2001, Andersson et al. 2004). Adult education at the upper secondary level, and particularly vocational adult education, is closely related to labour market measures. As a first step, the pilot project was aimed at recognising immigrants' vocational competence. The idea presented was that immigrants had knowledge that could be assessed and credited in relation to the curriculum. Consequently, they would not have to study as many years as they otherwise would have had to do to acquire a Swedish upper secondary diploma. This policy measure and pilot project were part of the creation of rules that now allow anyone to have their prior learning assessed and get a grade that is equal to grades from the corresponding course in municipal adult education. Further, validation centres that focus on assessing people's prior learning have emerged. RPL at this level has become a policy measure that focuses on the relation between education and the labour market. However, the labour market policy of the present government has been focused on getting people into the labour market, and education and validation have been seen as the long way round compared to being employed without such measures. In the present economic situation, however, it seems likely that new labour market measures including education and validation could be introduced.

RPL for immigrants at university level[4]

Recognition at university level is a system separate from that at the upper secondary level. Here, we will focus on RPL targeting immigrants. Sweden has a national system for evaluation and recognition of foreign qualifications, whereby foreign degrees are assessed in terms of their equivalence to Swedish counterparts. The National Agency for Higher Education evaluates higher education programmes leading to the recognition of a qualification of at least two years in length. This evaluation does not mean that a Swedish qualification is awarded, but guidance is offered to employers. The process of assessment and evaluation is only open to those who have complete and documented qualifications. Those who have not—for example, refugees who have fled from their native country—are not included. Additionally, an evaluation does not guarantee that a qualification is recognised in terms of a Swedish qualification. On the contrary, it is only seen as a recommendation for employers and higher education institutions, and the actual recognition depends on processes in these specific communities of practice.

If one requires recognition in terms of a Swedish qualification, one first has to be admitted to and become a participant in the required programme in question at a university or university college. These institutions are obliged to assess the actual competences[5] of applicants who lack formal eligibility. A right to the recognition of this actual competence in relation to admission requirements (eligibility) has been introduced nationally by the government. However, even this first step of assessment in terms of admission can be problematic for foreign professionals. The requirement for eligibility is to be able to study at higher educational institutions, which is normally assessed via high school (upper secondary level) records rather than professional experience and credentials. An assessment of 'actual competence' means that proof other than Swedish school records should be recognised, but it is still normally necessary to speak/read Swedish as most courses are in Swedish, which is an obstacle for immigrants.

Second, for those who are admitted, recognition for credit is also possible. An evaluation of foreign credentials and/or other proof by the National Agency of Higher Education might be used as the basis for decisions concerning credit. This can make the path to a Swedish qualification shorter, but the evaluation from the National Agency is no guarantee for credit: as mentioned, it is only a recommendation. Further, there is no system for assessment and recognition of professional competence developed in working life. Working life competence is not necessarily equivalent to the requirements of higher education, and is more or less excluded in this system.

The system for recognition of foreign qualifications in Sweden described above is mainly for 'non-regulated' professions. In certain 'regulated professions' where formal authorisation, certification etc. are required (e.g., teachers, physicians and attorneys-at-law), the qualifications are subject to the review of the responsible professional and regulatory authorities: the relevant community of practice is not the university but a certain professional community. For example, the National Board of Health and Welfare assesses foreign qualifications of physicians and other professions in the health care sector, and the qualifications of teachers are assessed by the National Agency for Higher Education. This system of recognition is somewhat different in that it looks at the requirements of the workplace to a greater extent than the system for non-regulated professions described above.

Challenges when recognising immigrants' vocational knowledge

What central challenges have emerged in the practice of RPL for immigrants? In this section, we will discuss parts of results from prior studies we have conducted of RPL projects. The aim is to raise some important questions in relation to RPL targeting immigrants. We will focus on the importance of the vocational language, the sorting mechanisms inherent in RPL, and the problems of transfer of knowledge between contexts.

Importance of vocational language skills

When recognising immigrants' prior learning, one is also more or less explicitly assessing the language skills of the immigrants. In one of our studies of pilot projects (Andersson *et al.* 2003a), where we focused on recognition of vocational competences at the upper secondary level, we noticed how Swedish language skills of the immigrants were seen as important. Even though an immigrant might be a vocational expert, she or he is entering the community of practice (the vocational practice in Sweden) as a newcomer in terms of language skills. As language is one of the important tools we use to learn in the social context of which we are part (cf. Vygotsky 1978), special attention needs to be focused on how language skills are defined and mobilised within practices of RPL. Here, questions of power become important. Who defines what language skills need to be assessed, and how is the assessment conducted? Are there measures taken to enhance the opportunities to enter the new community of practice?

In our interviews with teachers and project leaders, there were clear references to the need for good Swedish language skills in the Swedish labour market, as it is important to be able to communicate with colleagues and customers. Without sufficient language skills, it is argued, we risk being excluded from the work community, and there is a risk that we will not be able to do good work. Through such statements, we can see how power operates and through its operation, it defines what is necessary and not necessary to know. Here, there are assumptions about the need to know good Swedish as a vocational worker. Further, definitions that exclude at the same time as they intend to include can be seen in the criteria used for gaining access to the RPL process. In our studies, language skills were often used as criteria when selecting those who were allowed to enter the practice of RPL. One main reason used to argue for such criteria was that the assessors needed to be able to understand the ones they were assessing. Otherwise, they would not be able to see what the persons actually know (Andersson *et al.* 2003a).

However, in our studies we could also see that language demands were typically flexible and therefore unpredictable; that is, there were no fixed criteria (such as a written curriculum or written guidelines) for what language knowledge was required to gain access and the demands were not the same in each practice. However, what was more or less stable was the idea that different vocations need different kinds of language skills, i.e. there is a distinction made between general language skills and vocational language skills. What seemed to be important in the validation process in general was the vocational language skills, e.g. if you were a hairdresser, you needed to know the Swedish terms for different hairstyles, for different scissors, etc. Based on our interviews with immigrants, teachers and project leaders, a picture was outlined that those with good Swedish vocational language skills could more easily express their knowledge, while those with poor vocational language skills had problems in expressing their knowledge. A consequence of this was that the assessment of prior learning also included an assessment of the vocational language skills. In other words, those with poor vocational language skills (newcomers in terms of language skills) did not get a fair assessment in full in terms of their vocational skills as they might have more knowledge and competences than they were able to illustrate during the assessment process.

When interviewing the immigrants being assessed, language was the main problem raised by them (Andersson *et al.* 2003a). Not only did they feel that their language skills were not sufficient, they also heard it from their surroundings, teachers and supervisors. Consequently, many of them wanted to have more language training parallel with the process of validation. As an immigrant, you are offered language training in courses in Swedish directed at immigrants specifically. However, another context where language training could take place, which was argued for by some of the project leaders we interviewed, was the workplace. Being in a workplace was seen as helping the immigrant to learn the Swedish language of a certain vocation. Each vocation has specific terms that need to be learned if the immigrant is to be able to fully express her/his vocational knowledge. In one way, this could be seen as being in line with a situated view of knowledge and learning. Being in such the context of a newcomer in terms of language, one becomes part of a certain community in which one interacts with values, language and knowledge produced in this context (Wenger 1998). However, according to our interviews, the workplace where the immigrant should learn the language should not be a place where her/his countrymen work as this would not be a good environment for learning Swedish. There were examples in our study where this was the case and it resulted in immigrants mostly speaking their native language instead of Swedish.

So far, we can see how vocational language skills seem to be important when recognising immigrants' prior learning at the upper secondary level. Even though language skills are still important when recognising immigrant academics' prior learning, there do not seem to be the same problems when it comes to learning Swedish. In another study in which we focused on immigrant academics and their validation process (Andersson et al. 2003b), we noticed how the problem of language was not as large as that of the immigrants having their knowledge recognised at upper secondary level. The reason seemed to be that the academics were more used to studying, and thus more easily picked up the Swedish language; that is, they were more familiar with the practice of studying, although in another cultural context.

To conclude this section, we can see how power operates to exclude as it includes. Language is construed as a major concern in the process of RPL, especially vocational language skills. The need for good Swedish language skills is seen as a way to be able to make a fair assessment of the immigrant's knowledge, and as a way to judge whether someone is able to enter the Swedish labour market. Opportunities for learning Swedish are offered in the form of courses and workplace placements. However, even though such ways of reasoning might be based on wishes to be supportive, there is also exclusion. Diffuse and differing language criteria might lead to exclusion in several ways. The immigrant might not be allowed to enter the process of RPL; s/he might not be fairly assessed in relation to the vocational competences; s/he may not be able to enter the Swedish labour market. Thus, language differences act as a gatekeeper that might lead to marginalisation and exclusion. Consequently, in the practices of RPL, there is a need to take into account and find different ways of approaching the issue of language. One starting point could be to acknowledge that the immigrants are newcomers to the vocational practices in terms of language skills, even though they might be experts in terms of their vocational knowledge.

RPL as a sorting mechanism

Further studies of three Swedish urban validation centres (Andersson, Hult and Osman 2006, Andersson and Osman 2008) show how recognition of prior learning is used as an instrument for sorting, classifying and including or excluding immigrants in/from vocational communities in the Swedish labour market. The sorting mechanism inherent in RPL is identified in different ways. It is not only a matter of the formal assessments made via the validation process, there is also a sorting mechanism on a structural level; that is, certain vocations are chosen and included in the RPL opportunities, a choice not primarily based on what vocational competence immigrants have but on the demands of certain vocations in the labour market. From the perspective applied in the present article, this is about opportunities of entering relevant communities of practice where prior learning could be used and recognition acquired.

Another example of the sorting mechanism in the system is the de-grading of competence that was enacted in some vocational areas. In some cases, teachers with teacher training from another country were included in a validation process—not to get a teaching certificate of the type mentioned above but to be assessed as child minders. In this case, the validation was made in the vocational area of the candidate (here, pedagogical work) but on a lower level, resulting in what we have referred to as a 'descending vertical mobility'. This structural problem is related to the fact that municipalities run these validation centres, and they can only provide vocational education and validation at the secondary level, while teacher education is provided by universities and university colleges. The result is that these teachers are included in the community of pedagogical work but they are not allowed to participate fully as professional teachers.

A final example of the sorting mechanism is the informal aspect of the assessment process. The validation results not only in formal documents—grades, certificates, etc.—the assessments also have an informal dimension. Teachers making the assessments often have close relations to local labour market actors, and their informal recommendations are often important to get, from the candidates' perspective, the most important recognition: employment.

These studies show how, in different ways, the practices of validation contribute to a 'mis-recognition' of immigrants' vocational experiences and knowledge that affects the incorporation of immigrants in their areas of competence—the relevant communities of practice—in the Swedish labour market.

Transfer of knowledge from one context to another

One main problem related to mobility and raised in several of our studies (see e.g. Andersson *et al.* 2003a, 2003b, 2004) is the question of transferability and comparability of knowledge between contexts. How does one assess vocational knowledge created in one country/specific context in relation to the knowledge required and deemed essential in another country and context? For example (Andersson *et al.* 2003a), if a person has learned construction work in a country according to traditional standards and in relation to country-specific kinds of buildings, what value does such knowledge have in relation to the standards of construction work in Sweden? Here, we can draw further on socio-cultural theories of learning and their focus on the importance of the context of learning (e.g. Wenger 1998, Vygotsky 1978). As we have shown, such theorisation is helpful for understanding the problem of recognising immigrants' vocational knowledge. The community of practice of which they have been part differs from other communities. Their knowledge and values are most likely somewhat different. Thus, when they are being assessed in Sweden, the assessors represent another community of practice with other values and knowledge highlighted. The immigrants are not really assessed on their own terms as we could see in the former section concerning language skills. Here, we could further argue that the criteria for assessment in the vocational curriculum (e.g. in construction work) is defined in terms of Swedish conditions and traditions. Thus, even though the immigrant being assessed might be an expert in terms of construction work, this is related to another community of practice.

This problem is particularly relevant when we discuss refugees compared to working-class immigrants. As we have seen, in the 1950s and 1960s, many working-class immigrants came to Sweden due to a labour shortage, and the recognition problem was not important. There was a demand of their competence and they were employed even if they had a background in a somewhat different community of practice. But later, when immigrants have mainly been refugees, the recognition challenge and the problem of transfer is evident. There is no particular demand for the refugees' knowledge in the labour market, and refugees come regardless of unemployment or labour shortages. In addition to this, they often belong to visible minorities, which makes the issue of racial discrimination relevant as a dimension of the recognition problems, even if this is beyond the particular scope of this article.

Would it then be possible to tackle this challenge differently? Could knowledge be assessed in the practice where it has been acquired? In one way, this would be difficult, as it would require a system of assessment where individuals are assessed in their workplaces in their native countries. A more feasible way to do this might be to make the assessment context as 'authentic' as possible. One could ask the people being assessed to carry out tasks they normally do in their workplace in their native country, and the assessor could be a person who is well versed in the vocational knowledge of specific countries. However, the challenge of recognition is even more complex. Vocational knowledge is strongly related to the ideas of the labour market, which is its context. Consequently, even if immigrants are assessed and get recognition based on the vocational practice where they have been members, this does not necessarily mean that their knowledge has use or exchange value in the new (in this case Swedish) labour market. For example, construction work is and has to be different in different countries/contexts—the way houses are built is not only a matter of culture, but also a matter of the local climate, which places specific demands on the construction to make it possible to live in a house all the year around. A possible way forward in order to overcome this dilemma at least to some extent is discussed in the final section of this article.

Discussion

In this article, our aim has been to describe and analyse how immigration has developed in Sweden and what policy measures have been taken to tackle such immigration in terms of recognition of the immigrants', and among them in particular refugees', prior learning. We have also discussed some of the problems faced in RPL practices in relation to immigrants' prior learning from a perspective of learning as being situated in specific communities of practice. As illustrated, migration and mobility have in the last decade become an important issue in Sweden and in policymaking in education. As one of the solutions proposed for dealing with high unemployment rates among immigrants, the Ministry of Education has initiated the development of systems and methods of RPL. The idea of RPL has, among other things, been to handle the transfer of knowledge between contexts, i.e. to recognise knowledge acquired in another country in relation to Swedish grades and diplomas.

Through such a process, immigrants will, according to policy texts, be able to shorten their Swedish education.

However, such an ambition is not without problems. Transferring knowledge from one context to another is a challenge. Drawing on theories of situated learning, we conceptualise knowledge as context specific, while we acknowledge issues of power and power relations. Recognising knowledge developed within a vocation in another country is, as we have argued based on our previous studies, problematic. Firstly, the context in which the person is being assessed is different as it is a new community of practice the immigrant is entering (in terms of vocational practice and language skills), and therefore their knowledge is valued in relation to other kinds of knowledge demands and another practice compared to those demands and the practice in which their own knowledge was developed. Secondly, the one making the assessment most likely participates in other communities of practice and has the power to decide what counts as good and bad knowledge. As we could see in the example of language skills, the requirement is not clear and differed between RPL practices depending on who made the assessment. Thus, there is to some extent an incompatibility from the very beginning. Further, if you cannot express yourself with terms used in the vocation in which you are being recognised, there is a risk that you will not get a fair result in the recognition process.

Accordingly, we argue that there is a need for people involved in practices of RPL to acknowledge that the immigrants are newcomers in terms of language, and to the specific Swedish vocational practice, while they might be experts in relation to the vocational practice where they have developed their knowledge. In such way, it might be possible to find different solutions and ways to re-shape the assessment procedures and practices in ways that lead to inclusion rather than exclusion. Other exclusionary practices created in the intersection of mobility, knowledge and recognition are, for example, the definition by the labour market of which vocations should develop RPL opportunities, or the problem of the degrading of knowledge when an immigrant academic is only given the opportunity to become recognised at an upper secondary school level. The last example is related to the separation of and differences between upper secondary and university level presented earlier in the article. Different levels of bureaucracy have different rules and regulations and do not always work together, which causes problems for the individuals.

How would it be possible to handle these problems in a way that makes it easier for immigrants/refugees to have their prior learning recognised? One possible way forward could be to try to avoid seeing RPL mainly as a process whereby immigrants and Swedes have their knowledge recognised in relation to grades from upper secondary school or in relation to university degrees, i.e. RPL as a separate activity. Instead, one could see RPL as an integrated aspect of a learning process where the focus is on the knowledge and competences the person has in the specific work context in which s/he works. The latter definition is described as 'rpl' as opposed to 'RPL'—recognition of prior learning as an integrated aspect of a learning process as opposed to Recognition of Prior Learning as a separate activity (Breier 2005). With such a focus, it would be possible to integrate the educational system with the workplace. This can, for example, be seen in one of our studies (Fejes and Andersson 2009) where we analyse how healthcare assistants (HCAs) in the elderly-care sector had their knowledge, which they had developed through years of working in elderly care, recognised during working hours. Through collaboration between the funder of elderly care (a municipality), the employers (a municipality or a private company) and educational providers, the curriculum for the healthcare programme at the upper secondary school level was mobilised with the participating HCAs during working hours. Through group discussions under the supervision of a teacher, and through written essays, a HCA's prior learning was recognised, in relation to the curriculum. Thus, they were able to receive a diploma from upper secondary school in a much shorter time than would otherwise have been the case.

If this kind of RPL process were used more generally within other vocations, there would, of course, still be the problem of recognising knowledge developed in another context. However, by being in the work context—during a period of practical training or, if possible, employment—the immigrant would have the opportunity to become part of a new community of practice where prior learning could be recognised and integrated with the learning process, which takes place as a result of being in a new practice. In this way, the vocational part of lifelong education would move from mainly being part of the educational system to becoming part of working life. Such a shift in practices of RPL in Sweden would be in line with a shift from speaking of 'lifelong education' to speaking about 'lifelong learning'. Even though such a shift and use of language is problematic in many ways (e.g. Fejes and Nicoll 2008), it could be fruitful to use them when speaking about how to face the challenge of the mobility of knowledge. Furthermore, processes helping immigrants to enter new communities of practice could contribute to reducing discrimination based on misrecognition or non-recognition as well as on other factors.

Notes

1. For a deeper and broader analysis of RPL, see Andersson and Harris (2006).
2. The description of Sweden in this section of the article is based on work previously presented by Guo and Andersson (2006), Andersson and Osman (2008) and Andersson and Guo (2009).
3. The Sami population in the northern part of Sweden should not be forgotten, but it has had little influence on the main culture of society.
4. This section of the article is based on the Swedish part of a study presented by Andersson and Guo (2009).
5. Actual (in Sweden named 'real') competences include all competences a person has, as opposed to the formal competence that only includes what is formally documented.

References

ANDERSSON, P. and FEJES, A. (2005) Recognition of prior learning as a technique for fabricating the adult learner: a genealogical analysis on Swedish adult education policy. *Journal of Education Policy*, **20**, 595–613.

ANDERSSON, P., FEJES, A. and AHN, S.-E. (2004) Recognition of prior vocational learning in Sweden. *Studies in the Education of Adults*, **36**, 57–71.

ANDERSSON, P., FEJES, A. and HULT, Å. (2003a) *Att visa vad man kan – erfarenheter från ett regionalt nätverk för validering av yrkeskompetens* [To show what you know – experiences from a regional network for recognition of vocational competence] Vuxenutbildarcentrums skriftserie nr 18 (Linköping: Linköpings universitet).

ANDERSSON, P., FEJES, A. and HULT, Å. (2003b) *Validering av invandrade akademikers yrkeskompetens: Erfarenheter från Nätverk Sörmland* [Recognition of immigrant academics' professional competence] Integrationsverkets rapportserie 2003:04 (Norrköping: Integrationsverket).

ANDERSSON, P. and GUO, S. (2009) Governing through non-recognition: the missing 'R' in the PLAR for immigrant professionals in Canada and Sweden. *International Journal of Lifelong Learning*, **28**, 423–437.

ANDERSSON, P. and HARRIS, J. (eds.) (2006) *Re-theorising the Recognition of Prior Learning* (Leicester: NIACE).

ANDERSSON, P., HULT, Å. and OSMAN, A. (2006) *Validering som sortering – hur värderas utländsk kompetens?* [Validation as sorting and selection: how is foreign vocational competence evaluated?] (Norrköping: Integrationsverket and Valideringsdelegationen).
ANDERSSON, P. and OSMAN, A. (2008) Recognition of prior learning as a practice for differential inclusion and exclusion of immigrants in Sweden. *Adult Education Quarterly*, **59**, 42–60.
BARRETT, A. and DUFFY, D. (2008) Are Ireland's immigrants integrating into its labour market? *International Migration Review*, **42**, 597–619.
BERGGREN, K. and OMARSSON, A. (2001) *Rätt man på fel plats – en studie av arbetsmarknaden för utlandsfödda akademiker som invandrat under 1990-talet* [The right man in the wrong place – a study of the labour market for academics born abroad who immigrated during the 1990s] (Stockholm: Arbetsmarknadsstyrelsen).
BEVELANDER, P. (2000) *Immigrant employment integration and structural change in Sweden 1970–1995.* Lund Studies in Economic History 15 (Södertälje: Almqvist & Wiksell International).
BILLETT, S. (2006) Work, subjectivity and learning. In S. BILLETT, T. FENWICK and M. SOMMERVILLE (eds.) *Work, Subjectivity and Learning: Understanding learning through working life* (Dordrecht: Springer), pp. 1–20.
BREIER, M. (2005) A disciplinary-specific approach to the recognition of prior informal experience in adult pedagogy: 'rpl' as opposed to 'RPL'. *Studies in Continuing Education*, **27**, 51–65.
BUZDUGAN, R. and HALLI, S.S. (2009) Labor market experiences of Canadian immigrants with focus on foreign education and experience. *International Migration Review*, **43**, 366–386.
CONTU, A. and WILLMOTT, H. (2003) Re-embedding situatedness: the importance of power relations in learning theory. *Organization Science*, **14**, 283–296.
EKBERG, J. and ROOTH, D.-O. (2000) *Arbetsmarknadspolitik för invandrare* [Labour market politics for immigrants] (Växjö: Växjö University, School of Management and Economics).
FEJES, A. and ANDERSSON, P. (2007) Historicising validation: the 'new' idea of validation in Sweden and its promise of economic growth. In R. RINNE, A. HEIKKINEN and P. SALO (eds.) *Adult Education – Liberty, Fraternity, Equality? Nordic Views on Lifelong Learning* (Turku: Finnish Educational Research Association), pp. 161–184.
FEJES, A. and ANDERSSON, P. (2009) Recognising prior learning: understanding the relations among experience, learning and recognition from a constructivist perspective. *Vocations and Learning: Studies in vocational and professional education*, **2**, 37–55.
FEJES, A. and NICOLL, K. (eds.) (2008) *Foucault and Lifelong Learning: Governing the subject* (Routledge: London).
FULLER, A., HODKINSON, H., HODKINSON, P. and UNWIN, L. (2005) Learning as peripheral participation in communities of practices: a reassessment of key concepts in workplace learning. *British Educational Research Journal*, **31**, 49–68.
GUO, S. and ANDERSSON, P. (2006) The politics of difference: non/recognition of the foreign credentials and prior work experience of immigrant professionals in Canada and Sweden. In: P. ANDERSSON and J. HARRIS (eds.) *Re-theorising the Recognition of Prior Learning* (Leicester: NIACE), pp. 183–203.
GUSTAFSSON, B., HAMMARSTEDT, M. and ZHENG, J. (2004) Invandrares arbetsmarknadssituation – översikt och nya siffror [Immigrants' labour market situation – overview and new figures]. In SOU 2004:21, *Egenförsörjning eller bidragsförsörjning? Invandrarna, arbetsmarknaden och välfärdsstaten, Rapport från Integrationspolitiska maktutredningen* [Supporting oneself or receiving benefits? The immigrants, the labour market and the welfare state. Report from the investigation on power and integration policy.] (Stockholm: Integrations- och jämställdhetsdepartementet) pp. 15–55.
HÄRNQUIST, K. (2003) Educational reserves revisited. *Scandinavian Journal of Educational Research*, **47**, 483–494.
KÖPSÉN, S. (2008) *Från revolution till reträtt: Lärande i en fackförenings vardag* [From revolution to retreat: Everyday learning in a local trade union] (Linköping: LiU-Press).
LAVE, J. and WENGER, E. (1991) *Situated Learning: Legitimate peripheral participation* (Cambridge, UK: Cambridge University Press).
LEGRANDE, C., SZULKIN, R. and EKBERG, J. (2004) Kan diskriminering förklara skillnader i position på arbetsmarknaden mellan invandrare och infödda? [Can discrimination explain differences in labour market position between immigrants and natives?] In SOU 2004:21, *Egenförsörjning eller bidragsförsörjning? Invandrarna, arbetsmarknaden och välfärdsstaten. Rapport från Integrationspolitiska maktutredningen* [Supporting oneself or receiving benefits? The immigrants, the labour market and the welfare state. Report from the investigation on power and integration policy.] (Stockholm: Integrations- och jämställdhetsdepartementet), pp. 185–220.
MINISTRY OF EDUCATION (1996) *En strategi för kunskapslyft och livslångt lärande* [A strategy for adult education and lifelong learning] SOU 1996:27 (Stockholm: Regeringskansliet, Utbildningsdepartementet).
MINISTRY OF EDUCATION (1998) *Validering av utländsk yrkeskompetens* [Validation of foreign vocational competence] SOU 1998:165 (Stockholm: Utbildningsdepartementet).
MINISTRY OF EDUCATION (2001) *Validering av vuxnas kunskap och kompetens* [Validation of adults' knowledge and competence] SOU 2001:78 (Stockholm: Utbildningsdepartementet).

NAKHAIE, M.R. (2007) Ethnoracial origins, social capital, and earnings. *International Migration & Integration*, **8,** 307–325.

NATIONALENCYKLOPEDIN (1991) Emigration. In *Nationalencyklopedin, Femte bandet* [Swedish national encyclopedia volume 5] (Höganäs: Bokförlaget Bra Böcker).

NYSTRÖM, S. (2009) *Becoming a professional: A longitudinal study of graduates' professional trajectories from higher education to working life* (Linköping: LiU-Press).

RENAUD, J. and CAYN, T. (2007) Jobs commensurate with their skills? Selected workers and skilled job access in Québec. *International Migration & Integration*, **8,** 375–389.

SOROKIN, P.A. (1959) *Social and Cultural Mobility* (Glencoe, IL.: Free Press).

STATISTISKA CENTRALBYRÅN [STATISTICS SWEDEN] (2009a) Befolkningsstatistik i sammandrag 1960–2008 [Statistics about the Swedish population 1960–2008] (online) http://www.scb.se/Pages/TableAndChart___26040.aspx (accessed April 27, 2009).

STATISTISKA CENTRALBYRÅN (2009b) Statistikdatabasen [Statistical database] (online) http://www.ssd.scb.se/databaser/makro/start.asp (accessed April 27, 2009).

TANGAARD, L. (2006) Situated gendered learning in the workplace. *Journal of Workplace Learning*, **18,** 220–234.

VYGOTSKY, L.S. (1978) *Mind in Society. The development of higher psychological processes* (Cambridge, Massachusetts: Harvard University Press).

WENGER, E. (1998) *Communities of Practice: Learning, meaning and identity* (Cambridge: Cambridge University Press).

Transnational migration, social capital and lifelong learning in the USA

MARY V. ALFRED
Texas A&M University, USA

At the beginning of the twenty-first century, immigration continues to be a powerful force that shapes the US demographic landscape and hence influences all aspects of US lifeways. Unlike past waves of immigration, communication, media and transportation technologies enable today's immigrants to maintain strong ties and relationships with their homeland while they live and work in the host country. The transnational identities of today's immigrants have implications for lifelong learning across both nations. In their attempts to adapt in the new society, they form new networks and relationships with members of the host country and other kinfolks who preceded them in the border-crossing venture. At the same time, they continue to maintain relationships and ties with the homeland, drawing from social capital resources from both contexts. The purpose of this paper is to examine the intersection of immigration, transnationalization and lifelong learning through the lens of social capital theory. More specifically, drawing from the literature, it examines how networks and relationships inform learning and acculturation among today's ethnic minority immigrants. Findings from the literature suggest that ethnic minorities have strong bonding networks with members of their cultural and racial groups but weak bridging networks with those outside their group, which has implications for accessing funds of knowledge inherent in other network groups.

Introduction

A glimpse at the history of the USA reveals that immigration has always been at the core of that society. According to Pedraza (1996: 1), 'Americans are immigrants—people whose origins were various but whose destinies became Americans.' However, unlike prior waves of immigration, the majority of today's immigrants are not drawn from Europe as it was in the past, but from non-Western nations, primarily Asia, Latin America and the Caribbean making the American population more non-white and more diverse than ever before (Schuck 1998, Portes and Rumbaut 2006). This wave of immigrants is perhaps more controversial than earlier ones because it is dominated by ethnic and linguistic minorities, thus contributing to a major demographic shift in the diversity and racioethnic makeup of the US population. In addition, the transnational nature of today's immigrants suggests that they draw from the funds of knowledge from both countries through their participation in networks and relationships. This article examines how social capital, inherent in these relationships, influences learning and acculturation in the new nation.

Methodological approach: a review of the literature

The approach used for the collection of the data that informed this work was a thorough review of literature that would help explore the interplay of migration, transnational identities, social capital and lifelong learning. Using single and combined keywords such as 'immigration', 'immigrant learners', 'lifelong learning', 'social capital', 'immigration and social capital', 'acculturation and assimilation', 'social capital theory' and 'transnational migration' to name a few, I conducted a search for relevant literature. Among the academic databases accessed for relevant literature were electronic catalogs of published books at the university library, Google Scholar, Proquest Research Library Plus, Academic Search Premiere, EBSCOhost, ERIC and other internet sites to include that of the United States Bureau of the Census. As a result, literature from journal articles, published books and census data were reviewed, analyzed and organized in the production of this article.

Commenting on the review of literature as a research methodological approach, Kennedy (2007: 139) notes, 'Although the literature review is a widely recognized genre of scholarly writings, there is no clear understanding of what constitutes a body of literature. Each reviewer must decide which specific studies to include or exclude from a review and why.' Therefore, the bodies of literature selected for this manuscript were deemed important to build and present an argument on how migration and social capital intersect to inform lifelong learning among immigrant adults. It also examines factors that influence social support among racial and ethnic minorities. To give a broad view of the migration experience and the role of social capital in lifelong learning and acculturation, the paper is organized in the following sequence:

(a) a profile of US immigrant population;
(b) the motivational forces of migration;
(c) literature in support of the transnational orientation of some of today's immigrant groups;
(d) concepts of social capital and findings from related research; and
(e) conclusion with an examination of social capital, adult education and lifelong learning.

Profile of the US immigration population

According to Terrazas and Batalova (2008), as of December 2007, the estimated foreign-born population of the USA was 38.1 million, representing 12.5% of the overall population. This is a stark increase from 32.5 million or 11.4% at the end of March 2002 that Schmidley (2003) reported. The increase is even more pronounced when we examine the 1990 foreign-born population that was reported at 19.7 million or 7.9% of the US population (Larsen 2004). This number is an increase of 18.4 million over the 17-year period, nearly doubling the immigrant population. This dramatic increase is primarily the result of immigration from Asia and Latin America (Camarota 2002). According to Schmidley (2003), as of March 2002, 52% of the immigrants in the USA were from Latin America (made up of the Caribbean, Central America, and South America) and 25% from Asia (Schmidley 2003). The Latin American countries with the highest representation of immigrants in the United States were Mexico, Cuba, the Dominican Republic and El Salvador. The Asian countries with the highest immigrant rates included China, the Philippines, India, Vietnam and Korea (Camarota 2002). In contrast, only 14% of the foreign-born population came from Europe, a significant shift from the 62% recorded in 1970.

Overall, according to population reports (Camarota 2002, Schmidley 2003, United States Bureau of Census 2003, Larsen 2004, Terrazas and Batalova 2008), the largest wave of immigrants arrived between 1985 and 1990, when 75% of the Salvadoran immigrants, more than 50% of the Korean, Vietnamese and Chinese immigrants, and nearly 50% of the Mexican and Filipino immigrants arrived. They continue to come in large numbers. As a result, the racial and ethnic composition of the foreign-born population now consists of more than 78% people of color (Larsen 2004), thus transforming the ethnic makeup of the US foreign-born population and that of the country as a whole.

Moreover, according to the US Bureau of the Census Report (2003), many of the newcomers speak a language other than English in the home. In fact, over 95% of Mexicans, Cubans and Salvadorans speak Spanish in the home, and 95% of the immigrants from China, Korea, the Philippines and Vietnam speak an Asian language. In addition, about 80% of those from Italy and 58% of those from Germany speak a language other than English. It is also worth noting that over 43% of foreign-born immigrants fall between the ages of 25 and 44. Of those over 25 years of age, 67.3% are likely to have graduated from high school compared to 87.5% of the native-born population (Larsen 2004). The highest percentage of high school graduates was found among Asians (83.8%) and Europeans (81.3%), compared to Latin Americans (49.6%). Immigrants from Latin America, including those from Mexico, have the lowest rate of high school completion at 37.3% (US Census Bureau 2003).

Additionally, as many scholars have noted, a defining feature of today's immigrant population is the diversity of their socioeconomic backgrounds. Today's immigrants come from both rural and urban backgrounds, from underdeveloped regions of the Western hemisphere, as well as from industrially developed areas of East Asia (Alba and Nee 1999). Occupationally, the new immigration encompasses the full spectrum of jobs, from migrants who perform unskilled labor to skilled immigrants who hold professional and technical jobs, including engineers, mathematicians, computer scientists, natural scientists, teachers and health workers (Alba and Nee 1999). Therefore, today's immigrant population reflects a pattern of demographics that reveals deep polarization between the most educated and wealthiest and the least educated and poorest.

This emergent pattern of adaptation seems to follow a new hourglass segmentation found in the US economy and society (Suarez-Orozco and Suarez-Orozco 2000). Noticeably, there are those immigrants who are quickly achieving upward mobility, primarily through education and high-tech jobs, while on the opposite end of the hourglass, large numbers of low-skilled workers find themselves locked in low-wage service jobs. Those in between approximate norms of the majority culture and disappear into US cultural institutions without much notice (Sparks 2003). This concept of the hourglass segmentation raises questions not only about education and lifelong learning but also about race and racial locations. Which immigrants are at one end and which are at the opposite end, Sparks asks. Are white Europeans found more often in the upwardly mobile end? Are Latinos/as more often found in the low-wage jobs? Understanding the motivation and the conditions under which individuals migrate will help shed light on these questions and on the learning and adaptation experiences of immigrant groups.

The forces of migration

A variety of motivational forces encourage people to cross the borders from their homeland to a foreign country. In the case of immigrants to the USA, most are pulled in search of a better standard of living, either through education or through work. While the majority come voluntarily, others are pushed from their homelands because of political, social and economic conditions that cause them to seek refuge in a new country. Despite the conditions under which one migrates, Portes and Rumbaut (1996) theorize that the motivation to leave one's homeland has to do with a 'push and pull' factor that fuels a major life-altering decision. They note:

> The basic reason why immigrants come to America is the gap between life's aspirations and expectations and the means to fulfill them in the sending countries. Different groups feel this gap with varying intensity, but it clearly becomes a strong motive for action. (Portes and Rumbaut 1996: 12)

The concept of the push and pull factors of migration must also be understood in relation to the material consumption of the Western world. According to Portes and Rumbaut (2006), the United States and other industrialized countries play a double role in promoting the process of migration. First, through the media, they are portrayed as a source of much of the modern culture and material goods consumed worldwide. Second, the same process of media attention has taught an increasing number of people about economic opportunities in the developed world that are absent in their own countries. Seen from these perspectives, much of today's immigration can be viewed as a direct influence of the materialistic culture of Western societies. Overall, most people migrate to fulfill their dreams of a better life (as defined by Western standards) that cannot be realized in their home country. Today's media technology helps to accentuate the gap between the conditions that exist at home and those of the receiving country.

As an immigrant from a small Caribbean island, I too left the homeland in the late 1970s to join my Caribbean husband who was then serving in the US Army. Prior to my departure, I, like many island residents, saw the US as an opportunity for a better education and, most importantly, for a better life economically. Watching the one-station television during the 1960s and 1970s, the message that came across and the images that we conjured were those that depicted the USA as a nation where opportunities for self-improvement were plentiful and as a place where anyone who was capable and willing could achieve upward mobility. Although we witnessed the dark side of America on the television screen during the many African-American-led protests for civil rights in the 1960s, we held steadily to the image of America as the Promised Land, a land of opportunities and a country where we could fulfill dreams of a better life. Therefore, despite the negative images, we came to America. However, the pathways to the Promised Land are just as diverse as those who came, and hence significantly influence lifelong learning participation patterns among the new comers.

While all immigrants share a history of leaving their homeland, the conditions under which they migrate are often diverse and therefore result in different sets of expectations of the receiving country. Portes and Rumbaut (1996: xxiii) eloquently captured the diversity among the different immigrant groups, noting:

> Today's immigrants come in luxurious jetliners and in the trunks of cars, by boat and on foot. Manual laborers and polished professionals, entrepreneurs and refugees, preliterate peasants and some of the most talented cosmopolitans on the planet—all are helping to reshape the fabric of American society.

While these groups are helping to shape the fabric of American society, they are also reshaping the culture and structure of communities of learning within which they take membership. In their attempts to learn the life ways and mores of the new society, they form new networks and relationships with members of the host country and other kinfolks who preceded them in the border-crossing venture. At the same time, they continue to maintain relationships and ties with the homeland. Their lifelong learning experiences must therefore be understood from the perspectives of transnational migration and social capital.

Beyond assimilation: the transnational orientation of contemporary immigrants

Earlier conceptualizations of immigration portrayed immigrants as persons of disparate backgrounds, associational ties and cultural histories that learned to identify with the collectivity of the US (Goldin 1999). They were portrayed as individuals who were ruptured from the home country to take on permanent residency in new territories that were often vastly different from their own, with little intention of returning home. More common of the early European immigrants, these individuals were presented as those who had broken all ties with their country of birth and had learned to assimilate the cultures, values and mores of the new country (Glick Schiller 1999).

The assimilation model assumes a total absorption into the dominant culture and that the goal of the assimilation process is for the individual to become socially accepted by members of the dominant culture (Pedraza 1996). Therefore, according to LaFromboise, Coleman and Gerton (1993), the underlying assumption of the assimilation model is that a member of one culture loses her original cultural identity as she acquires a new identity in the second culture. The immigrant experience, through the lens of this model, is seen as a process of permanent displacement and loss of prior personal and cultural identity and history. As a result, many scholars have found this model to be inadequate to capture the adaptation experience of today's immigrants who come from collectivistic cultures, where the group culture is a core element of the individual's identity. Accordingly, Pedraza (1996: 11) notes:

> [Immigrants] have experienced another whole life in another country, another culture, yet they will live out a whole new set of choices and experiences...in the new society to which they migrated. And very often during the immigrant generation, they remain extremely involved with the country, village, and family they left behind.

As a result of this extreme involvement with the home country among many of today's immigrants, a growing number of scholars are arguing that the process of learning to identify with the host country has meant that the individual must understand not only who she is but also who she is not. According to Glick Schiller (1999), this process of Americanization has been and continues to be simultaneously a process of racialization and transnationalization. Therefore, as part of this process, Glick Schiller, Basch and Blanc-Szanton (1992), Kearney (1995), and Glick Schiller (1999) argue that contemporary immigrants have identified with both the US and their country of origin in ways that are not captured in traditional theories of immigration that emphasize a process of rupture, permanent displacement, and assimilation.

These scholars argue for theories that acknowledge the transnational identities of today's immigrants and reject the view of immigrants as people who have uprooted themselves from their country to settle permanently and totally assimilate in a new land. Instead, they call attention to the fact that a significant number of today's immigrants maintain strong ties with their home country and resist total assimilation into the new culture. Rather, according to Kearney, they go through a process of acculturation where they hold on to elements of the country of origin while they acquire the values, mores and life ways of the new culture.

LaFromboise *et al.* (1993) note the major difference between the assimilation model and the acculturation model of adaptation is with the assimilation process, the individual gives up her minority cultural identity and assumes the cultural identity of the majority group. The acculturation model, on the other hand, assumes that the individual becomes competent in the majority culture while retaining and identifying with her minority culture. Alba and Nee (1999) found that one of the primary characteristics of the acculturation model is its involuntary characteristic. Most often the new immigrant is forced to learn the behaviors and practices of members of the new culture in order to survive economically. This economic survival in the new country is one of the primary reasons for migration and one that allows for the financial resources to participate in activities of the home country.

That is particularly important as many of today's immigrants continue to travel back and forth between the homelands and participate in social, cultural, and political activities in both countries. An important characteristic of today's immigrant groups is the financial and material support they provide to their family and to their community left behind, thus allowing them a voice and a presence in the building of the society. In addition, modern day transportation and communication technologies have facilitated the movement between the country of origin and the host country and immigrants' participation in the affairs of both countries.

To capture the essence of the back and forth movement across national borders, these authors propose the term 'transnational migration' or 'transnationalism' to characterize the bicultural identities of these immigrant groups. According to Glick Schiller (1999: 94):

> this new approach makes visible the networks of immigrants that extend across international borders. It posits that even though migrants invest socially, economically, and politically in their new society, they may continue to participate in the daily life of the society from which they emigrated but which they did not abandon.

Theorizing immigration from a transnational perspective provides a better understanding of the impact of the phenomenon on the lives of those involved in the border-crossing experience (Basch, Glick Schiller and Blanc-Szanton 1994, Goldin 1999). It has been established that immigrants are not a monolithic group; therefore, the transnational process also makes visible which individuals take on a transnational identity and how race, class, socioeconomic status and the border-crossing experience influence such identification. Having a transnational identity means that the immigrant sees himself as a member and participant of both cultures, meaning that the individual acculturates to the new culture while maintaining relevant values and practices of the old.

Moreover, some researchers have found a distinct relationship between race, education, and the mode of adaptation into the new culture. Alba and Nee (1999) found the earlier waves of immigrants, primarily white Europeans, were found to assimilate more quickly as they had easier access to majority white institutions and the workplace. This supports Hans' (1999) notion that in order for assimilation to take place, the immigrant must be given permission to enter the 'American' group or institution. As Hans (1999: 162) notes, 'Since discrimination and other factors often lead to denial of that permission to the immigrant...assimilation will always be slower than acculturation.' One of the conclusions that can be drawn from Hans' statement is that those immigrants who have been given permission to enter into 'American' society and its institutions will assimilate more rapidly into that culture, whereas those who are denied access will cling more readily to their ethnic groups at home and in the US and acculturate rather than assimilate. Such acculturation would, therefore, promote a transnational self-identification.

According to Basch *et al.* (1994: 7), 'Transnational processes are characterized by cultural and social fields in which actors take actions, make decisions and develop subjectivities and identities embedded in networks of relationships that connect them simultaneously to two or more nation states'. Accordingly, the multiplicity of the immigrant's involvement in both the home and host societies is a central element of transnationalism. In other words, transnational migrants maintain a dual-place orientation (Sutton and Chaney 1994) and acculturate rather than assimilate into the mainstream culture.

For example, Monkman's (1997) study of learning among Mexican-American immigrants in California clearly demonstrates the transnational dynamics that shape some immigrant people's lives in the new nation. The Mexican-Americans in her study had strong ties with networks, both at home and in the host country, and these cultural interactions shaped their identities as transnational immigrants. Many of her study participants spoke of life in Mexico and in California in dual terms and even while in California, their networks included friends and family members from Mexico (Monkman 1997). As a result of these transcultural networks and interactions, they continue to maintain Mexican culture and traditions while they participate in America's cultural systems. Their close proximity to their homelands in Mexico further helps to facilitate a system of supportive networks across both regions. One could also argue that they maintained strong ties and networks in Mexico because, as a group, the US public has not accepted their presence and instead has marginalized them as the 'Other', the 'Outsider'. As a result, they hold on to their ethnic networks and identities for a sense of belonging.

Other studies (Basch et al. 1994, Monkman 1997, Alfred 2003) have found that the identities of many migrant groups continue to be rooted in their nation states while they live and work in the host country. For example, Basch et al. note that the USA recognizes the Haitian population as Haitian-Americans while the island of Haiti recognizes them as Haitians. Some will argue, however, that many US citizens see Haitians as poor blacks who invaded the US in full force during the 1980s and landed on the welfare rolls. Like the Mexican immigrants, they are generally viewed as unwelcome guests on US shores. No matter how they are viewed by members of the host country, their social networks at home continue to recognize them as viable members of the Haitian community, particularly for the financial, political and educational contributions they make for the development of individuals and communities.

Similarly, Alfred's (2003) study of learning and development among Anglophone Caribbean immigrant women in the United States revealed the transnational identities of the study participants. The study found that the women navigated the borders of the home and host countries, maintained strong social and family networks in both cultures and participated in the social, cultural and political activities of both nations. When asked to define who they were in terms of their cultural identity, several participants had trouble separating their African-Caribbean identity from their American identity. As one participant noted:

> I am an American with Caribbean roots; I am active in both worlds, and they both continue to influence me.... I look forward to going home [to the Caribbean] every year or so, but I always look forward to coming home [to the US]. Today, I am a product of both worlds and a citizen of both. (Alfred 2003: 251)

It is no surprise, then, that many immigrants continue to maintain membership in the country of origin while they live and work in the new nation. To that end, our understanding of the voluntary immigrant experience must be situated within the context of transnational migration. However, the traditional approach to education tends to be defined and organized within national boundaries (Monkman 1997) rather than from a more global or transnational context. Not surprisingly, courses in adult and higher education are no exception. As Monkman (1997: 26) observes:

> The content of courses in most regions of the world are reflective of the cultural, social, and political values and relations at the national level, sometimes with an effort to reflect the realities of particular groups within a country, but rarely acknowledge the issues relevant to transnational individuals and families.... These courses are focused on facilitating the transition of the immigrants to life in the United States with little attention to how transnational issues are experienced.

This view of immigrants as transnational nomads who maintain cultural traditions of the home and host countries must be considered in the planning and delivery of educational programs. This planning must take into consideration the lifelong learning experiences of these immigrants, as such prior learning influences learning in the host country. Taking into consideration the lifelong experiences of the newcomers can assist them in affirming their ethnic identity as well as fulfilling their need to learn, to survive and to cope within the new environment. In that sense, the education experience can become meaningful and relevant to the new immigrants who seek to embrace both cultures. Similarly, the immigrant experience can also be meaningful to the native-born citizen as she learns from the experiences of the newcomer. After all, the learning that takes place in the formal education classroom determines how the immigrant will be received and positioned in the larger spheres of life, work, career and community. While there is a tendency to acknowledge and value only the learning that takes place in institutional classroom environments, we must also consider learning that takes place beyond formal schooling (Jarvis 2007). Learning is recursive and multidimensional and must therefore be understood within broader social, cultural, and structural contexts.

The issues worth exploring, then, are how do immigrants learn to navigate the cultures of the new country and how do their early socializations prepare them for the transnational experience. The concepts of social capital and funds of knowledge provide a lens through which we can understand the significance of social networks and kinship relationships in the acculturation and wellbeing of individuals and groups.

Social capital, acculturation and lifelong learning

According to Field (2005), much of our life is passed in the company of others, and as we go through life, we acquire new relationships and lose old ones. Similarly, the meanings we give to these relationships can change over time. Field further suggests that these social relationships and the patterns they assume influence our capacity to learn across the lifespan, help us secure goods and services, and provide opportunities to give and receive affection. Embedded in these relationships are resources that have been referred to as social capital.

One of the pioneers of social capital theory is Pierre Bourdieu (1986) who became interested in the ways in which members of the middle and upper class were able to capitalize on material and human resources inherent in networks and social groups to advance their own interests and positional advantage. He articulated a clear interconnection between social capital and social inequalities and found social capital to be a source of power to advance one's interest and leverage one's position within a given context.

Unlike Bourdieu, Coleman (1998) employed the concept of social capital in educational research. From his research on the educational attainment among students in public and private schools, Coleman concluded that students in private schools performed better than those in public schools because there was a stronger sense of community and norms that the parents, teachers and students embraced. Drawing from his further research on educational attainment in poor urban communities, he concluded that social capital could convey significant benefits to poor and marginalized communities through civic engagement. Therefore, Coleman viewed social capital as a resource embedded in family and community that could be harnessed for the wellbeing of individuals and groups.

Another major contributor to the theory of social capital is Putnam (1995) who posits that social capital serves both as a bonding and a bridging function. As a bonding function, it tends to reinforce community values, cultures and group homogeneity. As a bridging function, Putnam suggests that social capital can provide linkages to networks and acquaintances that are external to one's immediate community, thus widening the pool of available resources and social networks. However, Putnam failed to account for factors such as race, class and nationality, (among others), which tend to serve as barriers among minority populations to other white-dominated networks or social groups, thus denying them the bridging opportunities that he speaks of.

Despite its limitations, social capital has been found to influence the way people acquire new skills, knowledge and behaviors throughout their lifespan. Since learning is recursive and continuous, the knowledge, skills and behaviors acquired through social capital networks become funds of knowledge (Hernandez-Leon and Zuniga 2002) that influence future learning. Social capital and lifelong learning are, therefore, interconnected and must be examined within the context of each other. According to Jarvis (2007: 1), lifelong learning is:

> *the combination of processes throughout a lifetime whereby the whole person—body (genetic, physical and biological) and mind (knowledge, skills, attitudes, values, emotions, beliefs and senses)—experiences social situations, the perceived content of which is then transformed cognitively, emotively or practically (or through any combination) and integrated into the individual person's biography resulting in a continually changing (or more experienced) person.* [Italics those of the author]

Lifelong learning is mediated through social interactions and must be viewed within the context of the lived experience. In the case of transnational migrants, lifelong learning must be understood within the socio-cultural contexts of the traditional home, the motivation to migrate, the conditions under which various groups make entry and the acculturation experiences in the new country. Each of these life events takes place within social networks and personal relationships, and social capital theory provides a framework to understand lifelong learning among transnational immigrants.

Social capital as a conduit for lifelong learning

'It is not what you know, it is who you know.' According to Woolcock and Narayan (2000), this common adage sums up much of the conventional wisdom regarding social capital. They note:

> It is a wisdom born of experience—that gaining membership to exclusive clubs requires inside contacts, that close competitions for jobs and contracts are usually won by those with friends and family who constitute the final safety net. (Woolcock and Narayan 2000: 226)

To the new immigrant, networks and relationships create opportunities for learning the culture and life ways, and social capital theory provides a lens through which to observe the interactions that facilitate such learning. Through these lenses, we see how accumulation of social capital is deployed and reinvested in the new homeland, thus facilitating the adjustment of the newly arrived immigrants.

Falk and Kilpatrick (2000) suggest that social capital results from learning interactions that take place in a social, political and cultural context. Fundamental characteristics of these interactions are reciprocity, trust, shared norms and values. The more frequent the learning interactions, they theorize, the greater the capacity to accumulate social capital resources. Accordingly, Falk and Kilpatrick posit that a precondition to building social capital is the existence of a sufficient quantity and quality of learning interactions. In designing adult learning programs, for example, instructors can plan to maximize learning interactions, thus helping learners build social capital resources within and outside the immediate learning community.

Similarly, Field (2005) notes that social capital theory calls for a constructivist view of learning and brings attention to the ways in which people learn and construct knowledge as a result of their interactions with homogeneous and heterogeneous network communities. He distinguishes between learning from everyday social interactions and formal education. Field (2005: 3) writes, 'The concept of learning is very different from the concept of education, and people's active engagement in the wider social context is an extremely important aspect of the distinction between the two.' In order to understand how immigrants learn and construct knowledge from their interactions with social networks and ties, it is necessary to broaden our view of learning to one that goes beyond formal, institutional learning to include learning that takes place in networks and communities. Social capital theory assumes that these networks and communities are made up of a person's family, friends and associates, and these are important assets that can be capitalized in times of need, leveraged for capital gains or enjoyed purely for the human interactions it affords (Woolcock and Narayan 2000).

Studies of migration have used the notion of social capital to explain how and why individual and household decisions about migration are highly dependent on access to social capital stored in support networks (Portes and Sensenbrenner 1993, Hernandez-Leon and Zuniga 2002). According to Hernandez-Leon and Zuniga, learning from social capital interactions plays a significant role in producing particular outcomes among immigrant groups; for example, social mobility, types of assimilation and incorporation and educational achievement.

Social capital, funds of knowledge, and immigration adaptation

While the concept of social capital emphasizes the capacity of social actors to draw resources from networks, Hernandez-Leon and Zuniga (2002) suggest that, as a methodological tool, we also include the concept of 'funds of knowledge' to further explore immigrants' learning and adaptation. According to Hernandez-Leon and Zuniga (2002: 6):

> The notion of funds of knowledge refers to information, expertise and skills—frequently incorporated as individual human and cultural capital—but which are collectively created as part of the adaptive strategies of low income populations…. Elements and pieces of these funds of knowledge are developed and exchanged through social networks of kin or residentially clustered households.

These exchanges, however, are guided by expectations of reciprocity and trust, and access is primarily based on group and network membership. Therefore, it can be argued that understanding the geographic implications of social capital and funds of knowledge provide insights about the ongoing process of settlement and dispersion. As immigrants make entry to geographic locations with a high concentration of members from the sending country, 'a time compression takes place because new comers do not have to start accumulating social capital from scratch.... They can, in fact, use those transplanted or drawn from reservoirs of social capital' (Hernandez-Leon and Zuniga 2002: 9) embedded within ethnic enclaves and transnational communities.

Hernandez-Leon and Zuniga (2002) conducted a study to determine how Mexican immigrants mobilize social capital and funds of knowledge acquired from the homeland and other large metropolitan regions in the US to facilitate their adaptation in a small southern town. Using qualitative and descriptive quantitative data collected among the migrant settlers, the study found that social capital and previous funds of knowledge facilitate settlement at both the individual and group levels. At the individual level, the study found a rapid increase of entrepreneurial ventures among those who migrated originally to labor in low-wage industries such as poultry farming and the carpet industry. Drawing from traditions and knowledge acquired from home and prior settlement experiences, they ventured into business as this was seen to provide better economic returns and upward mobility than low-wage employment. They also observed significant gains in terms of professional development and community engagement among individual actors. At the group level, the study found a compression of the migratory cycle as the settlement in the small southern town progressed more rapidly through the various stages of community formation and incorporation (Hernandez-Leon and Zuniga 2002). Overall, the study found that Mexican-American immigrants were deploying and transplanting social capital and funds of knowledge acquired in the homeland and other settlement regions in the US to facilitate their adaptation in the new location.

With much relevance to the US, Anucha, Dlamini, Yan and Smylie (2006) examined social capital within the context of gender, immigrant status and race by exploring how associational networks are created in the city of Winsor, Canada, and the ways in which four ethnic groups—Eastern Asian, African/Caribbean, South Asian, and West Asian/Middle Eastern—participate in such networks. For the purpose of that study, the authors conceptualized community organizations as the core element of social capital. They examined the structure and types of social capital among immigrant groups; how elements of positionality, such as gender, race/ethnicity, age and socioeconomic status mediate access to social capital; and the outcomes or return from women's access to social capital resources.

The study found community organizations to be an important source of social capital and lifelong learning opportunities for immigrant women, but the benefits were hampered by the limited financial resources available for these organizations to promote networking and learning opportunities among group members. The results indicated that the elements of positionality among immigrant groups influence their access to certain networks and hence employment opportunities in the marketplace. These same elements also influenced one's access to the funds of knowledge available within the group. The African Caribbean immigrants, for example, were found to have the least access to networks and social capital resources because of the small representation among that group. The findings suggest that the larger the ethnic group population within a given geographical region, the more access group members have to each other's capital. They also found that the relationships that were formed and the learning that took place were concentrated primarily with members of the same ethnic groups and that across group relationships were not widely fostered. The knowledge gained from informal learning, therefore, was limited to the funds of knowledge of the in-group members.

In line with the findings from the study reported above, Campbell and McLean (2002) found that ethnic identity was a significant factor in African Caribbean women's perception of the role of interpersonal networks in their acculturation and labor-force participation in the UK. While there was a strong African-American community, African Caribbean immigrants were found to be at a disadvantage and often felt excluded from such networks. The authors found evidence that despite the role of people's interpersonal networks, African Caribbean identity often served as a source of social exclusion in other spheres of community life. This is no surprise because as Sutton and Chaney (1994) reported in the book *Caribbean Life in New York City*, black Caribbean immigrants in the US experience both voluntary and involuntary exclusion.

Voluntarily, many isolate themselves from American blacks and Puerto Ricans, two minority groups with whom they are socially categorized. In referring to their voluntary isolation from black Americans, Sutton and Chaney explain that black Americans have experienced more downward than upward mobility, a general deskilling, cultural denigration and continued separation from the resources and rewards of mainstream society. They had the lowest income and the highest school dropout and unemployment rates in the city. As a result, since their minority status places black Caribbean immigrants in the same minority status as American blacks, some selectively isolate themselves from that group in order to maintain what they perceive as their higher social status and economic positions (Sutton and Chaney 1994).

Similarly, research has found that African-American blacks in general have not readily forged coalitions with their foreign-born Caribbean black counterparts. While both groups have much in common based on their experiences with race and racism, Rogers (2004: 294), speaking from the context of New York City, notes, 'Afro-Caribbeans and African-American New Yorkers thus far have been unable to establish a stable coalition'. Because of the tension that exists between native- and foreign-born blacks, the opportunities for building networks and support systems across the two groups are significantly minimized. It is important to emphasize that the discussion here is not meant for broad generalizations but to help understand why these two ethnic groups, both of African descent with similar experiences of racism and discrimination, often experience problems with bridging networks across the two groups.

While problems with bridging networks have been identified among ethnic groups, limitations with bonding networks have also been explored. For example, Sanders, Nee and Semau (2002) analyzed the relationship between job changes and use of personal networks during the job search process among Asian immigrants in Los Angeles. The study found that ethnic ties contributed to the employment of immigrants; however, such employment was limited to low-wage jobs with low prestige; and that immigrant women were more inclined to fall prey to these segments of the labor market. Since immigrant women engage in more social bonding within their ethnic groups than social bridging across groups, this could account for their limited exposure to employment and other training and development opportunities that would facilitate employment beyond low-wage jobs. According to Bourdieu (1986), social inequality is caused by the unequal access to and interaction of symbolic, cultural and social capital. Because low-income immigrants are often at the margins of the wider society, the quality of their networks is indeed compromised.

Overall, despite the positive outcomes associated with the concept of social capital (Coleman 1998, Hernandez-Leon and Zuniga 2002), there is a growing recognition that there are downsides to the processes that build and maintain it, especially among ethnic minority groups who live on the fringes of society. The data suggest that one's access to social capital and the nature of the capital resources are structurally determined by one's social position (Bourdieu 1986, Portes and Landolt 1996) and the degree to which one has received permission to enter and participate in a network group or community. However, for transnational immigrants, participating in social networks within the ethnic community hastens the acculturation process as the novice immigrant acquires knowledge, skills and practices to help facilitate the adjustment from the home country to the receiving country. They participate in bonding networks rather than bridging networks, although across group relationships have been found to provide more learning opportunities that are not possible within the ethnic community alone. What remains to be explored is how adult education can facilitate the growth of networks in communities, thus enabling participants to form bridging relationships and to have access to the funds of knowledge inherent in the wider learning community.

Conclusion: social capital, adult education and lifelong learning

In order to understand how immigrants construct knowledge from their interactions with social networks and ties, it is necessary to broaden our view of learning to one that goes beyond formal, institutional learning to include learning that takes place in networks and communities. Community education is a well accepted context for adult learning, and the concept of lifelong learning has taken education beyond the formal institution and into other less formal settings. It would be important then to explore the ways in which social networks influence access to and participation in adult learning programs. For example, Field (2005: 5) asks:

> How do social networks help us create and exchange skills, knowledge and attitudes that in turn allow us to tap in to other benefits? If we have more social capital—stronger and more extensive network ties—then are we more likely to learn new things than people with less social capital? And is our learning affected by the types of network that people have—are they qualitatively different in nature?

To Field's questions, I would add the following: How do the power dynamics inherent in social networks provide educational access to certain groups while they serve to exclude others? What is the impact of adult learning on the community? We often speak of learning communities and communities of practice; therefore, these questions are central to the discourse on learning communities consisting of social networks and the dynamics of interactions. They beg us to consider whether some social arrangements are better than others at promoting learning and, also, what kinds of arrangements are more suitable for different learners and contexts. Despite the unanswered questions, there is the general agreement that adult education can promote learning communities and can create avenues for the development of social capital and the promotion of lifelong learning.

According to Balatti and Falk (2001), using and building social capital are both outcomes of learning as well as the processes by which learning occurs. For learners to develop social capital in the classroom, they note, they must be able and willing to interact in new ways, in new contexts and with new people. The argument being made here is that an individual's knowledge and skills are not enough to develop social capital relationships and that the norms of the group within which the resources circulate play a crucial role.

Building a classroom community that emphasizes shared norms, mutual respect and collaboration that foster bridging relationships across differences holds promise for developing of social networks that can benefit participants in both psychosocial and instrumental ways. An example that comes to mind is that of learning groups, a common feature of adult learning pedagogy. What often begins as a learning activity at times extends into supportive networks in and out of the classroom. Many career opportunities have resulted from relationships that begin as a result of collaborative learning arrangements. For example, in a study of social capital among women learners in 10 adult education programs in Australia, Balatti and Falk (2001) found that for all the sites they investigated, the program, consisting of faculty, staff and students, became fertile ground for social capital development. The programs deliberately set out to create the conditions that encouraged participants to develop the building blocks—namely, trust, norms, and relationships—required for social capital to develop.

Adult education can also help learners develop linking ties with other networks and capitalize on the funds of knowledge inherent in these bridging relationships. As an example, faculty can expose students to related professional organizations through professional meetings and conferences, thus providing them with opportunities to form bridging relationships with other professionals beyond their immediate circles. These relationships can provide instrumental benefits in terms of career and other learning opportunities.

In summary, there are inherent risks with social capital networks, but with deliberate intent, instructors and program planners can foster social capital development whereby learners can capitalize on the resources to improve their living conditions and those of partner members. After all, the gains from social capital networking should be bi-directional, in that all members have opportunities to give and to share of the resources embedded within the community.

References

ALBA, R. and NEE, V. (1999) Rethinking assimilation theory for the new era immigration. In C. HIRSCHMAN, P. KASINITZ, and J. DEWIND (eds.) *The Handbook of International Migration: The American experience* (New York: Russell Sage Foundation), pp. 137–160.

ALFRED, M.V. (2003) Sociocultural contexts and learning: Anglophone Caribbean immigrant women in US postsecondary education. *Adult Education Quarterly*, **53**(4), 242–260.

ANUCHA, U., DLAMINI, N., YAN, M. and SMYLIE, L. (2006) *Social Capital and the Welfare of Immigrant Women: A multi-level study of four ethnic communities in Windsor* (Ottawa, Ontario: Status of Women Canada).

BALATTI, J. and FALK, I. (2001) *Socioeconomic contributions of adult learning to community: a social capital perspective*. CLRA Discussion Paper D10-2001. Tasmania University, Launceston, Australia:. Center for Learning and Research in Regional Australia.

BASCH, L., GLICK SCHILLER, N. and BLANC-SZANTON, C. (1994) *Nations Unbound: Transnational Projects, Postcolonial Predicaments, and Deterritorialized Nation-States* (Longhorn, PA: Gordon and Breach).

BOURDIEU, P. (1986) The forms of capital. In J.G. RICHARDSON (ed.) *The Handbook of Theory and Research for Sociology of Education* (New York: Greenwood), pp. 241–258.

CAMAROTA, S.A. (2002) *Immigration in the United States—2002: A snapshot of America's foreign-born population* (Washington, DC: Center for Immigration Studies). Available online at: http:/www.cis.org/articles/2002/back1302.html (accessed 29 May, 2007).

CAMPBELL, C. and MCLEAN, C. (2002) Ethnic identities, social capital, and health inequities: factors shaping African-Caribbean participation in local community networks in the UK. *Social Science and Medicine*, **55**, 643–657.

COLEMAN, J.S. (1998) *Foundations of Social Theory* (Cambridge, MA: Belknap Press).

FALK, I. and KILPATRICK, S. (2000) What is social capital? A study of rural communities. *Sociologia Ruralis*, **40**(1), 87–110.

FIELD, J. (2005) *Social Capital and Lifelong Learning* (Bristol, UK: The Policy Press).

GLICK SCHILLER, N. (1999) Transmigrants and nation states: Something old, something new in the US immigrant experience. In C. HIRSCHMAN, P. KASINITZ and J. DEWIND (eds.) *The Handbook of International Migration: The American experience* (New York: Russell Sage Foundation), pp. 94–119.

GLICK SCHILLER, N., BASCH, L. and BLANC-SZANTON, C. (1992) Transnationalism: A new analytic framework for understanding migration. In N. GLICK SCHILLER, L. BASCH and C. BLANC-SZANTON (eds.) *Toward a Transnational Perspective on Migration: Race, class, ethnicity, and nationalism reconsidered* (New York: New York Academy of Sciences), pp. 1–24.

GOLDIN, L.R. (1999) Transnational identities: The search for analytical tools. In L. R. GOLDIN (ed.) *Identities on the Move: Transnational processes in North America and the Caribbean Basin* (Albany, NY: University of Albany), pp. 1–9.

HANS, H.J. (1999) Toward a reconciliation of 'assimilation and pluralism': The interplay of acculturation and ethnic retention. In C. HIRSCHMAN, J. DEWIND, and P. KASNITZ (eds.) *The Handbook of International Migration: The American experience* (New York: Russell Sage Foundation), pp. 161–171.

HERNANDEZ-LEON, R. and ZUNIGA, V. (2002) *Mexican Immigrant Communities in the South and Social Capital: The case of Dalton, Georgia* (University of California, San Diego: The Center for Comparative Immigration Studies).

JARVIS, P. (2007) *Globalization, Lifelong Learning and the Learning Society*, Vol. 2 (London: Routledge).

KEARNEY, M. (1995) The local and the global: The anthropology of globalization and transnationalism. *Annual Review of Anthropology*, **24**, 547–565.

KENNEDY, M.M. (2007) Defining literature. *Educational Researcher*, **36**, 139–147.

LAFROMBOISE, T., COLEMAN, H.L. and GERTON, J. (1993) Psychological impact of biculturalism: evidence and theory. *Psychological Bulletin*, **114**, 395–412.

LARSEN, L.J. (2004) The foreign born population in the United States: 2003. *Current Population Reports* (Washington, DC: US. Census Bureau). Available online at: http://www.census.gov/prod/2004pubs/p20-551.pdf (accessed 3 July, 2009).

MONKMAN, K. (1997) Transnational or immigrant learners: re-drawing the boundaries of socio-cultural context in understanding adult learning. Paper presented at the Comparative and International Education Society (CIES) Annual Meeting, 19–24 March (Mexico City, March). ERIC Document No. 408123.

PEDRAZA, S. (1996) Immigration, race, and ethnicity in American history. In S. PEDRAZA and R. G. RUMBAUT (eds.) *Origins and Destinies: Immigration, race, and ethnicity in America* (Albany, NY: Wadsworth Publishing), pp. 1–20.

PORTES, A. and LANDOLT, P. (1996) The downside of social capital. *The American Prospect*, **26**, 18–24.

PORTES, A. and RUMBAUT, R.G. (1996) *Immigrant America: A portrait*, 2nd edn (Berkeley: University of California Press).

PORTES, A. and RUMBAUT, R.G. (2006) *Immigrant America: A portrait*, 3rd edn (Berkeley: University of California Press).

PORTES, A. and SENSENBRENNER, J. (1993) Embeddedness and immigration: Notes on the social determinants of economic action. *American Journal of Sociology*, **98**(6), 1320–1350.

PUTNAM, R.D. (1995) Bowling alone: America's declining social capital. *Journal of Democracy*, **6**(1), 65–78.

ROGERS, R.R. (2004) Race-based coalitions among minority groups: Afro-Caribbean immigrants and African-Americans in New York City. *Urban Affairs Review*, **39**(3), 283–317.

SANDERS, J., NEE, V. and SEMAU, S. (2002) Asian immigrants' reliance on social ties in a multiethnic labor market. *Social Forces*, **81**(1), 281–314.

SCHMIDLEY, D. (2003) The foreign-born population in the United States. *Current population reports* (Washington, DC: US Census Bureau).

SCHUCK, P.H. (1998) *Citizens, Strangers, and In-betweens: Essays on immigration and citizenship* (Boulder, Colorado: Westview Press).

SPARKS, B. (2003) A sociocultural approach to planning programs for adult learners. *Adult Learning*, **12**(4), 22–26.

SUAREZ-OROZCO, M. and SUAREZ-OROZCO, C. (2000) Some conceptual considerations in the interdisciplinary study of immigrant children. In H. TRUEBA and L. BARTOLOME (eds.) *Immigrant Voices: In search of educational equity* (New York: Rowman & Littlefield Publishers), pp.17–36.

SUTTON, C. and CHANEY, E. (1994) *Caribbean Life in New York City: Sociocultural Dimensions* (New York: Center for Migration Studies).

TERRAZAS, A. and BATALOVA, J. (2008) US in focus: the most up-to-date frequently requested statistics on immigrants in the United States. *Migration Information Source* (Washington, DC: Migration Policy Institute).

UNITED STATES BUREAU OF THE CENSUS REPORT (2003) Estimates of the unauthorized immigrant population residing in the United States: 1990 to 2000. Available online at: http://www.dhs.gov/xlibrary/assets/statistics/publications/Ill_Report_1211.pdf (accessed 25 May, 2007).

WOOLCOCK, M. and NARAYAN, D. (2000) Social capital: implications for development theory, research, and policy. *World Bank Research Observer*, **15,** 225–250.

Learning through social spaces: migrant women and lifelong learning in post-colonial London

SUE JACKSON
University of London, UK

This article shows how migrant women engage in learning through social spaces. It argues that such spaces are little recognised, and that there are multiple ways in which migrant women construct and negotiate their informal learning through socialising with other women in different informal modes. Additionally, the article shows how learning is shaped by the socio-political, geographical and multicultural context of living in London, outlining ways in which gendered and racialised identities shape, construct and constrain participation in lifelong learning. The article shows that one way in which migrant women resist (post)colonial constructions of difference is by engaging in informal and non-formal lifelong learning, arguing that the benefits are (at least) two-fold. The women develop skills (including language skills) but also use their informal learning to develop what is referred to in this article as 'relational capital'. The article concludes that informal lifelong learning developed through social spaces can enhance a sense of belonging for migrant women.

Lifelong learning, a catchphrase of modern governments, is not a new concept, although it has been differently named across a century, including as recurrent (Kallen and Bengtsson 1973, Istance *et al.* 2002), popular (Crowther *et al.* 2005), adult (Wilson and Hayes 2000), continuing (Jarvis 1983), liberal (Van Doren 1943) and lifelong education (Yeaxlee 1929). Whatever the term, the concept includes learning across the lifespan (Field and Leicester 2000) although more often than not current government policy, both in the UK and elsewhere, has focussed on learning across the *working* lifespan (Burke and Jackson 2007). Whilst lifelong learning includes formal as well as informal and non-formal learning, this article is particularly interested in the informal and non-formal learning that is undertaken by the migrant[1] women with which this research is concerned.

Although boundaries between informal and non-formal (and indeed formal) learning are fluid and can only be meaningfully drawn in relation to particular contexts and for particular purposes (Colley *et al.* 2002), I am taking informal learning to be the unstructured learning which most of us do on a daily basis. It arises from our encounters with others as well as with the cultural artefacts of our daily lives. Non-formal learning includes non-accredited learning that is nevertheless structured and intentional and that often takes place in more formal contexts such as adult learning centres or workplaces. This article shows how migrant women engage in non-formal and informal learning through social spaces, arguing that although social spaces are little recognised as sites of learning there are multiple ways in which migrant women construct and negotiate their informal learning through their experiences of socialising with other women in different informal modes and semi-formal associations.

In addition, the article shows how learning is also shaped by the socio-political, geographical and post-colonial context of living in London. In considering *post-colonial* London, it is not arguing that colonialism no longer has relevance. On the contrary, the histories and experiences of colonialism continue to impact on the (previously) colonised and the (previous) colonisers. Whilst 'post' can suggest something which supersedes, or comes after, the preffix 'post' can also be used to indicate a process of ongoing transformation or change (see e.g. Venn 2006), central to theorisations not just of post-colonialsm as well as post-structuralism and feminism (see e.g. Brooks 1997, for discussion of post-feminism). In considering the post-colonial, Couze Venn suggests that:

> The post-colonial can be understood as a virtual space, that is, a space of possibility and emergence. It is thus also potential becoming: it opens towards a future that will not repeat existing forms of sociality and oppressive power relations. (Venn 2006: 190)

In considering migrant women's lifelong learning, I am interested in spaces of possibility. Nevertheless, the post-colonial belongs to the virtual and discursive spaces and collective memories of the colonisers as well as the colonised. As McLintock (1995: 5) argues, 'imperialism…is not something that happened elsewhere—a disagreeable fact of history external to Western identity'. Both colonialism and imperialism construct 'difference' and therefore identity (Brah 2007) although this is not always recognised nor problematised.

The article develops understandings of ways in which intersected gendered, sexualised, racialised, ethnicised and diasporic identifications construct and constrain participation in lifelong learning. It argues that whilst identities are formed in part through individual agency, they are also constructed and constrained by gendered, racialised and sexualised social divisions. The article shows that one way in which migrant women resist post-colonial constructions of difference is by engaging in informal and non-formal learning, arguing that the benefits are (at least) two-fold. The women develop skills (including language skills) but also use their informal and non-formal learning to develop what is referred to in this article as 'relational capital'. The article concludes that learning developed through social spaces can enhance a sense of belonging for migrant women.

The research

The findings discussed in this article come from a larger research project conducted for the Economic and Social Research Council in the UK.[2] The project explored women's social spaces in post-colonial London and examined the ways in which women perform social identifications in private and public social spaces in London. Its aims were to:

- explore commonalities and differences in the ways in which women construct their gendered and sexualised, racialised and ethnicised identities within social spaces in post-colonial London;
- examine the ways in which women perform social identifications in private and public social spaces in London; and
- develop theoretical understandings of post-colonial intersected identities in urban social spaces in London.

It was developed through 42 in-depth interviews with 'white' and 'South Asian', 'straight' and 'queer' women in the different urban cultural spaces of some of the localities of London. Extensive contacts with diverse community groups were undertaken in order to locate particular groups with which the project could work. Local government websites were used to identify community projects and groups and extensive contacts were made with diverse community groups. Subsequently, the groups were visited on their premises and permission was sought to include them in the research sample. Groups selected were:

- an informal network for (mainly) young Asian women identifying as lesbian or bisexual;
- two older Asian women's groups that met under the aegis of local authorities;
- three mixed-ethnic reading groups: one run by a local library and the other two through informal networks;
- three mixed-ethnic groups who meet socially to knit, one of which is specifically for 'queer' women.

Prior to conducting the interviews, a team of three researchers spent some time as participant observers within the selected social groups, a key methodological aspect of work grounded in feminist research. A second team began the analysis by reading all of the interview transcripts and discussing the key themes that were emerging. It became apparent that post-colonial London was a key theme on which to focus analysis. Other key themes that emerged included, for example, 'locality', 'identity', 'friendship' and 'multiculturalism'.

Each theme was further coded and analysed through the sub-themes that were revealed. For example, 'identity' was further analysed through several sub-themes, such as 'belonging', 'diaspora', 'religion', 'sexuality', 'whiteness' and 'national identity'. Analysis was undertaken by the new team using Nvivo software for examining qualitative data. Nvivo provided an efficient way of managing data derived from loosely structured interviews, with the process allowing a methodical sifting and selecting of data that reinforced the theoretical debate. Names are coded throughout and ethnicities and sexualities (where stated) are self-identified.[3]

London: a city of migrants?

Women constitute around one half of the world's international migrant population, and international migration is one of the most challenging global policy issues of the twenty-first century. Although global migration is not new, the scale of it is. As a report by the UK's Home Office (2005) shows, around 175 million people worldwide live outside their country of birth, and almost 10% of people living in the developed world are migrants, of whom around 45% are women (European Women's Lobby 2007). Women in diverse geographical contexts and at different historical moments have been involved in various forms of migration, and understanding gender relations is key to the development of migration policies and theoretical concerns on issues such as employment, household organisation, identity, citizenship and transnationalism (Willis and Yeoh 2000). However, despite the global as well as national significance of migration, there is still a lamentable lack of gender analysis in most of the policy debates (Schiff *et al.* 2007), and theory, policy and practice that link gender equality concerns with migration are rare (Jolly and Reeves 2005). Discussions of migrants are often gender neutral, with experiences normally debated in relation to men's lives and employment, with nuances or analyses of gender and its intersections seriously lacking in European policy (European Women's Lobby 2007).

UNESCO defines migrants as 'those who move from one region or place to another'. The term migrant can be understood as 'any person who lives temporarily or permanently in a country where he or she was not born, and has acquired some significant social ties to this country' although a person can also be considered a migrant even when s/he is born in the country they inhabit (European Women's Lobby 2007). Although the majority of women interviewed whom I discuss in this article were not born in the UK, some were, and I shall be taking the broader UNESCO definition of migrants to include here women who were born in or partially identify with a country of generational origin or diasporic identification (see below). I do this through their self-definitions of ethnicity (e.g. British Asian, Asian British, East African Asian, etc) and their often complex constructions of cultural identities (Bhachu 1996, Buijs 1996), reflected through colonial pasts and post-colonial presents.

London, the site of this research, has been described as the post-colonial city *par excellence* (Cox and Narayan 2008). It should be understood through its histories and peoples as well as through its current economic and political climate. Its eight million plus inhabitants speak over 300 languages and there are at least 50 ethnic/national communities with over 10,000 members (Cox and Narayan 2008). London has the highest proportion of foreign-born people per head of population in the UK (Home Office 2005), and there is a foreign-born population somewhere in the region of two million currently living in London (Gordon *et al.* 2007: 3). Once in the UK, migrants tend to be more heavily concentrated in London than elsewhere: more than 40% migrants to the UK live in London, making up 26% of London's population. Migrants come from a wide range of both developed and under-developed countries, with recent migration from Eastern Europe seeing large growth. This follows earlier patterns of immigration to London in the 1960s and 1970s from primarily Commonwealth countries, and Jewish and Irish immigration at the turn of the century.

As a force of global power and a major port, London has long been a city of migrants, filled with tensions and complexities, as this interviewee shows:

> London [...] it's an amazing, it's just an amazing city. A city with such hard history to swallow and such a mix [...]. You forget that the city you live in is also

> this city that has had and still has this incredible kind of global significance in all sorts of ways. I have a really palpable sense of that and a really palpable sense of the history and that this is this city that's been kind of growing since Viking invasions, mmm, really, and exclusively through migration. This is a city of migrants and a city that kind of oppressed large sections of the world and a city that you know just so amazing and I really, the sense of history I think and that connection to history that's sometimes quite painful is a really big part of what makes me feel English and certainly what makes me feel comfortable in London. (KQKG8, White British, lesbian, 30s)

However, whilst this respondent recognises the 'hard history' of oppression and pain, she still feels 'comfortable in London'. London's (and England's) colonial past is also what makes it 'great' for her, and she seems to identify with the colonisers ('we're who showed up'):

> But I do like London because London, London is, is quintessentially English in the sense that we're who showed up. There's something great about that. (KQKG8, White British, lesbian, 30s)

Nevertheless, living in London (Cox *et al.* forthcoming) is not necessarily 'great' for all (Bellis and Morrice 2003) and some migrant women clearly experience isolation, both from people and from access to goods and services. The respondent below, who has lived in London for 42 years, still lives in a place of loneliness and isolation, a world far away from her 'own country':

> There was no one from my community whom I could meet, that was the first thing—as a housewife, I mean once you're done with your chores, what are you supposed to do? Where it's all/.... Europeans with their 'hello hi' formalities, they're hardly like people in our countries. It's not like in your own country where people ask how you are, if you need anything, so of course there will be isolation. (BC01, British Asian, 60s)

As she explains, it is difficult to see how feelings of separateness might be overcome, when real or apparent culture clashes make it appear impossible for different groups to 'mix'. London is filled with past, present and future possibilities; with the local, national and global; with stories and histories and collective memories; with gendered, sexualised and racialised identities. Identifications and categorisations develop through the conditions and relations that evolve through colonial and postcolonial histories and discursive spaces (Jackson 2008), with multiple axes of difference arising from the impact of colonialism (see e.g. Spivak 1996, Mohanty 2003), including migration. As the extracts below demonstrate, these axes include gender (shopping, child care) and possibly socio-economic circumstances (including lack of transport and ability to travel):

> the area where I live, I faced a lot of problems because it is a largely residential area, so I had to travel far for groceries and shopping.... Since now a lot more people have moved to the area, and the demand has increased, there are more things available, and my kids are also grown up now! (BC01, British Asian, 60s)

Other axes of difference include ethnicity ('Asians') and religion ('Muslims'):

> First of all, there's a clash between the people of both places— language, religion, they way we conduct our daily activities, our culture, everything of ours, i.e. of Asians, clashes with theirs, especially—I think—of Muslims, because we don't drink, there are a lot of things we don't do, restrictions, it's difficult to mix with them. Their compatibility of their concepts and communication is difficult, because what we consider wrong, they consider good, so there is a clash. How should we mix? (BC01, British Asian, 60s)

As Avtar Brah has shown, the 'problematic of identity' (Brah 2007: 136) continues to determine ways in which subjectivities and identities emerge and are submerged, and our sense of self is tied to our interactions with others through the everyday practices in which we locate ourselves (Venn 2006: 17). The intersections of gender, 'race', class and sexuality (Brah and Phoenix 2004), coupled with the power relations of post-colonialism, signal ways in which meanings of such everyday practices are constructed through multiple layers. As the interviewees show, perceived (or actual) cultural clashes are constructed through the intersections of religious, classed, sexualised, racialised and gendered identities. As this research has shown, intersected identities are also constructed through discourses of 'migrant'.

London is a major city of complex spaces. It is a post-strucutral world made up of structures derived from social, historical, economic, political, ideological and cultural conditions and power relations (Jackson 2008). It is through such conditions and relations that identities evolve. Stuart Hall (2000) conceptualises identity as a continual process of becoming through identifications:

> Precisely because identities are constructed within, not outside, discourse, we need to understand them as produced in specific historical and institutional sites within specific discursive formations and practices, by specific enunciative strategies. Moreover, they emerge within the play of specific modulations of power, and thus are more the product of the marking of difference and exclusion.... Above all...identities are constructed through, not outside, difference. (Hall 2000: 17)

Identities are borne through discursive spaces, including those of colonialism, post-colonialism and empire, and of the discursive and material spaces of migration and diasporic identifications. Whilst some of the women may not be first generation in the UK, they have a strong psychic and emotional connection to their generational memories of diaspora, developed through the stories and histories told to them of 'home'. However, whilst diaspora is about loss and exile, it is also about developing flexible and/or alternative ways of being (Rassool 1997). Diaspora is about movement that is emotional and psychic and well as physical, as new belongings and identities in new spaces are negotiated and constructed. Our sense of self varies according to our histories, shared experiences and identifications as well as the meanings we attach to them. I am interested in exploring a diaspora embedded in the everyday through considerations of the past, present and future, through the tensions between old and new relationships and social networks, and through changing meanings of identity and community (Jackson and Kiwan in preparation).

As this research shows, groups and individuals of unequal power and unequal access to resources and to dominant ways of being try to find liveable spaces, including through the social spaces in which I am interested in this article: women's social spaces in London. Mohanty (1992) has described a politics of location that is developed though the inter-relationship of social, cultural, political, historical and economic processes with personal biographies and collective stories or histories. The interviewees have shown how they belong in multiple locations simultaneously, with strong ties to localities in which they do not live because of ties of memory— including disaporan memories. The research identified ways in which social spaces enable women to negotiate and understand the multiplicity of diverse identities, including diasporan identities. In the next section, I explore ways in which informal and lifelong learning impacts onto such identity constructions, and in particular to examine ways in which learning takes place through social spaces.

Different spaces, different voices

Experiences of migration can provide new opportunities but can also entrench traditional roles (Jolly and Reeves 2005). For some migrant women, the search **for** social spaces is located with communities that confirm their ethnicised, gendered and sexualised identities:

> I enjoy a lot at communities centres that we Asians have...such as this community centre, or sometimes we go to other women's centres. I feel very relaxed and free, because it's our own people, and it's a carefree environment. (AWG1, British Asian, 60s)

In a post-colonial order characterised by fragmentation, tradition can be a strong pull in holding groups together. Rennie Johnston draws on Woody Allen's view that 'tradition is only an illusion of permanence' (Johnston 2003: 10), but sometimes an illusion can seem to be enough. If previous sources of collective identity are no longer available, alternative ways need to be discovered (see Beck 1992 in Field 2005: 17), and social spaces which confirm otherwise minoritised identities are highly valued:

> I think it's because, umm, a lot of the time sort of you can be in certain environments when you have white friends.

> Mmm

> And that's just fine. But there are just odd moments when you are aware of being Asian, or you're with straight friends and there are odd times that you are aware of being gay. But it's just one space where you don't have to think about your label at all. Quite often I don't, I'm not aware of it, but I think you just don't totally relax in an environment just because you are different. (SSG2, 20s, British Asian Indian, lesbian)

Rachel Silvey (2006) argues that gender differences need to be examined with regard to spatialities of power, including the gender dimensions of the socio-spatial production of borders. But as I have argued thus far, gender is not a homogenous category, and borders are constructed around and within gendered post-colonial configurations. This respondent problematises the primacy of 'white' social spaces, pointing instead to the benefits of finding social spaces that enable her to move through and beyond difference. SSG2 wants to move beyond the 'label' whilst AWG1 (above), in finding her own social spaces, prioritises at least two aspects of her identity, her 'Asianness' and her gender. There may also be other aspects of identity, including religion, that make her feel 'relaxed and free' amongst 'our people', yet which seem to set up barriers to communication with others, including language, as another respondent shows:

> We came here and I had very hard time, one year, I live alone, my English was not that good, although I speak English alright, I learned with my children when they go to school. But the English pronunciation of these white people and mine was vast different. I can't explain them what I am going to tell you, or I don't understand when they talk. I understand few words, but then, I thought...oh...I don't know what they are saying, I had very very difficult two years, after, slowly slowly I got my life back when my daughters grow...and everything. (AWG3, British Asian, 70s)

For AWG3, a particular type of 'English pronunciation' is associated with 'these white people', demonstrated an association of language with 'race' and hierarchical voices in a post-colonial world. Other respondents, too, express the difficulties that learning to communicate in a different language can bring:

> Yes, I did everything...after my husband died, I established myself. Nobody helped me. Nobody ever helped me. Nothing, not write a letter, I can't write still an English letter, official letter I can't write it. I can read and I can understand 90%, but 10% I don't understand. So I need a help, I need help, somebody's make me understand. The bills letters comes or some comes you know, then I have to ask somebody, 'Am I understanding alright or it's not alright?', my friend explain me what the letter is saying, and that's what is helping me sometime you know. (AWG4, British Asian, 50s)

Language can be a major obstacle to participation in knowledge societies, a concept I explore below. The emergence of English as the language of globalisation leaves little room for other languages (UNESCO 2005), or for speaking in different voices (Gilligan 1993). Tett *et al.* (2006) argue that adult literacy and language 'are part of social practices...and are patterned by social institutions and by power relations' (2). This may be particularly important in the UK currently with the introduction of citizenship tests for those seeking permanent status. Such tests include English language tests to demonstrate the ability to communicate in English. In their own research on language and identity for asylum seekers, Bellis and Morrice (2003: 85) argue that whilst learning English is an important aspect of developing a sense of citizenship and belonging, it is also linked to a sense of identity and self-esteem. However, attendance at an English language class by no means guarantees positive identity construction. In part, as AWG3 showed (above), power relations are embedded in the primacy of (particular) languages.

Feminist theorists and others have long questioned the extent to which it is possible for subordinated groups to issue challenges to language, when members of those groups are themselves constructed through the language structures of the dominant group. For example, both 'migrant' and 'woman' are understood in different voices and with differently knowledges. As early as 1973, for instance, Sheila Rowbotham was discussing how women are denied access to language, having instead to construct our identities out of silence, from a consciousness formed in a (white) man's world. In addition, as this respondent shows, consciousness is also formed in a (post)colonial world where moving from silence to speech (hooks 1989) is not always easy, and migrant women can be literally silenced: 'you can't speak':

> I joined in English classes, you know always I never wasted my time. When I came here, the very first thing I did is I joined English education classes to improve my language. I thought the education is not only for jobs and I believe that education is also used for socialising. Because if you don't know anything, you go anywhere so many friends you have whatever they discuss, but if you can't speak, if you can't take interest in the subject you just sit down like this only. So first of all I thought let me improve my language and everything so that I can talk, mix up about everything. (AWG4, British Asian, 50s)

For Paulo Freire (often considered a visionary in his work on education and social transformation) literacy is an essential step on the route to becoming a reflective thinker. Freire suggests that we can only achieve a sense of identity through language, and we can only take part in the struggle for transformation if we have an identity (Freire 2004). Through claiming or reclaiming language, people can critically engage in an analysis of their experience that enables them to transform and create the world. In his examination of language, Freire demonstrates the struggle between oppression and liberation—although, as others have shown, literacy itself can be viewed as a colonising process (Bowers and Apffel-Marglin 2005: 3). In considering literacy and oppressive practices, for example, Freire shows how Creole was viewed as an antagonistic force that threatened the privileged and dominant position of Portuguese (Freire 1985: 184/6). The colonisers, he says, had to convince people that the only valid language was Portuguese: they stated that Creole does not contain the necessary vocabulary to enable scientific and technical advancement, for instance, and that Portuguese is far superior as an 'educated' and advanced language (Jackson 2004: 24). The colonisers have the power of naming and of constructing those who 'know' and those who do not.

Throughout his life's work, Freire has viewed education as a political act (Jackson 2007). Teaching, he believes, can never be divorced from critical analysis of how society works, and teachers must challenge learners to think critically through social, political and historical realities within which they are a presence in the world. He says that:

> education makes sense because women and men learn that through learning they can make and remake themselves, because women and men are able to take responsibility for themselves as beings capable of knowing—of knowing that they know and knowing that they don't. (Freire 2004: 15)

However, the creation of 'knowledge' is neither impartial nor accidental. All knowledge is not equally privileged and what is 'known' and who are the 'knowers' is highly politicised. Some knowledges count whilst others do not, legitimising and de-legitimising beliefs and practices. Education is always a certain theory of knowledge put into practice, and it is therefore always political (Freire 2004: 71). Different realities and different ways of knowing and experiencing the world need to be acknowledged and understood. Nevertheless, current political interest in knowledge societies remains in the main unproblematised. Although knowledge societies are about identifying, producing and disseminating information to build and apply knowledge, it has been argued that they require an empowering social vision that encompasses plurality, inclusion, solidarity and participation (UNESCO 2005). There must be a recognition that 'knowledge' is partial and embedded in power relations. What can be 'known' and who can be a 'knower' creates both meaning and oppression:

> Different knowledges and their possibilities are differently distributed to different social groups. This distribution of different knowledges and possibilities is not based on neutral differences in knowledge, but on a distribution of knowledge which carries unequal value, power and potential. (Bernstein 1996: 8)

When power relations are masked, inequalities between social groups become legitimised. Bernstein (1996: 170) says that a central question to ask is who recognises themselves as of value, and what images are therefore excluded by the dominant image of value? However, the question is not just who recognises themselves as of value but also how this recognition occurs (or not), and how it is enabled or constrained. Nevertheless, as this respondent shows, different ways of knowing can develop more positively in 'safe' social spaces:

> It's just saying 'Oh, y'know I've thought through this and y'know where I'm coming from, it signifies this' and someone will say, 'Well actually, I can see what you mean, but from where I'm coming from, it signifies that' and I think it's really important to have those discussions 'cause I think that people are um shy of saying things that are opposing or different, and maybe they're worried about offending, so it's nice to have a nice safe, comfortable environment, to say your opinion and listen, and actively listen to someone else as well. And I often change my mind, that's what I like about it. (AWG12, 40s, British/Asian/Pakistani)

Possibilities for different voices and different spaces are important for the development of both learning and teaching, in speaking and in listening, especially when multiple identities are recognised and embraced. I shall explore this further in the next section by developing a concept of relational capital that can be accumulated, developed and shared.

Learning through social spaces

As I showed above, lifelong learning is a highly fluid and contestable concept (see e.g. Field 2000, Jackson 2003), with multiple overlapping and differing meanings. I have argued here that especially important for lifelong learning is informal and non-formal learning rather than the more formal and accredited learning that attracts government funding (Benn *et al.* 1998, Colley *et al.* 2003, Field 2005). As Frank Coffield (2000) has shown:

> [i]f all learning were to be represented by an iceberg, then the section above the surface of the water would be sufficient to cover formal learning, but the submerged two-thirds of the structure would be needed to convey the much greater importance of informal learning. (Coffield 2000: 1)

Whilst lifelong learning can mean all learning from cradle to grave, including formal, non-formal and informal learning, it is most frequently taken as synonymous with formal post-compulsory learning. Nevertheless, lifelong learning includes learning in educational institutions, in the workplace, in the home and in religious, voluntary and community organisations. For many women engaged in post-compulsory and informal and lifelong learning, the picture is complex. They are less likely than men to have received formal education, especially post-compulsory education (Jackson 2004), so social networks can be vital in developing learning opportunities for women. This may be especially true for migrant women moving between countries and cultures (Brine 1999, Heward and Bunwaree 1999), who are less likely to have received formal education than are their male counterparts. In the developing countries, an average of one woman in two cannot read, and two-thirds of illiterate people in the world are women (UNESCO 2005).

Naomi Sargent (1997) has shown that the less likely people are to have continued education whilst young, the less likely they are to participate when they are older. For many women, including migrant women, continuing at school or in further education was not considered an option (Jackson 1998). Although in formal educational institutions there is often little recognition of the past learning experiences, skills and resourcefulness of people of diverse cultural, social and ethnic backgrounds (Dadzie 1993), one way in which new opportunities can be developed is through informal and non-formal learning opportunities in the different social spaces and for the diverse voices and communities discussed above. London, with its large numbers of migrant communities, is very well placed to be able to offer some of those social spaces. However, learning opportunities differ widely and, as this respondent shows, are sometimes taken up regardless of whether or not there is a perceived need for learning:

> So, one day one of the ladies said hello, hello and she showed me that there is a community centre there on {name} Road and I went there. I come across {name}. She is sewing teacher.
>
> Okay
>
> She was very good to me and I started sewing. I knew sewing. But for just to pass the time, I joined the class from there got so many other classes. I used to go in {name} and everywhere. I did so many classes. To socialise I do go Saturday and Sunday to my friends in {name} and also in the community centres. [...] the community centres have become my parents like that. All my stay here in {name} has gone in this community centre. Because once a week, twice a week I am there in these community centres. (AWG4, British Asian, 50s)

The respondent shows that whilst she may have appeared to join a community centre to 'learn' a previously held skill (sewing), her primary reason was 'to pass the time', to become part of a community and to obtain some relief from her loneliness. The diverse communities and migrant groups of London give increased opportunities for discovering a sense of group belonging, for affirming diasporic identifications.

Although of secondary interest, AWG4 did move on to learn new skills and develop new interests, through doing 'so many classes'. However, learning was just a part of the importance she attaches to her involvement in the centre and perhaps most importantly she fulfilled her aim to become part of a community, replacing the loss of the generational knowledge ('the community centres have become my parents') left behind in her homeland.

As the quotations from AWG4 (above and below) show, the respondent has located herself in a discourse of domesticity, including her experience of a daughter learning from her parents. Women such as AWG4, often isolated in the 'private' realms of domesticity, may struggle to find new ways. They are more likely to suffer a loss of identity, often feeling rootless due to changing roles in the family as well as to societal perceptions of migrant women (Jackson 2008). In addition, for girls and young women, expectations of domesticity have formed and informed their prior experiences, and have often outweighed expectations of schooling and education:

> First of all, I was doing my schooling and everything in that age, other thing that I was looking after the house and everything and I was looking after my sisters and all they were younger to me as I am the eldest. (AWG4, British Asian, 50s)

Nevertheless, informal or lifelong learning is one way in which migrant women can network with others and affirm identities. In considering learning through social spaces, I turn to spaces where what is most important is those aspects of our identities which we have in common with others, where we find common understandings, traditions that are shared and traditions that are still to be made—the social spaces of community.

Community education is one educational arena that has often been attractive to women (Jackson 2006). It is rooted both in new policy directions linked to social cohesion, older philanthropic concerns with adult education for poor working-class people and more radical traditions of working class organisations which developed in counterpoint to upholding the status quo (Tett 2006: 1). Community education is a space where transformation can be acted out and defined through policy and practice and through ideological positionings. However, as Lyn Tett (2006) explains, although community education responds to concepts of 'community', this is a slippery concept that is difficult to define. However, it can be broadly divided into three elements:

- Place: this is the most common meaning and refers to people living in a particular geographic community such as neighbourhood or village.
- Interest: this refers to people who share the same interest or activity such as community activists or environmentalists or members of the same religious or ethnic group.
- Function: this refers to groups with the same profession, such as teachers, or the same role, such as community representatives, who acquire a common sense of identity despite not having the same physical locus (Tett 2006: 2).

The women in this study fall into all three categories, often in complex ways. Whilst they all share a geographic location—they all currently live in London—the project has demonstrated that London can be viewed as a series of urban villages in which its inhabitants live, work and establish themselves as part of smaller communities. As a major city of migrants (see above), London allows for the possibilities for multiple communities to develop and flourish. As this respondent shows, 'commonality' with others is as important as finding new ways of being:

> I do have a need in me to meet and to socialise with gay people. There is a commonality there. I mean, actually, [the social group] is that extra special cream on the top of the cake, isn't it? That they're not only just gay, but they are also Asian women. And you just think, oh fantastic. Because there is just that commonality and it just makes a huge difference. (SS01, 30s, Asian, bisexual)

For some of the women, centres such as the Asian Women's Centres fulfil a role of bringing together a community of women organised through religious, cultural and/or ethnic traditions:

> Since we live away from our homeland, we enjoy religious celebrations more, and of course the social ones too, because we get to meet each other, discuss things such as problems—consult each other for advice, just sit and chat. (AWG1 British Asian, 60s)

Social spaces can offer a meaningful context for problem posting and problem solving and community knowledge can provide a recognisable starting point for empowerment of minoritised individuals and groups (Johnston 2003), developing a relational understanding of different ways of knowing as well as replacing knowledge lost through depletion of familial networks:

> You already know that there are firstly these centres, there is the {name} Women's Centre and an Asian Community Centre. We are involved in a lot of activities here: classes, outings, a social club every Monday where we all sit together, have a laugh and a chat, discuss issues and give advice. Some take recipes, some teach knitting, ask for advice about their children, we have all sorts of discussions there which are very helpful because there are people from all age groups—old and young, so the atmosphere varies. There are young people, old women and very old women like me! It's very beneficial communicating with these different age groups. (AWG1 British Asian, 60s)

Yet communication can sometimes appear to happen in different voices (Gilligan 1993): voices emanating from multiple traditions, cultural origins and identifications.

When migrants arrive in a new homeland, they need to develop, or re-develop, what I am calling here relational capital. This in part refers to the capital that is acquired from familial networks, but also that which acquired from the development of a relational understanding of different realities, of the relationship between things and of different ways of knowing and experiencing sometimes competing worlds.

The concept of capital—whether it is material, social, cultural or so forth—is about its accumulation not just for a stock to exchange, but also to invest. An investment in social capital, for example, can pay off when networks are increased and benefits accrue for the future. Social networks therefore become a valuable asset (Field 2003) that enable people to commit to each other in order to accrue the benefits.

Whilst the development of social cohesion through social networks and relationships of reciprocity and trust is a key benefit of social capital, it can also lead to a tightening of the fabric of elite groups and exclusion of 'others' (Jackson 2006). That is not to say that those living in marginalised groups or communities cannot also develop the reciprocity, trust and networks demanded for the accumulation of social capital (Coleman 1988). Nevertheless, privileged groups maintain and use their networks, connections and relationships with other privileged groups, maintaining the status quo for the group and accruing individual benefits.

Whether for marginalised or elite groups however, the accumulation of capital is about an individualised notion of benefits. In setting out the case for relational capital, I am also arguing for a notion of capital that is about the accumulation of *shared* or collective stocks that may be developed through communities of practice. Communities of practice are formed when people come together who share a repertoire of resources and who engage in a process of collective learning that generates collective ideas, commitments and memories (Wenger 1998), particularly important for migrants seeking new ways of being without losing diasporic identifications. Learning in communities of practice may be non-formal and intentional, but is mainly informal and unintentional. According to Wenger (undated), for communities of practice to flourish they must contain three elements:

- an identity defined by a shared domain of interest, where members value their collective competences and understandings, even if they are little recognised or valued outside of the group;
- the development of a network of relationships where members interact and learn from each other; and
- the development of shared repertoires of resources, including shared experiences, stories and problem solving.

All three elements exist in the social spaces discussed here as can be seen, for example, in the Asian Women's Group. However, I am arguing for the importance of a fourth dimension, the development of relational capital, which enables the accumulation of collective stocks of understandings that arise from the relational understandings of and between the different voices, histories and memories discussed here, including those derived from post-colonialism and experiences of diaspora. Relational capital, then, is political, and relational understandings, *per se*, are about an investment in the development of shared consciousness. For some migrant women, centres such as the social support group play a central role in enabling women to organise around a common sense of identity, regardless of where they live in London, illustrating the formation of social bonds that extend beyond kinship and friendship to other forms of solidarity. Learning through social spaces in which they learn to recognise themselves and others, and to be recognised in return, enables the women to develop clearer knowledge and understandings about their relationships within their competing worlds.

Conclusions

In this article I have developed a concept of relational capital to expand my discussion of migrant women and lifelong learning in post-colonial London. This refers to the replacement of and addition to knowledge gained in familial networks often lost to migrants, but also the development of a relational understanding of different realities and of different ways of knowing and experiencing sometimes competing worlds. This has included gendered and racialised ways of being that result in appearing to speak in a different voice. In doing so, I have taken a broader explanation of migrancy that includes diasporic experiences and memories and recognises the complexities of identification for migrant women.

As has been seen from their own self-identifications and categorisations, these include multiple ways of understanding who they are, including affiliations and non-affiliations with nations, ethnicities, religions and sexualities. Cutting across these intersectionalities are the gendered experiences with which the women have lived and continue to live. The women's current experiences are acted out in London, a complex global and post-colonial city where identity and difference are constructed. These experiences are derived from social, historical, economic, political, ideological and cultural conditions and power relations. For many of the women, such a setting brings with it a loneliness constructed out of difference. One way in which the migrant women in this study resisted (post)colonial constructions of difference is by engaging in informal learning through social spaces they can claim as their own. Whilst not formally considered community education, and largely unfunded, communities of learning have nonetheless developed, and women also used their informal learning to develop relational capital.

The research showed that without spaces of affirmation it is not always possible for minoritised groups and individuals to recognise themselves, and they can become rendered invisible. Whilst some interviewees experienced a sense of belonging to neighbourhoods through their multiple identities, for others their prioritised identities led to exclusions and feelings of unbelonging. Whilst it was not always recognised as such, for most of the migrant women in this research, involvement in informal learning through women's social spaces has been involvement in a political act. The article concludes that non-formal and informal lifelong learning developed through women's social spaces in London can develop a greater sense of affirmation and belonging for migrant women.

Notes

1. Definitions of 'migrant' will be discussed later in this article.
2. ESRC RES-148-25-0022 Intersecting identities: Women's spaces of sociality in post- colonial London.
3. AWG: Asian Women's Group
   BC01: Book club 1
   BC02: Book club 2
   BC03: Book club 3

CLKG: Central London knitting group
KQKG: Klick Queer knitting group
NLKG: North London knitting group
SSG: Social support group

References

BACHU, P. (1996) Identities constructed and reconstructed: representations of Asian women in Britain. In BUIJS, G (ed.), *Migrant Women: Crossing Boundaries and Changing Identities* (Washington: Berg Publishers), pp. 99–118.
BELLIS, A. and MORRICE, L. (2003) A sense of belonging: asylum seekers, cultural difference and citizenship. In COARE, P. and JOHNSTON, R. (eds.) *Adult Learning, Citizenship and Community Voice* (Leicester: NIACE), pp. 73–91.
BENN, R., ELLIOTT, J. and WHALEY, P. (eds.) (1998) *Educating Rita and Her Sisters: Women and continuing education* (Leicester: NIACE).
BERNSTEIN, B. (1996) *Pedagogy, Symbolic Control and Identity* (London: Taylor and Francis).
BOWERS, B.A. and APFFEL-MARGLIN, FREDERIQUE, (eds.) (2005) *Re-thinking Freire: Globalisation and the Environmental Crisis* (New Jersey: Lawrence Erlbaum Associates).
BRAH, A. (2007) Non-binaried identities of similarity and difference. In WETHERELL, M., LAFLECHE, M. and BERKLEY, R. (eds.) *Identity, Ethnic Diversity and Community Cohesion* (London: Sage), pp. 136–145.
BRAH, A. and PHOENIX, A. (2004) Ain't I a woman? Revisiting intersectionality. *Journal of International Women's Studies*, 5(3), 75–86.
BRINE, J. (1999) *Under Educating Women: Globalising Inequality* (Bucks: OU Press)
BUIJS, G. (1996) *Migrant Women: Crossing Boundaries and Changing Identities* (Washington: Berg Publishers).
BURKE, P. and JACKSON, S. (2007) *Reconceptualising Lifelong Learning: Feminist interventions* (London: Routledge).
COFFIELD, F. (2000) *The Necessity of Informal Learning* (Bristol: Policy Press).
COLEMAN, J. (1988) Social capital in the creation of human capital. *American Journal of Sociology*, **94**, 95–120.
COLLEY, H., HODKINSON, P. and MALCOLM, J. (2002) Non-formal learning: mapping the conceptual terrain. A consultation report (Leeds: University of Leeds Lifelong Learning Institute).
COLLEY, H., JAMES, D., TEDDER, M., and DIMENT, K. (2003) Learning as becoming in vocational education and training: class, gender and the role of vocational habitus. *Journal of Vocational Education and Training*, 55(4), 471–498
COX, R., JACKSON, S., KIWAN, D. and KHATWA, M. (2010), Living London: Women negotiating identities in a post-colonial city. In WETHERELL, M. (ed.) *Identity in the 21st Century: New Trends in Changing Times* (Hampshire: Palgrave Macmillan), pp. 175–196.
COX, R. and NARAYAN, Y. (2008) Unravelling Britishness: 'Identity' and women's social spaces in post-colonial London. Paper presented at Empires, Diaspora and Identity Conference (Turlock CA, March).
CROWTHER, J., GOLLOWAY, V., and MARTIN, I. (2005) *Popular Education: Engaging the academy. International perspectives* (Leicester: NIACE)
DADZIE, S. (1993) *Working with Black Adult Learners. A Practical Guide* (Leicester: NIACE).
EUROPEAN WOMEN'S LOBBY (2007) *Equal Rights, Equal Voices: Migrant women in the European Union*. Available online at: http://www.womenlobby.org/ Site Resources/data/MediaArchive/Publications/ 1817%20BR% 20en%20MP01LR.pdf (accessed 15 October 2008)
FIELD, J. (2000) *Lifelong Learning and the New Educational Order* (Stoke on Trent: Trentham Press).
FIELD, J. (2003) *Social Capital* (London: Routledge).
FIELD, J. (2005) *Lifelong Learning and Social Capital* (Bristol: Policy Press).
FIELD, J. and LEICESTER, M. (eds.) (2000) *Lifelong Learning: Education across the lifespan* (London: RoutledgeFalmer).
FREIRE, P. (1985) *The Politics of Education* (Basingstoke: Macmillan).
FREIRE, P. (2004) *Pedagogy of Indignation* (Boulder: Paradigm).
GILLIGAN, C. (1993) *In a Different Voice: Psychological theory and women's development* (Harvard: Harvard University Press).
GORDON, I., TRAVERS, A. and WHITEHEAD, C. (2007) *The Impact of Recent Immigration on the London Economy* (London: City of London).
HALL, S. (2000) 'Who needs "identity"?' In DU GAY, P., EVANS, J. and REDMAN P. (eds.) *Identity: A reader* (London: Sage), pp. 15–30.
HEWARD, C. and BUNWAREE, S. (eds.) (1999) *Gender, Education and Development: Beyond access to empowerment* (London: Zed Books).
HOME OFFICE (2005) *Controlling our Borders: Making migration work for Britain: a five year strategy.* (Norwich: The Stationery Office).

HOOKS, B., (1989) *Talking Back* (Massachusetts: South End Press).
ISTANCE, D., SCHUTZE, H., and SCHULLER, T. (2002) *International Perspectives on Lifelong Learning: From recurrent education to the knowledge society*. (Bucks: Open University Press).
JACKSON, S. (1998) In a class of their own: women's studies and working-class students. *The European Journal of Women's Studies*, **5**(2), 195–215.
JACKSON, S. (2003) Lifelong earning: lifelong learning and working-class women. *Gender and Education*, **15**(4), 365–376.
JACKSON, S. (2004) *Differently Academic? Developing lifelong learning for women in higher education* (Dordrecht: Kluwer Academic Press).
JACKSON, S. (2006) Jam, Jerusalem and Calendar Girls: lifelong learning and the WI. *Studies in the Education of Adults*, **38**(1), 74–90.
JACKSON, S. (2007) Freire re-viewed. *Educational Theory*, **57**(2), 199–213.
JACKSON, S. (2008) Diversity, identity and belonging: Women's social spaces. *The International Journal of Diversity in Organisations, Communities and Nations*, **8**(3) 147–154.
JACKSON, S. and KIWAN, D. (in preparation) Encounters, intersections and multiplicity: women's identities in post-colonial London.
JARVIS, P. (1983) *Adult and Continuing Education: Theory and practice*. (London: RoutledgeFalmer).
JOHNSTON, R. (2003) Adult learning and citizenship: clearing the ground. In COARE, P. and JOHNSTON, R. (eds.) *Adult Learning, Citizenship and Community Voices* (Leicester: NIACE) pp. 3–21.
JOLLY, S. and REEVES, H. (2005) *Gender and Migration: Overview report* (London: Institute of Development Studies).
KALLEN., D. and BENGTSSON, J. (1973) *Recurrent Education: A strategy for lifelong learning* (New York: OECD Publications Center).
MCLINTOCK, A. (1995) *Imperial Leather: Race, gender and sexuality in the colonial context* (New York: Routledge).
MOHANTY, C.T. (1992) Feminist encounters: Locating the politics of experience. In M. BARRETT, and A. PHILLIPS (eds.) *Destabilising Theory: Contemporary feminist debates* (Cambridge: Polity Press), 74–93.
MOHANTY, C. (2003) *Feminism Without Borders: Decolonizing theory, practicing solidarity* (Durham NC: Duke University Press).
RASSOOL, N. (1997) Fractured or flexible identities? Life histories of 'black' diasporic women in Britain. In MIRZA, H. (ed.) *Black British Feminism* (London: Routledge), pp. 187–204.
ROWBOTHAM, S. (1973) *Woman's Consciousness, Man's World* (Harmondsworth: Penguin).
SARGENT, N. with FIELD, J., FRANCIS, H., SCHULLER, T. and TUCKET, A. (1997) *The Learning Divide* (Leicester: NIACE).
SCHIFF, M., MORRISON, A. and SJOBLOM, M. (eds.) (2007) *The International Migration of Women* (Hampshire: Palgrave Macmillan).
SILVEY, R. (2006) Geographies of gender and migration: spatializing social difference. *International Migration Review*, **40**(1), 64–81
SPIVAK, G. (1996) *The Spivak Reader* (London: Routledge).
TETT, L. (2006) *Community Education, Lifelong Learning and Social Inclusion* (Edinburgh: Dunedin Academic Press).
UNESCO WORLD REPORT (2005) *From the Information Society to Knowledge Societies* (Paris: UNESCO Publishing).
VAN DOREN, M. (1943) *Liberal Education* (New York: Henry Holt)
VENN, C. (2006) *The Post-Colonial Challenge: Towards alternative worlds* (London: Sage).
WENGER, E. (1998) Communities of practice Learning as a social system. *Systems Thinker*. Available online at: http://www.co-i-l.com/coil/knowledge-garden/cop/lss.shtml (accessed 10 April 2009).
WENGER, E. (undated) Communities of practice: a brief introduction. Available online at: http://www.ewenger.com/theory/ (accessed 10 April 2009).
WILLIS, K. and YEOH, B, (eds.) (2000) *Gender and Migration* (Cheltenham: Edward Elgar).
WILSON, A. and HAYES, E. (2000) *Handbook of Adult and Continuing Education* (New Jersey: Jossey-Bass).
YEAXLEE, B. (1929) *Lifelong Education: A sketch of the range and significance of the adult education movement* (London: Cassell).

Beyond deficit paradigms: exploring informal learning of immigrant parents[1]

YAN GUO
University of Calgary

Abstract

This study explores how immigrant parents construct and mobilize their knowledge through informal learning to support their children's education. The study reveals that many participating immigrant parents learned the meaning of parental involvement primarily through trial and error. They learned Canadian curricula by using the Internet, passed on their first-language knowledge, instilled the best values of both Canadian and country-of-origin cultures, and learned how to advocate on behalf of their children, who were often marginalized at school. The results of this study illustrate the significance of informal learning about parental involvement by immigrant parents and the need for teachers and school administrators to recognize and make use of parent knowledge.

Résumé

Cette étude examine comment les parents immigres construisent et mobilisent leurs connaissances par l'apprentissage informel en vue de soutenir l'éducation de leurs enfants. L'étude révèle que de nombreux participants ont appris leur role parental grâce à des pratiques d'essai et d'erreur. Ils ont appris les programmes canadiens en utilisant l'Internet, ont transmis leurs connaissances de leur langue maternelle, ont inculqué les meilleures valeurs des deux cultures, canadiennes et de leur pays d'origine, et ont appris à defendre les interers de leurs enfants, qui sont souvent marginalisés à l'ecole. Les résultats de cette étude illustrent l'importance de l'apprentissage informel sur fa participation parentale par les parents immigrants et de la nécessité pour les enseignants et les administrateurs scolaires à reconnaître et à utiliser les connaissances des parents.

Introduction

Parents' active involvement in schools is a desired norm in North America. However, parental involvement is mainly a North American concept. It is neither expected nor practised in many immigrants' countries of origin (Ogbu, 1995). Immigrant parents who attended a focus group discussion conducted by the British Columbia Teachers' Federation believed that parental involvement was a Western idea, leading the study author to conclude that immigrant parents "need more outreach to involve them" (Naylor, 1993, as cited in Guo, Y., 2006, p. 83). In fact, for immigrant parents, involvement may have negative associations (Wan, 1994); Wan explains that in Hong Kong, Chinese parents seldom attend school functions because a school's request to see parents means their children have gotten into trouble. Thus, negative social stigma associated with school communication may prevent some Chinese immigrant parents from interacting with schools and teachers when they come to Canada. Some research has suggested that whereas white parents are participating more in their children's education, immigrant parents' contacts with their children's schools are actually decreasing (Moles, 1993).

Regrettably, many teachers incorrectly interpret a lack of parental involvement as a lack of interest and concern (Delgado-Gaitan, 1990; Guo, Y., 2006). Teachers may come to believe that immigrant parents do not care about their children's education. Yet in studies, many immigrant parents indicate that they care passionately (Dyson, 2001; Guo, Y., 2007). Li (2002) concludes that cultural and linguistic differences prevent immigrant parents from intervening more often in their children's education. When parents successfully intervene, it is often because they have used informal learning to familiarize themselves with the Canadian education system (Foley, 1999; Liu, 2007; Livingstone, 1999, 2006). This informal learning may, however, be unrecognized by teachers and school administrators. Recognition of parents' informal learning is significant because it will help educators move beyond their deficit views of parents and understand the knowledge of immigrant parents.

Discourses on Immigrant Parents

For the most part, the literature on immigrant parents uses a deficit model, highlighting parents' inability to speak English and their difficulties communicating with schools (Gibson, 2000; Naylor, 1993, as cited in Guo, Y., 2006; Ng, 2005). In their study of Ethiopian parents in Australia, for example, Bitew and Ferguson (2010) concluded that immigrant parents have little knowledge about the education system of their host countries, and that few are able to help with homework or course selection.

Research shows that immigrant parents view education differently than Western teachers. Ran (2001) studied the interaction of four Mainland Chinese families with three British teachers in parent-teacher meetings. Ran found that Chinese parents and British teachers failed to connect with each other due to differences in educational philosophies. Chinese parents wanted more homework and emphasized accuracy and perfect scores – the micro aspects of learning-whereas British teachers viewed error as a normal part of the learning process and focused on problem-solving and other macro aspects of learning.

Research has also explored how cultural differences impact home-school communication. Dyson (2001) and Li (2006) found that Chinese parents are reluctant to challenge a teacher's authority because in Chinese culture, teachers are held in high esteem. Chinese parents see teachers as professionals with authority over their children's schooling. They believe that parents should not interfere with school processes. Yao (1988) explains that Asian parents usually do not initiate contact with schools because they see communication with teachers as a culturally disrespectful way of monitoring them. Espinosa (1995) found that most immigrant parents believe they are responsible for nurturing and educating their children at home, not at school.

Traditional models of family-school partnership include six types of parent involvement: parenting, communicating, volunteering, learning at home, decision making, and collaborating with community (Epstein, 2001). The conventional North American model for parental involvement in education involves forms of parental participation in school-based activities and events. This model intends to promote equal opportunity, but in practice has many failings (Dehli, 1994; McLaren & Dyck, 2004). Barriers such as class and race play a role in parent-school interaction. These include educators' cultural biases and generally low expectations of immigrant parents (Jones, 2003; Ramirez, 2003). As Cline and Necochea (2001) observed of the involvement of Latino parents in the Lampoc United School District in California,

> only parental involvement that is supportive of school policies and instructional practices are welcome here ... parents whose culture, ethnicity, SES [socioeconomic status], and language background differ drastically from the white middle-class norms are usually kept at a distance, for their views, values, and behaviors seem "foreign" and strange to traditional school personnel. (p. 23)

Probing further, Lareau (2003) found that middle-class white and black parents were more strategic in intervening in their children's schools than were black working class parents. Lareau also found that both middle- and working-class black parents were continually concerned with schools' racial discrimination. Perceived racial discrimination may have been a form of acquiescence among parents who were not strategic. In this regard, Canadian or U.S. models of parent involvement have tended to focus more on middle-class than working-class values and concerns and on experiences more relevant to parents of Anglo-Celtic descent than to those from non-English-speaking backgrounds. When immigrant parents do not conform to the dominant culture in their receiving country, schooling may end up undermining and subordinating parents' educative and child-rearing practices (Bernhard, Freire, Pacini-Ketchabaw, & Villanueva, 1998).

Knowledge Construction in Informal Learning

The knowledge that immigrants hold about their children is often unrecognized by teachers and school administrators (Jones, 2003). Non-recognition of immigrant parents can be attributed to misconceptions of difference and lack of knowledge about different cultures (Guo, S., 2009; Honneth, 1995). A deficit model of difference leads to the belief that difference is equal to deficiency, that the knowledge of others, particularly those from developing countries, is incompatible, inferior, and, hence, invalid (Abdi, 2007; Dei, 1996). If school staff members hold these attitudes, even tacitly, they may fail to recognize and make use of the knowledge of immigrant parents.

The extent to which informal knowledge is gained and used may be modelled as transcultural knowledge construction, whereby individuals in immigrant societies of the new world change themselves by integrating diverse cultural lifeways into dynamic new ones.

The resulting blended forms lead either to opposition and discrimination, or to cultural creativity and the integration of new knowledge within academic and societal positionings (Hoerder, Hebert, & Schmitt, 2006). For example, in her study of Chinese immigrants in Toronto, Liu (2007) reported that Chinese parents adapted to the Canadian way of educating children through informal learning.

Knowledge is power; knowledge is socially constructed, culturally mediated, and historically situated (McLaren, 2003). At the heart of the nature of knowledge as social relations is a notion of culture as a dynamic entity, as a way of using social, cultural, physical, spiritual, economic, and symbolic resources to make one's way in the world. Mobilizing such knowledge systematically in the classroom by teachers and administrators would promote insightful connections between curricular goals and immigrant students' experiences in countries of origin, in transition, and in residence in the local community, in turn making sense of transcultural flows and attachments to locality (Appadurai, 1996; Hannerz, 1992).

In addition to socially mediated forms of knowledge, immigrant parents' personal knowledge can play an important role in school relations. Personal knowledge refers to wisdom that comes with embodied meaning (Polanyi, 1958). A parent's personal knowledge is knowledge gained from lived experience in all aspects of life: at work, at play, with family and friends, and so on. It has temporal dimensions in that it resides in "the person's past experience, in the person's present mind and body, and in the person's future plans and actions" (Connelly & Clandinin, 1988, p. 25). Parental knowledge includes that drawn from their own educational backgrounds, their professional and personal experiences of interacting with schools in their countries of origin, their current understanding of the host country's education system, their own struggles as immigrant parents, and their future aspirations for their children (Pushor, 2008).

One way that immigrant parents construct their knowledge of parental involvement is through informal learning. Informal learning refers to any activity involving the pursuit of understanding, knowledge, or skill outside the curricula of formal and non-formal educational institutions (Livingstone, 1999). Informal learning occurs through everyday activities, and can be intentional or unintentional, explicit or tacit. Elsdon (1995) maintains that the most important and valuable forms of informal learning are unpremeditated learning leading to personal growth, including confidence, empowerment, making constructive relationships, organizational learning, and ability and willingness to shoulder responsibility. He further states that these changes are usually transmitted through families, friends, and neighbours.

Livingstone (1999) highlights three major criticisms pertaining to research on informal learning: individualistic bias, dominant class bias, and learning question bias. The first criticism challenges an often implicit assumption that people learn most of what they learn individually rather than in collective or relational contexts. The second criticism emerged because the vast majority of early research on informal learning was conducted with white, middle-aged, professional/managerial people and younger university students. Third, leading research questions related to informal learning were asked in biased ways from the dominant white, middle-class perspective. This study attempts to address these criticisms by exploring the informal learning[2] experience of immigrant parents in supporting their children's education.

Methodology

The parents were recruited through the Coalition for Equal Access to Education in Calgary, Alberta. This is a local umbrella organization of community agencies, groups, and individuals concerned with the current state of ESL instruction in the K-12 public education system and its consequences for immigrant children and families. The Coalition is committed to working with community, education, and government stakeholders to promote access to quality, equitable education for culturally diverse children and youth. With the assistance of the Coalition's staff member, the researcher sent a recruitment notice to the Coalition's e-mail list. The researcher also participated in several community functions and parent leadership workshops organized by the Coalition in order to recruit participants. Forty parents were targeted and 38 agreed to participate. The parents who participated in this study had arrived in Calgary from 15 countries, including China, Korea, Vietnam, Nepal, the Philippines, India, Pakistan, Bangladesh, Algeria, Ghana, Somalia, Sudan, Colombia, Belize, and Suriname. They spoke 23 different languages. All participants held credentials from their countries of origin. Twenty-five of these parents had bachelor degrees, 12 had master's degrees, and one had a high-school diploma. Occupations held in countries of origin included university instructor, teacher, engineer, social worker, principal, and manager. Once in Canada, most experienced downward mobility; they became community liaison workers, cashiers, production workers, or unemployed. Some parents volunteered in Canadian schools, participated in school councils, or worked in schools as lunch supervisors or teacher assistants. Some had observed teachers working with their children and were able to share these experiences.

Semi-structured, individual interviews with parents were used to elicit their perspectives on what teachers should know about their children. Several open-ended questions were used. These questions were designed to draw out rich descriptive data on parents' experiences with their children's teachers and schools, and their suggestions about what teachers need to know about their children, community, culture, and values to develop more effective home-school partnerships. Great care was taken in these interviews to inquire into how parents' knowledge of Canadian education was acquired, constructed, and activated. Each interview lasted from 60 to 90 minutes

An inductive analysis strategy was applied to the interview data throughout the study as the data were collected and processed (McMillan & Schumacher, 2001). This was accomplished by searching for domains that emerged from the data rather than imposing categories developed prior to data collection. Domains are large cultural categories that contain smaller categories/subcategories and whose relationships are linked by a semantic relationship (Spradley, 1980). Demographic information such as gender, level of education, and cultural background was also used to examine the emerging categories/domains. All findings were further analyzed in terms of different kinds of informal learning. These findings were not intended to generalize the experiences of all immigrant parents in Canada, but rather to provide insights into the complex cultural, linguistic, and religious issues that were salient for these particular participants.

Findings

Findings revealed that immigrant parents constructed and mobilized their knowledge in five aspects of informal learning: (1) learning school expectations by interacting with and observing other parents, (2) self-teaching curricula by using the Internet, (3) passing on first-language knowledge by informal teaching, (4) instilling hybridity of two cultures by informal teaching, and (5) advocacy and capacity building for immigrant students by using their parents' knowledge.

Learning School Expectations by Interacting with and Observing Other Parents

In the Canadian education system, teachers typically hold expectations that parents will participate in school events and show concerns for their children's educational success (Epstein, 2001). Many participants reported that they were unaware of the expectations held by teachers and public schools in Canada. For example, Tyrone,[3] a Sudanese parent, said:

> Like in my country, parents drop their kids in schools and then they study. Parents don't need to worry. They don't have to follow up with the teacher. We trust teachers and we trust schools. Here, education is 50 and 50, 50 for parents and 50 for teachers. You have to follow up with the school, you have to ask questions, and you have to volunteer.

Tyrone explained that many of the parents from Sudan, like him, simply did not know that parents ought to follow up with the school. Such unawareness was shared by many other participants. For example, in response to the researcher's question about volunteering in schools, Shaoli Ma, a Chinese immigrant, said, "I did not know. I did not understand it at all. When we first came, we didn't know anybody here." Both Tyrone and Shaoli reported that they learned the importance of communicating with teachers and volunteering in schools by interacting with and observing other parents. For these and other participants, these activities resulted in a big transformation in their beliefs about parents' presence in school. Daniel Yang said:

> I did not know that I had to volunteer in schools. Actually, I tried not to go to school. If my son's teacher asked me to go to school, I started to worry right away. My son might misbehave in school. I was thinking what was wrong with him.

Daniel explained that there are negative associations to parents' presence in schools in Chinese culture. Chinese parents seldom attend school functions because a school's request to see parents means their children have gotten into trouble. This finding was consistent with Wan's (1994) study of Chinese immigrant parents in the United States.

For some parents, efforts to become more involved were not positive experiences. After learning the importance of parent-teacher conferences, Nicole Liang initially went to every one. However, sometimes she felt she was not welcome by some teachers. She said, "Parents will meet the subject teacher individually. Some teachers are good and warm-hearted, but others are not. My son's arts teacher did not like to talk to me." After a while, Nicole stopped going to parent-teacher conferences. She explained that she wanted the teachers to give more homework to her child, but she felt "it is useless to go to these meetings ... because it can't solve the real problem." She did not feel encouraged by the school administrator. She cited one incident which took place in a meeting organized for the ESL parents:

> I want to be involved, but the principal said: "don't challenge the teachers." It was embarrassing. I remembered the last meeting they held particularly for ESL parents. The school invited the parents for suggestions. Chinese parents, nearly half of the immigrant parents, suggested that the teacher give more homework for the students and check the homework. But the school argued that they want the students to learn by themselves. Students should be encouraged and find homework themselves, or the parents should assign homework and monitor them.

Nicole explained that she, along with other parents in her son's school, viewed homework as a way of fostering good study habits for their children and communicating with schools (see Li, 2002 for a similar finding). Nicole reported that she did not feel the parents had challenged the teachers, as the principal had suggested, but were simply expressing their views of education, which differed from those of the teachers and the principal. She perceived the principal as having "an attitude problem."

Learning Canadian Curricula by Using the Internet

Many immigrant parents reported using the Internet as the most important means of learning about Canadian curricula. For example, Liming Wang described how she had relied on the Internet to learn Grade I math curricula to support her daughter:

> I did a Google search on the Internet. The key words I Googled was Grade 1 math or Grade 1 patterns. I was looking for teachers' instruction or some information from the Board of Education. I wanted to know what their expectations were ... In that way, I have some directions and how I can help Trish [her daughter].

Liming explained it was difficult for her to help her daughter since there were no textbooks and she did not know what her daughter was learning in school. She attempted to communicate with her daughter's teacher on a daily basis, but felt turned away by the teacher. Instead, she turned to the Internet for help. She went on to describe how she had to learn Canadian curricula in Chinese first before she could help her daughter:

> I did not know the geography of Canada. I went to the Internet and found the map of Canada. I had to learn it in Chinese first. Then I came back to the English website and read it again until I totally understood. We wouldn't expect the child to understand all of them. I just chose the easy part and explained it to Trish.

Liming also bought a puzzle of a Canadian map. She played the puzzle with her daughter. When her daughter started a magnet project, Liming bought three shapes of magnets. She explained:

> I went outside and got lots of soil, then used the bar magnet to attract all the iron chips, put them in the fabric paper, and clean them, but it was not successful. Later on, I thought maybe we can just play a game. I used a very huge cardboard and we drew a

lot of pictures on the cardboard. My design was a kind of animal adventure. You would leave from the start to the end, but on your way, there were some problems and you had to solve these problems. The first problem was that there was a dig. I just used the paper cup to dig a hole and there were some metal things in it. You had to use your bar magnet to pull them out. Another problem was that I used my daughter's plastic bows to make a necklace and then used a staple to stabilize it. That would be the metal.

The examples above illustrate how Liming Wang used her own resourcefulness to support her daughter's learning of academic language and content. At the same time, co-learning occurred, whereby she used her daughter's curricula to simultaneously develop and enhance her own learning.

Fangfang Li, a former teacher in China with a master's degree in science, on the other hand, used the Internet to peer behind the façade of school practices and curricula. She said:

Last month, my daughter had to write a report about space. She had no idea what the nine planets are, especially in English. She told me what they did in class was to look at some pictures. I Googled the curriculum in her grade and found out what they need to know about space in Grade 6.

From the Internet, Fangfang Li found that one of the requirements for students was to identify examples of differences among the nine planets. She saw contradictions between the documented official curriculum and the curriculum she heard about from her daughter. Unsatisfied with what her daughter learned in school, she took her daughter to an interactive science museum, taught her the concept of space in Chinese, listened with her to a guest speaker who was talking about space in English, and did many hands-on activities with her. In this way, Fangfang used her prior educational background to supplement what she perceived as lacking in her daughter's science class.

Passing on First-Language Knowledge by Informal Teaching

Thirty-six out of 38 parents in the study reported that their children's schools often ignore their children's previous language knowledge. Parents, therefore, informally taught their first languages to their children at home. The parents provided a number of reasons for passing on their linguistic values to their children. For some, teaching and preserving the first language at home was an important means of staying connected to relationships, cultural values, and identities forged in their home countries: "I want my children to keep up with Punjabi, so that they can talk to their grandparents" (Nim, Pakistan). "Language is culture. It is my language that makes my colour, who I am, and my culture" (Tamika, Somali).

Watching her children's gradual decline in the Somali language, Tamika felt the threat of her children losing their identity and culture, a concern echoed by most of the participants. Another parent, Kamal, went on to stress the political dimension that makes it even more powerful for the parent to stay connected with their first language:

> Bangladesh used to be part of Pakistan. At that time the ruler wanted to impose Urdu as the national language. We are speaking Bengali, so Bengali people fought for their right to speak Bengali. Many people were shot. People gave their lives for the language.[4]

Other parents listed more pragmatic reasons for keeping up the home language. Sana (Pakistan) said, "I think these days having more than one language is a good skill. You know our country is growing and there are many immigrants coming. I think most jobs will require additional languages." And Parveen (Nepal) offered, "One of the reasons I help him [her son] maintain Nepalese is that he can translate the concepts in Nepalese into English, so it will help him with his school learning." Sana perceived that acquiring different languages would be useful for future employment in a global world. Parveen realized the first language is an important learning tool for transferring the concepts from first- to second-language education.

Instilling Hybridity of Two Cultures by Informal Teaching

Beyond maintaining their first language, some Chinese parents in the study insisted that their children ought to retain their Chinese identity. Fangfang Xing put it nicely:

> That has to be Chinese identity. Even you are in Canada or whatever, the first thing is that you are Chinese. As Chinese, you have to know as much as possible about Chinese culture, literature, arts, every aspect, and Chinese lifestyle. That is the first thing. The second is how to combine two different things and how to bridge two cultures.

Fangfang Xing provided specific examples of good values of both cultures:

> The Chinese people are self-disciplined. They set up a goal and they will stick to that goal and work hard toward the goal ... The Canadian people are open-minded and creative. In China, the teacher intends to impose his or her values on the kids. But the teacher seldom says what is right and what is wrong. Whatever you said, the teacher will praise you. I think that is good to build kids' confidence.

Fangfang was comparing the good values of Chinese culture and Canadian culture. She hoped her daughter was able to "combine the good values of both cultures and to be a good person that influences the people around her."

Similarly, Mary Li wanted to pass on important values of both cultures to her children. She said:

> I like Canadian culture. People play hard, but they also work hard. It is the way to be responsible. I want them to learn the skills and to be independent. I also want them to have fun because my generation focus on working hard. I feel guilty if I enjoy myself. I think people need to find the passion about life ... I like the way that Chinese people maintain harmony with their family and community ... I don't want them to be too focused on individualism.

Fangfang and Mary hoped to instill in their children the best values of Chinese culture, such as self-discipline, work ethics, and maintaining harmony with the family and community, and to balance these with the best Canadian cultural values, such as open-mindedness, creativity, responsibility, and enjoyment of life. These parents showed awareness that part of their children's growth lay in their ability to draw on the best of both Chinese and Canadian culture.

Advocacy and Capacity Building for Immigrant Students by Using their Parents' Knowledge

Many participants reported that despite the promotion of multiculturalism in Canadian schools, their children continued to be the victims of demeaning treatment by some Canadian students motivated by ignorance and stereotypes. The participants learned different strategies to intervene in their children's schools. For example, Shin stated that in Korean culture, parents are not supposed to take the initiative to communicate with teachers. She learned from her neighbour that in Canada, if parents have concerns, they have the right to approach their children's teachers. Shin reported that although her English "was not good," she approached her daughter's teacher immediately when an incident happened to her daughter:

> When my daughter was erasing the board, behind her a student said to my daughter, "Korean student, you have to go back to your country. Why are you here?" She heard that because she was the only one in the classroom, but she couldn't recognize that voice. She turned around, but she couldn't find out who said that. She was very upset.

Shin explained to the teacher what happened and how upset her daughter was. She was satisfied that the teacher followed up with a whole class discussion about diversity and the harm of racism and anti-immigrant sentiments. Shin was willing to change a cultural practice from her country of origin and learned to advocate on her daughter's behalf.

Aneeka took a different approach. When her son was called "Osama bin Laden" by one of his peers in Grade 5, Aneeka advised her son to ignore such racist comments:

> My child told me, "Somebody called me Osama bin Laden." I asked him, "Are you?" "No, Mom." "Don't worry. You know you are not anything like that. You are a good Muslim boy. You believe in peace. You are not a terrorist. Don't let them make fun of you."

Aneeka stated how stereotypes and misconceptions about Muslim immigrants sometimes create low self-esteem among Muslim immigrant children, and she stressed the importance of building her son's confidence. She helped her son overcome adversity, teasing, and stereotypes from classmates by cultivating the child's spiritual (Muslim) identity. Unlike Shin, who learned to advocate for her daughter at school, Aneeka turned to her spiritual resources to develop her son's confidence at home.

Parveen encouraged her son, aged 12, to participate in the "Write Off Racism Poetry Contest" organized by ACCESS, Canadian Learning Television in Edmonton. She was proud that her son's poem (included below) ranked fourth among the 12–18 age group. She said, "He sometimes feels discriminated against as an ESL student. This poem is really related to what he is going through." The poem reflected on her son's actual experience of discrimination as an immigrant student. Her son was ridiculed about his phenotype and his English ability by his peers, who gave little thought to his character, personality, or feeling. She encouraged her son to think positively. She told her son: "You have visited so many countries and you know different languages. Respect what you have in a positive way." In this way, Parveen taught her son how to advocate not only for himself, but also for other ESL students who might share similar experiences.

Discussion

Impact of Prior Knowledge on Immigrant Parents' Participation in School Activities

The results of the study indicate that many immigrant parents learned the meanings of parental involvement primarily through trial and error practices. Both Tyrone and Daniel expressed that in their countries of origin, teachers assume full responsibility of children's education at school. Given this prior knowledge, they did not attend parent-teacher con-

---

Mirror Image

Whatever you call me,
Different could be my name;
The color you see in my skin-outside,
Might not be your same;
But don't create a wall in between
Thinking me a "creature new"
If you look deep down your heart-
You'll find-I'm you!!

You might be fair Snow-white of my fairy tale
I might be black demon or brown Gin,
but Oh well,
Skin is our armor; not what we really are,
Same red blood we have and salty tear.
Don't pull a curtain between us two-
If you wipe clouds of your eyes
You'll see-I'm you!!

I'm alien in your country;
so you'll be in mine.
English is my second language, but I've an open mind.
Don't hit me with Racism-thinking "Me" not "You"
If you ask alone with your heart
You'll find I'm you!!!

ferences, did not do volunteer work, and did not offer other assistance and support at school. Drawing from observations and informal learning from other parents, they started to follow up with the teachers. These examples support Hannerz's (1992) thesis that immigrant parents treat culture as dynamic and are willing to make changes to support their children's education. This finding is also consistent with Liu's (2007) study of Chinese immigrants in the Greater Toronto Area. Liu found that all immigrant parents in her study reported enormous learning in adapting to the Canadian way of educating children.

The Doublespeak of Parental Involvement in Canadian Schools

Other parents in our study engaged in more critical forms of learning. Nicole, for example, recognized a contradiction in schools: teachers and administrators encourage parental involvement, but ultimately hold on to knowledge and authority, positioning parents as receivers of knowledge (MacLure & Walker, 2000). Nicole learned that only certain types of questions are welcome by school administrators. The request of Nicole and other ESL parents for more homework was perceived as a challenge to teachers' authority. Parents learned that, unlike in their countries of origin, in Canada it is usually parents who take the initiative to contact the school if they have any concerns regarding their children. However, when they initiated parent-teacher meetings to express their concerns, they came to realize that frequent visits to the school are often unwelcome by teachers. Some parents in this study had to learn to navigate the doubles peak of the Canadian education system: parental involvement is encouraged, but only forms of parental involvement that support existing school polices and instructional practices are actually welcome in schools (Auerbach, 2007; Cline & Necochea, 2001). As Lopez (2001) notes, "parent involvement has become a privileged domain signified by certain legitimate acts," such as helping with homework, attending parent-teacher conferences, and participating in fundraising activities (p. 417). In activities such as attending parent-teacher conferences, "consensus and cooperation are assumed; parent involvement is treated as a social fact on neutral terrain rather than as a socially constructed phenomenon on the contested terrain of schooling" (Auerbach, 2007, p. 251). This alleged neutrality and universality fails to acknowledge immigrant parents' unique strategies for engaging in their children's education, and the broader social inequalities in which immigrant home-school relations are embedded. The unequal distribution of economic, human, cultural, and social capital, in addition to schools' devaluing of immigrant parent knowledge, constrains parents' relations with schools (Auerbach, 2007; Bourdieu, 1986).

Active and Skilled Agents of Parents' Own Learning to Support Their Children's Education

Moving beyond deficit models of immigrant parental involvement, the study findings reveal that immigrant parents are important constructors of knowledge about children, teaching, and learning. The immigrant parents' stories demonstrate how they were active and skilled agents of their own learning -learning they undertook to support their children's education. As highly educated professionals before immigration, many parents reported that the Internet was the most important source of learning about the school system, curricula, and services. This finding is consistent with the results of Liu's (2007) study, in which immigrants reported using the Internet as the most important means of learning and exchanging information on child education. Concerned with the lack of textbooks and other learning materials from the school, some immigrant parents in our study taught themselves Canadian curricula in their first languages, then used what they had learned to teach their children in both their first languages and in English. Participants sought to instill the best values of both Canadian and their country-of-origin cultures, continued to teach first languages to their children, and learned how to advocate on behalf of their children, who were often marginalized at school. In this sense, their learning was informal, intentional, and emancipatory (Cunningham, 2000; Freire, 1970; Livingstone, 1999).

Immigrant Parents Supporting Their Children to Combat Racism

Early studies have shown that immigrant parents' learning is self-directed and deliberate, incorporating definite goals to support their children's learning at home and to build their children's capacities for combating discrimination and racism (Dei, 1996; Tough, 1971, 1978). Parents in this study used a variety of approaches to help their children construct a counter-discourse to racial, cultural, linguistic, and religious forms of discrimination. For example, Shin's narratives speak powerfully and poignantly about the ways in which, despite her limited English-language skills, she attempted to advocate for more inclusive schooling practices for immigrant children (Dei, James, Karumanchery, James-Wilson, & Zine, 2000). She turned to her neighbour for strategies of approaching teachers and constructed her transcultural knowledge by integrating a Canadian way of communicating with teachers (Hoerder, Hebert, & Schmitt, 2006). Aneeka lamented that most of what the Canadian public and Canadian teachers and students know about Muslim immigrants is based solely on biased media coverage. Aware of the negative stereotypes of Muslims as terrorists, created by a post-9/11 narrative (McDonough & Hoodfar, 2005), she focused on countering these stereotypes by stressing the nature of peace in Islam. She stated: "My religion is Islam. Islam means peace. I teach my children to love peace, to respect elders, to respect teachers and parents." She activated her personal knowledge (Polanyi, 1958), particularly her spiritual resources, to help her son overcome discrimination. Parveen, with a master's degree in creative writing, used her parenting knowledge (Pushor, 2008) and her educational background to help her son develop a sense of resilience. Her son's poem illustrates how he learned to resist racism and its hostilities, and balance struggle with hope. Shin, Aneeka, and Parveen all demonstrated that advocating for their children and teaching their children to self-advocate in the face of racism was another focus of parents' informal learning about parental involvement.

The Significance of Informal Learning and of an Expansion of Parental Involvement

The results of this study illustrate the significance of informal learning by immigrant parents (Livingstone, 1999). The informal learning was adopted by some immigrant parents in the study as a way of coping with various barriers they faced in support of their children's education in the different cultural environment. For example, Liming Wang reported how she felt she was turned away by her daughter's teacher although she attempted to communicate with the teacher on a daily basis. This negative experience made her think about how to strike a balance between the invitation to be involved and the danger of over-involvement. This example demonstrates that knowing how to be involved is one of those subtle feats of cultural capital that Bourdieu (1986), Lareau (2003), and others have described as being at the heart of supporting a child through schooling.

Furthermore, the results of this study illustrate the significance of the need to expand conventional models of parental involvement to recognize immigrant parent engagement (Lopez, 2001). In the Canadian system of education, teachers typically expect parents to participate in school events and show concern for their children's educational success (Epstein, 2001). The study suggests that even though immigrant parents did not volunteer at school functions or attend school council meetings, they supported their children's learning at home in the form of passing on cultural and linguistic values. The transmission of cultural and linguistic values has rarely been documented in the literature as a type of parental involvement (see Lopez for an exception). Immigrant parents in Lopez's study took their children to work with them in the fields and taught them to appreciate the value of their education, thus transmitting appropriate socio-cultural values as a type of parental involvement. Building upon Lopez's study, this research suggests that the immigrant parents saw transmitting their first-language knowledge, negotiating the terrain of both home and school cultures, and helping their children combat various forms of racism as important forms of involvement that their children needed. These hidden forms of parental involvement expand narrow conceptions of parent-school relations that tend to reinforce and serve the interests of white, middle-class families. This significant expansion to parental involvement has important implications for Canadian schools and education practitioners.

Implications for Practice

This study contributes valuable information for any school administrators, teachers, or education policy makers interested in enhancing their ability to work sensitively and effectively with students and parents from cultures different from their own. Several practical recommendations for educational personnel are made to show how educators can connect to the cultural spaces and images of schooling and learning that are out there in communities of new Canadians.

In this rapidly changing social context, schools need to better address the needs of students and parents from a multicultural, multilingual population. Guo and Mohan (2008) suggest that educators and administrators need to recognize that educational tasks may be given culturally divergent interpretations; that is, teachers and parents may have culturally divergent views of the educational agenda such as homework. Schools need to learn immigrant parents' views on education and cultural differences on home-school communication (Dyson, 2001; Li, 2006; Ran, 2001). Schools need to understand that cultural differences in conceptions regarding schools, teachers, and education actually underlie often conflicting views of parental involvement between immigrant parents and North American educators. Schools, therefore, need to become learning organizations "where people continually expand their capacity to create the results they truly desire, where new and expansive patterns of thinking are nurtured, where collective aspiration is set free, and where people are continually learning how to learn together" (Senge, 1990, p.3).

Incorporating the home cultures of immigrant parents into the school curriculum challenges educators to rethink predetermined involvement typologies that cause immigrant parents to be labelled as unwilling or uninvolved (Dyson, 2001; López, 2001). For example, parents may visit the classroom to share their knowledge (Pushor, 2008) or students may be given homework assignments that require them to interview their parents or their grandparents about their communities or their immigration experiences. This kind of activity helps to acknowledge parents' cultural values and make parents feel they can provide valuable contributions. This also helps students make better connections between the school curriculum and their personal experiences, which in turn will help students succeed academically.

Validating the first languages of diverse families is another approach to engage immigrant parents. An example would be the use of dual-language books, where the text is in both English and another language. A kindergarten teacher, a graduate student in my course, invited parents from 11 different languages to be part of a family reading program in her classroom. Every Friday, she allocated 25 minutes at the drop-off time for parent volunteers to read to small groups of children, often from dual-language books, on their own or with a partner parent reading the English text (Sarah Harrison, personal communication, December 16, 2010). The teacher reported the increasing appreciation of the children toward their classmates' multilingual abilities, as well as how much the parents of these children valued the opportunity to share their first languages and be part of the learning community.

Conclusion

A more effective and inclusive model of parental participation would need to recognize a full range of socio-educational norms, values, and cultural knowledge in the school community, which includes comprehensive understanding of the contribution of immigrant parents to their children's education. Instead of trying to get immigrant parents involved in traditionally sanctioned ways, schools should recognize the unique ways in which immigrant parents are already involved in their children's education. Educators often focus on what is lacking in immigrant families rather than on the potential resources upon which they can build. Schools and teachers must take the initiative if the resource of immigrant parent participation is to be fully used. The work of achieving social justice must involve immigrant parents and immigrant parents' voices must be heard.

Notes

1 An earlier version of this manuscript was presented at the Sixth International Conference on Researching Work and Learning, June 2009, Roskilde University, Denmark. The author wishes to thank the Social Sciences and Humanities Research Council for funding the study, and the journal editor and two anonymous reviewers for their constructive comments.
2 Some schools in Calgary offered workshops to teach immigrant parents how to get involved in their children's education in Canada. These workshops could be considered as a formal way to learn parental involvement. This study, however, focused on parents' informal learning, which occurred outside these formal educational institutions.
3 All participant names in the article are pseudonyms.
4 Kamal was referring to the Bengali Language Movement. Bengali is the primary language spoken in Bangladesh. In 1948, when Bangladesh was East Pakistan, the Government of Pakistan ordained Urdu as the sole national language. This new law sparked extensive protests among the Bengali-speaking majority of East Pakistan, including a protest organized by student demonstrators in 1952. The movement reached its climax when police killed student demonstrators on

February 21. This day has been declared as International Mother Language Day by UNESCO. For Kamal, his native language represents his culture and identity, as well as a tribute to the ethno-linguistic rights of people around the world. Kamal argued that an individual's right to use and learn his/her own native language is a basic human right (Skutnabb-Kangas, 2006).

References

Abdi, A. (2007). Global multiculturalism: Africa and the recasting of the philosophical and epistemological plateaus. *Diaspora, Indigenous and Minority Education, 1(4)*, 1–14.

Appadurai, A. (1996). *Modernity at large: Cultural dimensions of modernity*. London and Minneapolis: University of Minnesota Press.

Auerbach, S. (2007). From moral supporters to struggling advocates: Reconceptualizing parent roles in education through the experience of working-class families of color. *Urban Education, 42*(3), 250–283.

Bernhard, J. K., Freire, M., Pacini-Ketchabaw, V., & Villanueva, V. (1998). A Latin American parents' group participates in their children's schooling: Parent involvement reconsidered. *Canadian Ethnic Studies, 30*(3), 77–99.

Bitew, C., & Ferguson, P. (2010). Parental support for African immigrant students' schooling in Australia. *Journal of Comparative Family Studies, 41*(1), 149–165.

Bourdieu, P. (1986). The forms of capital. In J. G. Richardson (Ed.), *Handbook of theory and research for the sociology of education* (pp. 241–258). New York: Greenwood Press.

Cline, Z., & Necochea, J. (2001). ,'Basta Ya! Latino parents fighting entrenched racism. *Bilingual Research Journal, 25*, 1–26.

Connelly, F. M., & Clandinin, D. J. (1988). *Teachers as curriculum planners: Narratives of experience*. New York: Teachers College Press.

Cunningham, P. (2000). A sociology of adult education. In A. Wilson & E. Hayes (Eds.), *Handbook of adult and continuing education* (pp. 573–591). San Francisco: Jossey Bass.

Dehli, K. (1994). *Parent activism and school reform in Toronto*. Toronto: Department of Sociology in Education, Ontario Institute for Studies in Education.

Dei, G. (1996). *Anti-racism education: Theory and practice*. Halifax: Fernwood Publishing.

Dei, G., James, M., Karumanchery, L., James-Wilson, S., & Zine, J. (2000). *Removing the margins: The challenges and possibilities of inclusive schooling*. Toronto: Canadian Scholars Press.

Delgado-Gaitan, C. (1990). *Literacy for empowerment: The role of parents in children's education*. New York: The Falmer Press.

Dyson, L. (2001). Home-school communication and expectations of recent Chinese immigrants. *Canadian Journal of Education, 26*, 455–476.

Elsdon, K. T. (1995). Values and learning in voluntary organizations. *International Journal of Lifelong Education, 14*(1), 75–82.

Epstein, J. L. (2001). *School, family, and community partnership: Preparing educators and improving schools*. Boulder, CO: Westview.

Espinosa, L. (1995). Hispanic parent involvement in early childhood programs. *ERIC Digest* (EDO-PS-95-3). Retrieved August 2, 2010, from http://ceep.crc.uiuc.edu/eecarchive/digestsl 1995/espin095.html

Foley, G. (1999). *Learning in social action: A contribution to understanding informal education*. London: Zeb Books.

Freire, P. (1970). *Pedagogy of the oppressed*. New York: Herder and Herder.

Gibson, M. A. (2000). Situational and structural rationales for the school performance of immigrant youth: Three cases. In H. Vermeulen & J. Perl mann (Eds.), *Immigrants, schooling and social mobility: Does culture make a difference?* (pp. 72–102). London: Macmillan Press Ltd.

Guo, S. (2009). Difference, deficiency, and devaluation: Tracing the roots of non/ recognition of foreign credentials for immigrant professionals in Canada. *The Canadian Journal for the Study of Adult Education*, 22(1), 37–52.

Guo, Y. (2006). "Why didn't they show up?": Rethinking ESL parent involvement in K-12 education. *TESL Canada Journal*, 24(1), 80–95.

Guo, Y. (2007). Multiple perspectives of Chinese immigrant parents and Canadian teachers on ESL learning in schools. *Diaspora, Indigenous, and Minority Education: An International Journal*, 1(1),43–64.

Guo, Y., & Mohan, B. (2008). ESL parents and teachers: Towards dialogue? *Language and Education*, 22 (1),17–33.

Hannerz, U. (1992). Flows, boundaries and hybrids: Keywords in transcultural anthropology. In A. Rogers (Ed.), *Working paper series* (WPTC-2K-02), Transnational Communities Programme, Oxford University. Retrieved August 5, 2010, from www.transcomm.ox.ac.uklworking%20papers/hannerz.pdf

Hoerder, D., Hebert, Y., & Schmitt, 1. (Eds.). (2006). *Negotiating transcultural lives: Belongings and social capital among youth in comparative perspectives*. Toronto: University of Toronto Press.

Honneth, A. (1995). *The struggle for recognition: The moral grammar of social conflicts*. Boston: MIT Press.

Jones, T. G. (2003). Contributions of Hispanic parents' perspectives to teacher preparation. *School Community Journal*, 13, 73–96.

Lareau, A. (2003). *Unequal childhoods: Class, race, and family life*. Berkeley: University of California Press.

Li, G. (2002). *"East is east, west is west?" Home literacy, culture, and schooling*. New York: Peter Lang.

Li, G. (2006). *Culturally contested pedagogy: Battles of literacy and schooling between mainstream teachers and Asian immigrant parents*. Albany, NY: SUNY Press.

Liu, L. (2007). Unveiling the invisible learning from unpaid household work: Chinese immigrants' perspective. *The Canadian Journal for the Study of Adult Education*, 20(2),25–40.

Livingstone, D. W. (1999). Exploring the icebergs of adult learning: Findings of the first Canadian survey of informal learning practices. *The Canadian Journal for the Study of Adult Education* 13(2),49–72.

Livingstone, D. W. (2006). Informal learning: Conceptual distinctions and preliminary findings. In Z. Bekennan, N. C. Burbules, & D. Sibennan-Keller (Eds.), *Learning in places: The informal education reader* (pp. 203–227). New York: Peter Lang.

Lopez, G. R. (2001). The value of hard work: Lessons on parent involvement from an (im)migrant household. *Harvard Educational Review*, 71, 416–437.

MacLure, M., & Walker, B. (2000). Disenchanted evenings: The social organization of talk in parent-teacher consultations in UK secondary schools. *British Journal of Sociology of Education*, 21(1),5–25.

McDonough, S., & Hoodfar, H. (2005). Muslims in Canada: From ethnic groups to religious community. In P. Bramadat & D. Seljak (Eds.), *Religion and ethnicity in Canada* (pp. 133-153). Toronto: Pearson Education Canada Inc.

McLaren, A. T., & Dyck, I. (2004). Mothering, human capital, and the "ideal immigrant." *Womens Studies International Forum*, 27,41–53.

McLaren, P. (2003). *Life in schools: An introduction to critical pedagogy in the foundations of education*. Boston: Pearson Education.

McMillan, J., & Schumacher, S. (2001). *Research in education: A conceptual introduction* (5th ed.). New York: Longman.

Moles, O. C. (1993). Collaboration between schools and disadvantaged parents: Obstacles and openings. In N. F. Chavkin (Ed.), *Families and schools in a pluralist society* (pp. 21–49). Albany, NY: SUNY Press.

Ng, R. (2005). Immigrant garment workers as embodiment of gender, race and class relations. In L. Biggs & P. J. Downe (Eds.), *Gendered intersections: An introduction to women's & gender studies* (pp. 204–209). Halifax: Fernwood Publishing.

Ogbu, J. (1995). Cultural problems in minority education: Their interpretations and consequences-Part two: Case studies. *Urban Review*, 27, 271–297.

Polanyi, M. (1958). *Personal knowledge: Towards a post-critical philosophy*. Chicago: University of Chicago Press.

Pushor, D. (2008, March). *Parent knowledge: Acknowledging parents.* Paper presented at the Annual Meeting of the American Educational Research Association, New York.

Ramirez, A. Y. (2003). Dismay and disappointment: Parental involvement of Latino immigrant parents. *The Urban Review, 35,* 93–110.

Ran, A. (2001). Travelling on parallel tracks: Chinese parents and English teachers. *Educational Research,* 43(3), 311–328.

Senge, P. (1990). *The fifth discipline: The art and practice of the learning organization.* New York: Doubleday Currency.

Skutnabb-Kangas, T. (2006). Language policy and linguistic human rights. In T. Ricento (Ed.), *An introduction to language policy: Theory and method* (pp. 273–291). Malden, MA: Blackwell Publishing Ltd.

Spradley, J. (1980). *Participant observation.* New York: Holt, Rinehart & Winston.

Tough, A. (1971). *The adult's learning projects: A fresh approach to theory and practice in adult learning.* Toronto: OISE Press.

Tough, A. (1978). Major learning efforts: Recent research and future directions. *Adult Education Quarterly,* 28(4), 250–263.

Wan, Y. (1994). *Immigrant Chinese mothers' involvement in K-6 United States schools: A participatory study.* Unpublished doctoral dissertation, University of San Francisco.

Yao, E. (1988). Working effectively with Asian immigrant parents. *Phi Delta Kappan, 70,* 223–225.

A changed context of lifelong learning under the influence of migration: South Korea

JIN-HEE KIM
Korean Educational Development Institute

The aim of this paper is to examine how Korean society is being changed under the impact of migration and the kinds of learning domains that are evolving through participation in social interaction between migrant workers and local citizens in South Korea. Employing a qualitative case study, participants' changed learning areas were investigated. Major findings revealed that continuous engagements in social activities developed people's learning domains such as 'self efficacy and esteem', 'intercultural capability', 'knowledge and awareness on cultural diversity', and 'democratic attitude and civic virtue'. Although multicultural society is an irreversible social condition in contemporary Korea owing to the influence of magnified migration, findings demonstrate that migration itself is not enough to facilitate human learning continuously. Instead, social engagements between different agencies in informal learning settings enable people to reconstruct their life experiences.

Introduction

This study investigates how learners reconstruct their experience and learn through social engagements under the prevailing migration flow. Indeed, the advent of globalisation is not confined to flows of trade, finance and technology, but also to the large-scale movement of workers (Castles and Miller 2003). Given that migrant workers seek to improve their lives by moving to highly developed countries in the North and newly industrialising countries in Middle-East Asia (Jordan and Duvell 2003), South Korea displays a specific regional context of migration influence.

Employing this background, this paper explores changed social conditions and learning practices in South Korea. In particular, to understand this phenomenon in detail, a qualitative case study anchoring a migrant workers' centre is conducted. This centre is conceptualised as a differentiated learning environment embracing a large diversity of nationalities, ethnicities and identities that enables migrant workers and local peoples to learn through participation in social activities.

Therefore, this paper begins with an examination of altered social conditions of South Korea under the influence of migration. Then, a theoretic framework and methodology will be suggested to interpret a specific case study. Finally, we can acquire the major findings of this study underlining the kinds of learning domains that evolve when people interact within a non-formal migrants' centre. In addition, a discussion and conclusion drawn from these findings will display recommendations of a lifelong learning policy. Through this process, we can gain an insight of lifelong learning at the periphery comprehending transnational adult learners and their interaction with local people in the age of migration.

Extensive migration, multicultural practice and changed social landscape: context

Korea has undergone economic development in earnest since 1962 and its economy has been rapidly liberalised since the mid-1980s. This rapid industrialisation had demanded considerable foreign labour and their manpower in the economic market, especially the manufacturing industry. Particularly, since the early 1990s, Korea has started to attract tens of thousands of migrant workers from developing nations for employment in the so-called '3D' (difficult, dirty and dangerous) jobs that are often eschewed by local people. The range and pattern of migration in Korea had centralised on the labour section to supply the demand of workforce for the demeaning manual jobs. Almost 95% of migrant workers in South Korea are classified as economic migrant workers (Korea Labor Institute 2004).

Migrant workers have been admitted under two major legal systems. One is the Industrial Trainee Program (ITP) system adopted in the early 1990s that enables small and medium-sized manufacturing firms to take on foreign nationals as trainees. The other is the Employment Permit System (EPS), which was introduced in 2004. By passing the EPS Act, Korean industry could fulfil its need for large numbers of migrant workers under a more comprehensive and effectively managed migration system. Korea became the first labour importing country in Asia to attempt to protect the rights of migrant workers through legislation (Asian Migration Center 2005).

Migration has an enormous influence on the demography, economy, culture, politics and social relations of both receiving countries and sending nation states (Eytan 2004). It is also assumed migration entails a transformation of the learning society.

Applying this view to Korea, the number of foreign residents including migrant workers now stands at over 1,066,291: approximately 2% of South Korea's total population of 49,130,000. The Korean government announced that the number of 'legal' foreign residents stood at 722,686 as of May 2007, which was a 35% increase compared to 2006 (Ministry of Government Administration and Home Affairs 2007). As it excludes the number of those who stay in the country for fewer than 90 days and undocumented migrant workers, the number of which is estimated to be around 344,604, the total number of foreigners is much larger. Migrant workers of all nationalities, from more than 103 countries such as China, Bangladesh, Uzbekistan and Sri Lanka have lived in Korea (Ministry of Justice 2007). It could be estimated that Korea is now a country of massive migration, especially as a regional hub of recruiting migrant workers in East Asia (Castles and Miller 2003: 197).

Table 1. The current number of migrant workers in Korea

2005		2006	
China	10685	China	12843
Thailand	5408	Thailand	5605
Indonesia	5084	Indonesia	4922
Philippines	4385	Vietnam	4154
Vietnam	3817	Philippines	3729
Uzbekistan	2169	Uzbekistan	2916
Pakistan	1886	Cambodia	1715
Sri Lanka	1690	Sri Lanka	1623
Mongolia	1110	Myanmar	1360
Cambodia	530	Mongolia	1345
Others	1024	Others	3779
Total	**37788**	**Total**	**43991**

Source: Ministry of Justice, Republic of Korea (2007).

The current phenomenon of increase of migrant workers is not simply about numbers. It reflects how the host nation is fast becoming a multicultural and multiethnic society, and importantly shows that adapting to diversity has become inevitable in Korea. Indeed, the surge of labour migration and its impact affects not only economic sectors but also social and cultural arrangements. In a similar vein, as an example of changed social arrangements, international marriages (which have increased 10 times within the last 15 years) are speeding up the changes. Besides, the number of multicultural households has already reached 10% particularly in rural areas (Ministry of Government Administration and Home Affairs 2007).

These social conditions reveal that a multicultural society is no longer a distant notion for Korea. Traditionally, Korea has been a closed society with the perception of a monoculture and a homogenous race and ethnicity (Shin 2006). Although it has been believed Korean has been a racially homogeneous nation, such beliefs are now incorrect because of extensive migration. Since Korea is gradually transforming into a multicultural and multi-racial society, the persistent ethnic nationalism has started to be challenged among Koreans. In addition, the birth rate of Korea is getting lower and the country is becoming an aging society, so the nation cannot survive without migrant workers. As a result, there is no alternative choice for Koreans but to mix with immigrants to form a nation (Seoul Statement 2005). It is seen that Koreans should get themselves over the barrier of ethnic nationalism.

Migration produces a significant opportunity for the whole society to realign for a new future that engages in multiculturalism. An influx of migrants to Korea has influenced a quantitative alteration of national demography as well as the classic concept of an ethnically homogeneous nation. The idea of 'multicultural Korea' is all the more credible if witnessing national statistics of soaring numbers of foreign residents, increased NGOs for migrant workers' advocacy, segregated residential areas and international food supermarkets. Both covert and overt interactions with migrant workers in the street, workplace and public places have become common, displaying a representative shape of the contemporary life-world in Korea. In essence, facing as it does an immense increase of migrant workers, Korean society has started to experience new social circumstances. These phenomena also represent how a foreign labour-receiving nation started to undergo multicultural practices engaging in a wide diversity of ethnicity, culture, class and identity.

This distinctively demonstrates Korean society's changing social configuration, which in turn has led to a differentiated context of lifelong learning. It calls for keen considerations for migrant workers' rights, democratic engagements and the ability to learn to live with various social groups. In this sense it should be acknowledged that the learning areas of migrant workers and local peoples evolve within this social context. Hence our attention will turn to peoples' transformed learning trajectories and their engagement in social interaction with different agencies.

Learning engaging in migration: theoretic framework

Issues and relations between migration and learning

Migration increases both opportunities and challenges. In terms of opportunities, by moving from an impoverished place to more prosperous locations across national, political and cultural boundaries (Eytan 2004), migrant workers incarnate the notion of the 'global village' in social practice. This magnifies the world's interconnectedness, interdependency and embracing of societal diversity. Migration provides people with more extensive selections of life through widening of a spatial realm. Conversely migration also generates complex challenges. Apart from highly qualified professionals, most migrant workers encounter social restrictions such as poor working conditions, discrimination and a segregated residential area within the host society. Indeed, it has been estimated that in East Asian labour-receiving countries such as Japan, South Korea and Hong Kong, approximately 2.64 million migrant workers live and work under such conditions (Annual Report of Asian Migration Center 2005). Given that a majority of local people view migrant workers as infringing upon their established social status quo, there is often social tension, collision and disjuncture within the host society.

These complex conditions enable us to observe a conceptual framework of migration and learning in the field of lifelong learning. The issues of migration and learning engage in multiple dimensions as follows:

- transnational learning environment;
- disjuncture and social connection/disconnection; and
- culture, diversity, marginalisation and their relation with human learning.

First, given that international migration produces changes both to a society and the lives of individual migrants, it also allows people to deal with different learning environments beyond the nation-state's boundary. Migration calls for people to adopt a new transnational learning environment and to reconstruct their learning trajectory to correspond with their reshaped lives.

Second, migration generates disjuncture and social connection/disconnection in the host society, which affects people's reactions to social changes. As migrant workers encounter different social and economic settings outside of their homeland, their learning path begins to reorganise in response to this disjuncture. While some migrant workers integrate their entity into that of the host society, others may remain disconnected and resist the adaptation process within the host society.

Lastly, throughout migration flow, the multiple issues of culture, diversity and marginalisation mean that people face a set of cultural, social and political alterations. When massive migration takes place, the majority populations will have to confront a series of cultural pluralism and political conflicts (Castles and Miller 2003: 296). This condition enables both migrant workers and local people to modify their own expectations and perceptions about social conformity. It also inevitably leads to reconfigure the horizon of learning for social change.

In summary, these conceptual relations and issues suggest that migration is a collective action that arises out of social change and that affects one's learning trajectory. Migratory experience urges people to modify the assumptions of societal norms, which entails transitions of the learning mode. In addition, local people start to experience different ethnicities, cultures, nationalities and social realignments. These changed social circumstances mean that people cannot adhere to the previous life patterns or principles and existing practices any more—they have to respond to their changed life mode. Hence it could be argued that migration serves as a reactive condition to reconstruct one's lifelong learning. Particularly, since learning is existential for all human beings, we could argue that learning seems increasingly to be a pivotal condition for migrant workers who confront high discontinuity in their host society.

By engaging in migration, one's life experience is differentiated and reshaped. Given that migration provokes alterations and adaptation processes both socially and individually, it leads people to reorganise their learning trajectory so that they can interact with a changed new society and attempt to maintain their pattern of life.

Multicultural learning settings and democratic deliberation

Major theoretical backgrounds to this study are the concept of multicultural learning context and that of lifelong learning, which focuses on the cultural transmission of society's core values and philosophies (Larsson 2001). Having recognised that the migration phenomenon presents that contemporary society is heterogeneous rather than homogeneous and that it produces hybrid communities and societal pluralisation, it should be noted that these more complex mixtures of social configurations must lead to engagement in multi-layered components of ethnicity, culture, nationality and class. In short, different ethnicities, languages and cultures form multicultural learning settings.

Migration encourages a multicultural locality. It also infiltrates people's life world disturbing the status quo in their host community. Local people start to encounter a multiculturalism not just in theory but in practice: in the workplace, street, market, school and public service sector. This situation realigns social arrangements and relations (Seoul Statement 2005) as local people are exposed to the culturally pluralised life world under the impact of migration. In this way, migration stimulates people to reconstruct existing perceptions about social configurations and their own perceptions of them. This means that migration apparently produces a social practice of cultural diversity in the field of lifelong learning.

This multicultural setting creates a wide range of dynamic learning processes from rejection or problematisation of cultural difference to the assimilation of cultural pluralism. It also leads to reflection on how different learning agencies evolve their learning experiences in the midst of a transformed world. Consequently a multicultural learning setting within the context of migration does not merely concentrate on the simple generalisation of ethnocentric discourse (such as Indian for 'curry' and Korean for 'kimchi'). Instead, learning within multicultural context involves diversity, disjuncture and difference crossing borders of ethnicity, class and life experience among various entities (Baubock and Rundell 1998). In this respect it could be conceptualised that migrants' transnational migratory experience and local people's reaction converge on a multicultural learning setting.

Meanwhile, investigations into multicultural learning reveal democratic deliberation of social justice engaging in ethnicity, race, gender and class. Acknowledging social harmony is not always merely based on homogeneity, contemporary defenders of multiculturalism as a precondition of social advancement also face heterogeneity and disjuncture throughout participation and engagement with various subjects (Baubock and Rundell 1998). Indeed, the multicultural setting represents a certain cultural heterogeneity that underscores reciprocal interactions with diverse individuals, groups and institutions. In a similar vein, in recognising that the role of adult education is to overcome inequity, discrimination and alienation embedded in multicultural conditions (Walters 1997), lifelong learning underlines the learner's capacity-building and empowerment as a counteraction against hegemony and oppression (Johnston 1999). This context offers social learning opportunities to people to involve in different life experiences and histories of various entities fulfilling democratic deliberation.

Although to some extent the multicultural learning context challenges build democratic decision-making while emcompassing a complexity of diversity, they can lead to a reconstruction of monoculture-oriented learning paradigms. Indeed, the diversity within the multicultural learning setting allows multiple voices and experience of different entities to be heard and recognised (Bagnall 2006). Intersection between diversity and democracy creates possibilities to shape a multitude of identities (Larsson 2001).

The use of a migrant centre for this case study was devised to examine how people reconstruct their own learning trajectory in the middle of cultural diversity. It can serve as an experimental sphere whereby learners get involved in a democratic practice interacting with others in search of discovering marginalised migrants' voice and their empowerment through learning. This setting emphasises cross-cultural dialogue, understanding and participation between migrant workers and local people.

The constant development of world affairs continues to encourage diversity and heterogeneity, a multicultural condition that demands democratic reflection and practice. It calls upon a democratic response and commitment to empowering underprivileged entities through learning. In this respect, lifelong learning within multicultural setting is more than the mere coexistence of difference. Instead, it should offer and stimulate continuous learning opportunities to nurture the co-evolution of both society and individuals through active engagements between various agencies.

Transformative learning theory and informal adult learning approaches

Theories relevant to migrant workers and local people's learning in a non-formal migrant centre should also be considered—these include transformative learning theory and informal adult learning approaches. After acknowledging that migration causes a series of altered processes for individuals as well as for the host society, it should be noted that migration also enables people to transform their learning trajectory to respond to changed social conditions.

Thus for this study, transformative learning is deployed to understand people's reshaped learning phenomena within the migration context. The core of transformative learning theory is the process of perspective transformation using a prior interpretation to gain a new understanding of one's experience to lead further action. According to Mezirow (2000), transformative learning happens through a series of phases such as disorienting dilemmas, reshaping frames of reference and integrating new perspectives into people's lives. It involves experiencing a deep structural shift in the basic premises of thought, feelings and actions (O'Sullivan 2003). Indeed, learning occurs beyond one's cognitive or psychological processes (Jarvis 2007).

Given that this transformative approach in adult learning is the extension of consciousness through the transformation of world perspectives and the capacities of the self, migrants who traverse national and social boundaries are directed to transform their view of the social world and critically analyse their social situation. In particular, transformative learning provides people with social awareness and empowerment, linking them more closely to the wider society. In addition, in confronting the influx of migration, local people also come to change their assumptions and perceptions, leading to new ways of defining differentiated societal configuration. This understanding captures how both migrants and local citizens react to their social circumstances.

Once the concept the power of transformative learning and its ability to create direction in learning experiences has been acknowledged (O'Sullivan 2003), the migration centre can function as a direct learning channel for participants. People can transform existing assumptions and expectations by sharing their own narratives, knowledge, emotions and values there. This transformative learning theory throws a light on migrants' and local people's learning dynamics in a non-formal setting.

In terms of informal learning, Jordan and Duvell (2003) state that most migrants retain old social links and networks, relying more on informal systems such as friendship groups and community- and faith-based associations. This suggests that a great deal of migrant workers' learning occurs within informal settings as a reaction to their altered social world. Since migrant workers' learning is situated outside adult educational settings in the host land, it is essential to employ informal learning theory as a theoretic lens to understand their learning in a non-formal centre. For the local citizens, given that daily interactions with migrant workers are not rare situations, their informal learning occurs in a variety of places as a natural function of everyday life. In this context, the framework of informal adult learning leads us to gain access to interpret migrant workers' and local peoples' learning trajectories in the community.

Clearly, the heart of informal learning indicates that learning is not formally organised or recognised within a curriculum or educational settings. Instead, it takes place unconsciously in an incidental way. It does not necessarily follow a specified curriculum or systematic subjects, but rather originates sporadically in association with certain occasions (Bennetts 2003). Informal learning is multilayered learning that occurs in daily lives as part of a lifelong process. In this regard, informal learning occurs in a wide variety of places: at home, work, leisure, community centres and through daily interactions with others. For many adult learners, an informal setting transmits a wide range of narratives, norms, thoughts, knowledge and manners within social relationships.

Accommodating this notion into the migrant workers' centre, an informal learning approach reveals how participants develop their learning trajectory in the collective community through sharing informal experiences that include instant casual messaging, incidental performance, spontaneous meeting and daily life stories. This represents how informal learning happens when knowledge has not been externalised and promotes the development of participants' commitment and competence as well as their perception of self and others (Bennetts 2003). As such, adult informal learning theory contributes to our understanding of learning features in the migrant centre. Overall, these examined conceptual frameworks lead us to comprehend the essence of a changing context of lifelong learning engaging in migration.

Method

This study was conducted by employing a qualitative case study design to examine how migrant workers and local people learn from each other through participating in the migrant workers' centre. The qualitative research approach involved 'building a complex and holistic picture, analyse words, reports detailed views of informants and conducts the study in a natural setting' (Creswell 1998) rather than an artificial research setting created by a researcher.

To justify the qualitative research approach for this case study: qualitative methodologies were deployed to understand people's learning domains within a non-formal community. The Sung-Dong District Migrant Workers' Centre in Seoul served as a research field. The centre presents a condensation of interaction between migrant workers and local citizens at a local level, so it was hoped that it could be used to interpret a transformed figure of lifelong learning within the migration context.

In order to conduct in-depth interviews, informants were selected as a focus group. Employing the strategy of participant selecting (Herbert and Irena 1995), focus interviewees were chosen among those who were willing to share their narratives and learning experiences and investigate their learning journey with a researcher. Consequently, five undocumented migrant workers who have stayed for over eight years and participated in social activities enthusiastically, and five devoted Korean volunteers who served voluntarily in the migrants' centre for over three years were invited to be interviewed.

For this study, wide ranges of qualitative data were analysed to examine the learning phenomena. Afterwards, diverse data were collected from in-depth interviews with 10 participants, participation observation of social activities and an analysis of relevant documents including migrant centre monthly newsletters, guidebooks and brochures of regular programmes.

The interviews were done five times for two to three hours over a period of a six-month observation. All interviews were audio tape-recorded and transcribed. Pseudonyms were applied to all participants. In the pilot interviews, given the subtle and tacit nature of informal learning, open-ended questions were used to obtain participants' views about their learning paths in the migrant workers' centre. While espousing semi-structured in-depth interviewing approaches (Eisner 1997), this study encouraged participants to express their own experiences, feelings and attitudes, which led us to extract related research categories contextually.

In terms of observation, field observation was conducted every weekend, taking field notes during participants' regular meetings and occasional events such as membership training, international festivals and voluntary work sessions. Throughout the different avenues of observations, researchers attempted to note all verbal and non-verbal communication among participants and their responses and, interactions within the various circumstances in the centre.

Furthermore, for this study, given that interviews and participatory observation were all conducted in Korean, the translation process was crucial for the precise presentation of data. When dealing with transcriptions of the recordings and repeatedly listening to the tape recording, translation into English was done between the lines of the same transcript. Several participants who could speak English as a second language were also asked to review the translations and give feedback. In order to conserve coherence between the collected data in Korean and the presented data in English, peer review was adopted. The reviewer acknowledged that the domain of translation was generally precise after she checked over the whole original set and the translated version together. Overall, throughout the continual screenings and reflections processes of data collection, learning domains were investigated to understand the context in which migrant workers and local people learned from each other.

It was important during the research to explore the research questions and re-check emerging categories about migrant workers and local people's learning experiences. Multi-layered data based on interviews, observation field journals and documentary evidences were contextualized according to this research framework and related themes of people's learning trajectory. In particular, open coding forming contextualized concepts was used to analyse the data, but the final analytical process used theoretically selective coding, deploying a higher level of abstraction. This qualitative study also used several other analysis processes such as descriptive coding, theoretical memos, theoretical sampling and triangulation to maintain the validity of findings.

In summary, observing, questioning, checking, theorising and validating were used to cross-check. Accordingly, the overall methodology of this study was developed to explore informal and social learning between migrant workers and local people by continuously reshaping research categories about learning domains. It enabled us to draw out the changed contexts of learning of migrant workers and local people.

Findings

This study assumed that labour migration has an influence on learning areas of both migrant workers and local people. Major findings are presented by what they learn through participation in the non-formal migrant workers' centre. The centre is an autonomously organised community founded in 2001 by Sung-Dong District in Seoul. The total membership comprises over 250 people from 34 different nations, ranging from Africa to Central and South America. A few Korean volunteers are allowed to join if they are keen to learn about cultural diversity and interact with migrant workers in the community. Migrant workers and local people meet each other normally every Sunday (and occasionally Saturday) as well to participate in diverse activities such as:

- sharing their weekday life experiences;
- world culture study classes;
- debating social issues;
- volunteering with local minorities;
- IT education;
- civic campaigns; and
- multicultural festivals.

Self efficacy and self esteem

Most participants stated that they acquired self efficacy and confidence by participating in activities at the migrant workers' centre. In particular, migrant workers reported that they strived to express their voices by interacting with local people. By engaging in social practices, they overcame a crisis of self esteem in the host society. One of migrant workers explained as follows:

> I think I have grown and developed myself so much in this Centre. It puts forth my strength discovering my potential skills once again. By socialising with many Koreans, I became to regain my lost confidence and the ability of managing situations independently. Even if my tough social condition can't easily change, now I knew how to improve self skills and cope with difficulties. Just doing something toward better direction—that's what I learned through this experience.

There was considerable evidence from the data that migrant workers gained a new self-respect. By participating in the social activities at the centre they accessed learning opportunities that reflected their identities and capacities. If poor living conditions in Korea (usually presented as something of a 'working machine') have hindered migrants' self-efficacy, continual social interactions with other Koreans have enabled them to regain self-efficacy. This was acquired from reciprocal engagements with others, producing renewed self governance to cope with daily dilemmas and wider social disjuncture.

Local people also stated their changed learning areas through interacting with migrant workers in the migrant centre. A female Korean volunteer commented:

> As a volunteer teacher, I've been coming to this centre for three years. Participation itself is incredibly worthwhile for me. To meet lots of international people and culture in local community is a fantastic experience because I don't have to travel to enjoy cultural diversity. We study together, learn from

each other and do meaningful works together such as voluntary services, organising a world culture class and international food festivals. You know...all activities require a great deal of self-organisational ability for us.

Participants run a world culture class by themselves every Sunday, which features international culture, global issues, language and so on. Both migrant workers and local people who were willing to join the class were invited. They were encouraged to develop self competency by presenting their own materials and critically exploring taken-for-granted assumptions about the collective activity. This focused participants' responsibility to engage with specific roles. Because people took an active leadership when they prepared and presented their culture or world issues, decision-making ability was essential so as to take a share by dividing roles or portions. Thus it developed participants' self-efficacy, facilitating a multicultural experience. A male migrant worker said:

> Whenever I take a role to arrange world culture class, I think that I am such like a culture messenger or diplomat who leads people to understand my country's distinctive cultural assets. This activity enables me to break the long silence in the factory during whole weekdays. Now I've got self-confidence to realise that I have a capability to teach something about my country and culture for others. That boosts my confidence, which I never experienced in workplace in Korea.

Indeed, most migrant workers interviewed used these social experiences to develop their own leadership skills in their host society. For local citizens, the activity allowed them to broaden their understanding about world culture and global issues. A Korean volunteer confessed that:

> Although I am an original Korean, in my generation, I didn't have many chances to reflect my cultural assets sincerely. Moreover, learning different world cultures with foreigners is a totally new experience. This involvement offered me a sense of delegate of my country, Korea. Even though my presentation skill and communication ability is not perfect still, I believe the more I participate in this activity, the more I can learn lots of knowledge developing myself.

It can be recognised that most participants acquired their self efficacy and self esteem through participation in the migrant centre's activities. While they engaged with each other in social practices as active participants, migrant workers and local people could restore self confidence in reshaping their life experiences. It displays one of major learning domains in the non-formal centre.

Intercultural capability

The migrant workers' centre in the local community stands for a social setting of multiculturalism, which is constituted from multiethnic members who also have different socio-cultural backgrounds. Interaction with ethnically and culturally diverse agencies stimulates participants to reconstruct and deconstruct their own experiences constantly. A series of learning paths such as encountering, observing, clashing, understanding, reflecting and reconstructing evolve within this multicultural context. During interviews, most Korean volunteers told how their intercultural capabilities including behaviour, skills, and knowledge were limited so far. They confessed that they had a narrow view of the world, which caused them to reorganise previous perceptions to adjust a new multicultural society. One volunteer recounted:

> So far I considered myself that I am a global citizen who has an open mind toward any kinds of world cultures. However, through continual interaction with migrant workers, I should have realised that my global capacity is still very rough. The more I communicate with them, the more I should admit that my international competency is poor. Sometimes I can't understand informal codes of communication. Confronting weird mood and certain of clash, I came to reflect my taken for granted perspectives.

In some sense, the multicultural learning setting of the migrant centre produces abundant learning resources and subjects embracing cultural diversity, which likely induces a dynamic learning trajectory among participants. Yet it is also acknowledged that there are persistent disparities, conflicts of reciprocal interest and miscommunication owing to the centre's culturally heterogeneous elements. Migrant workers and local people are driven to reconstruct their existing expectations in order to correspond with enlarging multicultural circumstances. In this sense, intercultural capability was underlined by many participants. The voice of a Korean participant represents it as follows:

> For four years, interactions with migrant workers changed me a lot in terms of open mind, global knowledge, and communication skill with foreigners. Above all, through this opportunity I precisely learnt what multiculturalism is and gradually gained my intercultural potential.

Clearly, intercultural capability is a crucial area of learning for participants. International understanding is certainly appreciated to be one of essential learning domains in the contemporary world. In the migrants' centre, migrant workers and local citizens started to expand their learning trajectories, reshaping a mono-culture-centred life experience. This revealed a multicultural practice under the impact of migration. One Korean participant mentioned:

> Through continual participation and face-to-face interaction with migrant workers, I acquired different cross-cultural skills, which I couldn't experience before, even in school. One of my lessons is that any comments based on prejudiced view of particular religion, despite a friendly ice-breaking joke, would be highly rude manners. For me, it's experiential learning. If all Korean are invited to experience this learning opportunity exploring 'what is multicultural', there will be no discrimination or abuse against migrant workers or any other minority groups in Korea.

The research revealed that local citizens acquired a perception of multicultural assets, intercultural skills and attitudes, while interviews with migrant workers also emphasised intercultural capabilities through participation in the social activities:

> Although I have lived in Korea nearly nine years, multicultural reality has not been much welcomed in this society. Instead, I thought most Koreans hated it or dislike poor migrants just like me. That's why I didn't pay attention to learn certain of intercultural skills. Given that 13 hours daily work I was too busy to manage tough lives in Korea. But participating in this centre, I recognised how international competencies and cross-cultural understanding are significant to live well in Korea.

Migration allows Korean society to confront the intercultural learning environment. Indeed, UNESCO (2005) designated an intercultural learning competency based on cross-cultural dialogue as a key learning area in a lifelong learning society. Having recognised that enlarged migrant groups make Korean society more multicultural and multiethnic, such an increment in intercultural capability is noteworthy. It manifests the phenomenon of multicultural learning between migrant workers and local people within an informal social learning setting.

Knowledge and awareness of cultural diversity

We acknowledge that our life world is now multicultural (Jarvis 2007: 25). In this regard, lifelong learning calls for us to learn cultural diversity by engaging with different social entities. Considering Korea's changed multicultural conditions under the influence of migration, learning about cultural diversity is a social necessity. One Korean participant stated this:

> Although we heard about arising international labours and multicultural families from media, many Koreans were not aware of the serious influence of the multicultural phenomenon. Look at this migrant centre! We can't help admitting of such as changed social reality! There are lots of thing to learning from this cultural diversity. It makes our local community more dynamic.

Most participants viewed participation in the centre's activities as enabling them to envisage the notion of cultural diversity. However, for some local citizens, a sense of pure-blooded nationalism has prohibited them from adapting multiculturalism and cultural diversity. One Korean volunteer explained:

> Although Korean 'relatively' maintained one language, same ethnic backgrounds, similar appearances and distinctive tradition for thousands years, I think we now have to discard sort of notion of the ethnic nationalism. This classic view generated lots of discrimination against racial minority groups in our society. Wherever we go such as streets, workplaces, supermarkets and shopping centres, it is not difficult to find different-coloured migrant workers. Learning a new cultural fusion is necessary.

Indeed, the persistent concept of a pure-blooded nation has become rooted in Koreans' pride in their nation's ethnic homogeneity. It has produced various forms of discrimination against so-called 'mixed-bloods' in employment, marriage, housing, education and ordinary social relations (Shin 2006). However, facing extensive numbers of migrant workers, many Koreans started to doubt the validity of their nationalistic ideology. During interviews, this awareness was revealed. A male Korean volunteer said:

> Frankly speaking, I was one of the people who avoided or disliked encountering migrant workers because I felt uncomfortable to see them. As an old-fashioned typical Korean chap, I was not accustomed to mingle with foreigners. But by chance, I began to participate in this centre, which transformed my view and attitudes. For instance, when I read about frequent discrimination and racism against migrants in newspapers, I feel very ashamed. Are we qualified to be a member of the global community on earth?... Now, I gained a faith in self-power to manage my life and local community happier with cultural diversity.

This comment describes one way in which participants' learning domain of cultural diversity and global awareness was expanded through informal and social interactions. They believed that the multicultural practices of the migrant centre yielded rich fruits of cultural diversity such as intercultural understanding, valuable global knowledge and skills. In a similar vein, one female migrant worker also explained:

> While I get involved in different episodes and activities such as the world culture class and voluntary aid services for local elders, I began to open my eyes toward cultural diversity. Of course, if I were in my home country, I wouldn't perceive the importance of multiculturalism. Communicating with different people I learnt how our world is diverse indeed. This helped me to dissolve prejudices such as Korean customs and the Muslims' religion and then re-build up a new perspective to understand others.

She explicitly perceived her learning areas in social practice. However, this is not simply the extension of learning contents about global awareness. Instead, it displays the importance of the experiential process to understand cultural difference within a multicultural learning setting. A male migrant spoke of his changed perceptions about diversity:

> Before joining this activity, I couldn't realise the power of social interactions with others who have totally different backgrounds. It stimulated me to perceive the range and depth of global society. I knew now I am at the heart of cultural diversity in Korea. I got both social role and confidence to foster advanced multicultural society.

These findings reveal that migrant workers and local people have expanded their learning domain of knowledge and awareness of cultural diversity through engagement in the migrant centre. They came to develop knowledge based on different cultures and increased interest in global issues. Clearly, social interactions with different cultural agencies are good channels to enhance learners' global awareness and knowledge about cultural diversity (Selby 1994). They enable learners to reconstruct their taken-for-granted perceptions by reacting to a changed social context.

Democratic attitude and civic virtue

A feature of the migrant workers' centre is its wide cultural diversity. In spite of a disjuncture of ethnicity, race and class regarding migration, this non-formal setting means that all participants are welcome to embrace their own identities and backgrounds. By participating in collective practices in the centre, migrant workers and local people endorse their positions as subjective learners regardless of nationality, race and class, since they come to reflect and reorganise their own experiences continuously. This entails a certain level of democratic flow of decision-making, horizontal engagement and building reciprocal concession across activities. One migrant stated:

> Since I joined here, I often thought over a notion of democracy. All participants have different nationalities, races, languages and personalities, which represents multiculturalism itself. Sometimes this situation challenges us to accept a wide spectrum of diversity and reaching to common good. I think paradoxically the more we hold a great deal of diversity, the more we seek a democratic order to manage the situation properly.

Most Korean participants also pointed out that they learned democratic values by social engagements with migrant workers. For example:

> Sometimes we respect each other, help each other and also we often face a clash of viewpoint in collective conversations. You know...anything that can happen in this migrant centre. But the important thing is to try to manage a situation in democratic way. We should consider others' equal rights to involve a decision-making, communication process. That is what I learnt from this experience. I think diversity and difference could be welcomed only if we just take up democratic attitude.

The migrant workers' centre can be conceptualised as a dynamic democratic experiment. Participants sought ways toward common good for the local community, engaging in social activities such as voluntary aid services for local people and holding co-operative donation events via international festivals. Accordingly, their learning areas evolved into reciprocal concessions beyond self interest to make a better society. One migrant worker recounted:

> This experience is meaningful to fulfil myself. It gives me a sense of membership in Korea. Although I couldn't afford to consider others' concerns, my narrow view entirely changed after joining this centre. Step by step I started to listen to people's narratives, engage in conversation and co-operate with Korean people helping local minorities. Through these opportunities I got to know what is going on in society. Now, I wish to involve for public good, not just for selfish interest.

This reveals that the learning domain of participants surpassed individual concerns or interests, and reconstructs their perceptions about the mutual good for the community. These participants acquired more than skills and knowledge. In this sense, it appears that they gained more democratic attitudes. A Korean volunteer remarked:

> This participation is a kind of social education for me. I learned an attitude and value as responsible citizen. As we study together global issues, political system and different cultures, it is alive and face-to-face learning. Collective discussion with migrant workers led Koreans to gain various information and knowledge. They are really good teachers for us! Besides, we explore and criticise different socio-cultural phenomena including migration issues to figure out hidden meanings. This offered me a broader lens to perceive social context as an active citizen.

It is notable that participants could gain a sense of active citizenship and civic virtue with a critical view through this social participation, which indicates broadened learning areas. During interviews, similar findings were revealed from many migrants' remarks:

> Although I'm not a regular citizen in this society and moreover my legal working visa has been expired, I can contribute my ability and resource during the centre's various activities such as publishing newspapers, cleaning the local street, international festivals and volunteering services. So, I have played a certain role for the local community as a 'half-citizen' throughout those participations. Indeed, I am willing to do something for me and for others as well.

One Korean volunteer mentioned:

> Despite some difficulties or conflicts during collective activities with migrant workers, I gradually learnt how to co-operate with others beyond my own interests, how to understand social phenomena critically and how to democratically engage in society as an active citizen to make a better world.

Clearly, engaging in social practices enabled migrant workers to become 'participants' not merely bystanders in Korean society. Furthermore, other data demonstrated that many migrants perceived their identity as a social factor beyond societal marginalisation.

Briefly, migrant workers and local people came to incarnate democratic attitudes and civic virtue through the participation in the centre. Particularly, for migrants, in spite of social restrictions and mundane disjuncture in the host society, they learned how to engage with Korean society as active actors by this informal and social learning opportunity. Participants evolved their expanded learning domains within interpersonal and intercultural participation. Overall, it could be argued that social engagement with different agencies in the migrant centre enabled people to reorganise their view and practice.

Discussion and conclusion

This paper examined the meaningful issue of lifelong learning through a migration context. Findings revealed a transformed social landscape in Korea and reshaped learning domains of migrant workers and local people via migration. The influx of migrants produced not only an alteration of demography and multicultural practice in the host society but also changes in life experiences and learning trajectories.

Indeed, this paper revealed that a multicultural society and a multicultural nation are no longer distant concepts for Korea. The number of foreigners residing has been estimated to reach 2,539,000 in 2020 (Korea National Statistical Office 2006). Such statistics indicate the portion of foreigners could increase to about 5%. If we consider the low birth rate and the lack of a domestic labour force for demeaning jobs, the surge of migrant workers will surely continue. Inevitably a multicultural society is an irreversible social condition in Korea.

The findings of this case study suggest that migration is at the heart of transformation of an individual's life world. It can serve as a learning condition that enables people to reconstruct their perceptions and expectations by responding to altered social configurations. In this case, participation in social activities within the migrant workers' centre evolved people's skills, including their self efficacy and esteem, intercultural capability, knowledge and awareness of cultural diversity and democratic attitude and civic virtue. This indicates that, but for the continual social interaction and engagement with local people, migrant workers who moved across borders were likely to fall into disjuncture from social ties in the host society.

Korea, as a major labour-recruiting country in East Asia, still has a long way to go to build a comprehensive multicultural society embracing the salient entity of migrant workers. It requires diverse experiences and engagements to combat social exclusion of marginalised groups both in terms of policy and practice, and should seek ways of encouraging groups to live together. Government should envision a society in which different social groups such as migrant workers can live together as equal citizens of a democratic polity.

In addition, long-term perspectives and systemic readiness on learning and educational policy is also needed. This paper makes several recommendations for educational policy makers and lifelong learning facilitators in Korea:

(a) Expansion and provision of informal and social learning opportunities addressing cultural diversity;
(b) Support for education for underprivileged groups, regardless of individuals' nationalities, races and ethnic backgrounds;
(c) A citizenship learning programme to develop intercultural competency; and
(d) Promotion of adult learning focusing on learning to live together with different groups.

Migration as a changing social practice offers an insight into the understanding of the nature of human learning and its social context in a lifelong learning field. Thus, this paper contributes to broaden the horizon of learning in the age of migration.

Acknowledgements

I appreciate all the participants who have given me permission to conduct research. Their contributions and inspirations truly provide me with a meaningful learning journey.

References

ASIAN MIGRATION CENTER (2005) *Migration in Asia* (Hong Kong: Asian Migration Center Press).
BAGNALL, R.G. (2006) Lifelong learning and the limits of a tolerance. *International Journal of Lifelong Education*, **25,** 257–269.
BAUBOCK, R., and RUNDELL, J. (1998) *Blurred Boundaries: Migration, ethnicity, citizenship* (London: Ashgate).
BENNETTS, G. (2003) The impact of transformational learning on individuals, families and communities. *International Journal of Lifelong Education*, **22,** 457–480.
CASTLES, S. and MILLER, M.J. (2003) *The Age of Migration* (3rd ed) (London: Palgrave).
CRESWELL, J.W. (1998) *Qualitative Inquiry and Researcher Design* (California: Sage).
EISNER, E. (1997) *Enlightened Eye, the Qualitative Inquiry and the Enhancement of Educational Practice* (2nd edn) (New York: Prentice Hall).
EYTAN, M. (2004) *International Immigration Policy* (London: Palgrave).
HERBERT, J., and IRENA, S. (1995) *Qualitative Interviewing* (London: Sage).
JARVIX, P. (2007) *Globalisation, Lifelong Learning and the Learning Society* (London: Routledge).
JOHNSTON, R. (1999) Adult learning for citizenship. *International Journal of Lifelong Education*, **18,** 175–190.
JORDAN, B., and DUVELL, F. (2003) *Migration* (London: Polity).
KOREA LABOR INSTITUTE (2004) 이주노동자 현황 조사 연구 [Survey on Migrant Workers' Present State] (Seoul: Korea Labor Institute Press).
LARSSON, S. (2001) Seven aspects of democracy as related to study circles. *International Journal of Lifelong Education*, **20,** 199–217.
MEZIROW, J. (2000) *Learning as Transformation* (San Francisco: Jossey Bass).
O'SULLIVAN, E. (2003) Bringing a perspective of transformative learning to globalized consumption. *International Journal of Consumer Studies*, **27,** 326–330.
PAREKH, B. (2006) *Rethinking Multiculturalism* (London: Palgrave).
REPUBLIC OF KOREA, KOREAN NATIONAL STATISTICAL OFFICE (2006) 경제활동 인구조사 [Economically Active Population Survey] report 1. (Seoul: Korean National Statistical Office).
REPUBLIC OF KOREA, MINISTRY OF GOVERNMENT ADMINISTRATION AND HOME AFFAIRS (2007) 인구동향백서 [National Census White Paper]. (Seoul: Ministry of Government Administration and Home Affairs).
REPUBLIC OF KOREA, MINISTRY OF JUSTICE (2007) 외국노동자 현황. [Current Report of Migrant Workers] report 1. (Seoul: Ministry of Justice).
SELBY, D. (1994) Kaleidoscopic mindset: New meaning within citizenship education. *Global Education*, **2,** 20–31.
SEOUL STATEMENT (2005) *10 years of Migrant Forum in Asia* (Seoul: Chang Jin).
SHIN, G.W. (2006) *Ethnic Nationalism in Korea* (California: Stanford University Press).
UNESCO (2005) Available oline at: http://publishing.unesco.org/details.aspx?Code_Livre=4400
WALTERS, S. (ed.) (1997) *Globalization, Adult Education and Training* (London and New York: Zed Books).

Conclusion: toward transnational lifelong learning for recognitive justice and inclusive citizenship

SHIBAO GUO
University of Calgary, Canada

To build inclusive and socially just lifelong education, this article proposes transnational lifelong learning for recognitive justice and inclusive citizenship as a promising alternative to distributive and retributive approaches to lifelong learning. Informed by recognitive justice, this framework questions the claim that a universality of citizenship transcends cultural difference and particularity. It suggests 'pluralist citizenship' as an alternative form of citizenship that recognises transnational flows of migration and concomitant diasporic allegiances and affiliations. In rejecting the deficit model of lifelong learning, this framework acknowledges and affirms cultural difference and diversity as positive and desirable assets. Transnational lifelong learning seeks to balance freedom of mobility with protection, recognition and membership.

To build an inclusive and socially just lifelong education and one that im/migrants feel they belong, I propose the framework of *transnational lifelong learning for recognitive justice and inclusive citizenship* (*transnational lifelong learning* [TLL or TL^2] for short). Before I proceed to elaborate on this new framework, it is necessary to revisit the concept of social justice.

In the past decade or so, social justice has become a 'buzzword' for critical lifelong educators. However, many people use the term without fully understanding its meaning and implications. Social justice can be classified into three categories: *distributive, retributive* and *recognitive* (Gale and Densmore 2000). *Distributive justice* is best known to us through the liberal-democratic principles of individual freedom and the equal distribution of material and social goods. On this view, social justice is about who gets how much of the social good. For Rawls (1971), fairness is justice, which advocates a culturally neutral state where citizens deal fairly with each other and the state deals equally with all, regardless of how we conceive our ends. Rawls' 'justice as fairness' was criticised as 'unrealistic', 'unacceptably thin' and 'unfair' because governments cannot be culturally neutral; indeed, all states are culturally biased (Taylor 1994, Tamir 1995, Bloemraad 2000). As Bloemraad notes, one fatal flaw in Rawls' theory is that he predicated his whole discussion on a closed society that members neither leave nor enter. It is clear that there is no explicit place for immigration in his theory. One manifestation of distributive social justice in lifelong learning is the 'sameness' approach that assumes that lifelong learners are all the *same* with the *same* learning needs, and therefore treating them as the *same* will erase issues of inequity and injustice. This approach seemingly values all individuals equally. In fact, it negates the histories, backgrounds and experiences of diverse cultural groups, and thus represents an assimilationist ideal. Such an ideal means that cultural differences are viewed as deficits and deficiencies, and immigrants' knowledge is deemed inferior and hence devalued. The deficit model leads to solutions such as the implementation of remedial lifelong learning programs to bring immigrant individuals into line with dominant norms. This approach ignores differences in capacities, cultures and values, an illusion that sustains the status of privileged groups and perpetuates oppression and inequality (Young 1995).

Retributive justice favours market-individualism and is based on the claim that individuals deserve and are entitled to differential rewards in accordance with their differential contributions to productive and competitive processes (Gale and Densmore 2000). In educational contexts, entitlement is measured by students' academic merit and is thus ranked and rewarded according to their academic performances. A fatal flaw of this approach lies in the logic of markets that dictates the competition process and perpetuates economic subordination. *Retributive justice* is evident in both transnational migration and lifelong learning. In migrant selection, for example, many countries adopted a market-driven approach, putting in place a set of criteria for admission and exclusion that gives priority to property rights (of those with assets and skills) over moral claims (of those with vulnerabilities and needs) (Jordan and Düvell 2003). As Jordan and Düvell note, these criteria consolidate the hierarchical structure of global economies by reinforcing divergences between the opportunities and lifestyles of a nomadic global elite and those of migrants from developing countries who are seen as natural subordinates. As a handmaiden of the market, lifelong learning has been co-opted by the market state to serve its interests in preparing a more educated and flexible workforce to enhance global competiveness (Crowther 2004). It privileges practical and scientific knowledge at the expense of theoretical and indigenous knowledge (Jarvis 2007). In this context, learning has become vocational and an extension of work. Furthermore, responsibility for learning has been shifted solely to individuals, undermining common welfare and displacing blame for systemic failure onto individuals. The fairness dreamed of under this meritocracy, however, is never delivered because *retributive justice* privileges those from advantaged social and economic status who also represent dominant cultural norms.

Recognitive or *recognitional justice* represents a promising alternative to distributive and retributive approaches. It provides an expanded understanding of justice that insists that we must rethink not only what we mean by social justice, but also to acknowledge the place of social and cultural groups within this (Gale and Densmore 2000). It is a radical response to the restrictive conceptions of justice grounded in a narrow focus on material and economic goods. *Recognitive justice* seeks to increase the potency of social justice by extending its scope to include social goods (e.g., opportunity, position, and power) as well as institutional inequities. With its intent to recognise differences and areas of commonality among social and cultural groups, *recognitive justice* advocates three necessary conditions for social justice: the fostering of respect for different social groups through their self-identification, opportunities for self-development and self-expression and the participation of groups in decision-making through group representation (Gale and Densmore 2000). Since a society without group differences is neither possible nor desirable, recognising the validity of social and cultural groups is essential for their identity, sense of worth and self esteem (Taylor 1994, Fraser 2000, Honneth 2008). Notions of equality and liberation that entail ignoring difference merely perpetuate cultural imperialism and disadvantage groups whose experience, culture and socialised capacities are different from those of privileged groups (Young 1995, 2008).

It is this notion of recognitive justice that informs the notion of *transnational lifelong learning for recognitive justice and pluralist citizenship* put forward here. My sense is that lifelong learning reconceptualised in this way offers the broadened perspective on migration that recognises its transnational flows and concomitant diasporic allegiances and affiliations. It seeks to balance freedom of mobility with protection, recognition and membership. In agreement with Jordan and Düvell (2003), *transnational lifelong learning* holds that individuals should not only be free to choose where to live and work, but that they should be able to do so as bearers of substantial rights to those benefits and services that they need in order to participate as equal and autonomous members in whatever society(ies) they choose to join. Also, following Young (2008), this framework emphasises that granting equal rights to disempowered migrants is insufficient to ensure equal status because the ideal of a culturally neutral state cannot be achieved. Instead, it advocates minority group rights such as language assistance and other subsidies to help migrants overcome obstacles to integrating into the host society. Furthermore, it questions the claim that a universality of citizenship transcends particularity and difference. Consistent with 'differentiated citizenship' (Young 1995) and 'multicultural citizenship' (Kymlicka 2008), this framework proposes 'pluralist citizenship' as an alternative form of citizenship that recognises migrants' multiple attachments to specific traditions, values, languages and other cultural practices and that, furthermore, fosters plural ways of belonging. *Transnational lifelong learning* rejects the deficit model of lifelong learning that seeks to assimilate migrants to the dominant social, cultural and educational norms of the host society. Alternatively, it proposes to build an inclusive education that acknowledges and affirms cultural difference and diversity as positive and desirable assets. These assets are seen as a means of ensuring the participation of individuals from socially and culturally differentiated groups in social, political and educational institutions. It challenges Eurocentric perspectives, standards and values, and accepts presently marginalised knowledges as valid and valuable expressions of the human experience.

It is important to note, however, that this shift to *transnational lifelong learning* does not mean abandoning our interest in material conditions and distributive matters. As a bivalent collectivity 'by virtue of *both* the political-economic structure *and* the cultural-valuational structure of society [original italics]' (Fraser 2008: 190), migrants suffer both socioeconomic maldistribution and cultural misrecognition. Therefore, Fraser suggests, an ideal remedy requires both redistribution and recognition (Fraser 2008). Furthermore, it is important to recognise that the inequities in lifelong learning are a reflection of injustices in the wider global society. Therefore, lifelong learning should be taken as neither the sole perpetrator of inequities past and present, nor as the panacea for all social ills. Rather, as *transnational lifelong learning*, it can take on a new collaborative approach in building alliances with other marginalised groups in global civil society in working collectively to create a socially just and inclusive learning experience.

References

BLOEMRAAD, I. (2000) Citizenship and immigration: A current review. *Journal of International Migration and Integration*, **1,** 9–37.
CROWTHER, J. (2004) 'In and against' lifelong learning: Flexibility and the corrosion of character. *International Journal of Lifelong Education*, **24,** 125–136.
FRASER, N. (2000) Rethinking recognition. *New Left Review*, **3,** 107–120.
FRASER, N. (2008) From redistribution to recognition? Dilemmas of justice in a 'postsocialist' age. In S. SEIDMAN and J. ALEXANDER (eds.) *The New Social Theory Reader* (London: Routledge), pp. 188–196.
GALE, T., and DENSMORE, K. (2000) *Just Schooling: Explorations in the cultural politics of teaching* (Buckingham: Open University Press).

HONNETH, A. (2008) Personal identity and disrespect. In S. SEIDMAN and J. ALEXANDER (eds.) *The New Social Theory Reader* (London: Routledge), pp. 43–49.

JARVIS, P. (2007) *Globalisation, Lifelong Learning and the Learning Society: Sociological Perspectives* (Routledge: London and New York).

JORDAN, B. and DÜVELL, F. (2003) *Migration: The boundaries of equality and justice* (Cambridge: Polity).

KYMLICKA, W. (2008) Multicultural citizenship. In S. SEIDMAN and J. ALEXANDER (eds) *The New Social Theory Reader* (London: Routledge), pp. 270–280.

RAWLS, J. (1971) *A Theory of Justice* (London: Oxford University Press).

TAMIR, Y. (1995) Two concepts of multiculturalism. In Y. TAMIR (ed.) *Democratic Education in a Multicultural State* (Oxford: Blackwell Publishers), pp. 3–14.

TAYLOR, C. (1994) The politics of recognition. In A. GUTMANN (ed.) *Multiculturalism: Examining the politics of recognition* (Princeton, New Jersey: Princeton University Press), pp. 25–73.

YOUNG, I. (1995) Polity and group difference: A critique of the ideal of universal citizenship. In R. BEINER (ed.) *Theorizing Citizenship* (Albany: State University of New York), pp. 175–207.

YOUNG, I.M. (2008) Justice and the politics of difference. In S. SEIDMAN and J. ALEXANDER (eds.) *The New Social Theory Reader* (London: Routledge), pp. 261–269.

Index

Page numbers in *Italics* represent tables.

3D jobs (difficult, dirty, and dangerous) 4, 125
accreditation of prior experiential learning (APEL) 55
advocacy work 39
Alba, R.: and Nee, V. 77, 78
Alfred, M.V. 3, 72–88, 79; social capital and lifelong learning 4
Anderson, B. 10
Andersson, P.: and Fejes, A. 3, 54–71

Balatti, J.: and Falk, I. 86
Barrett, A.: and Duffy, D. 60
Basch, L.: *et al* 78, 79
Batalova, J.: and Terrazas, A. 73
Bellis, A.: and Morrice, L. 96
Bernstein, B. 98
Bitew, C.: and Ferguson, P. 107
Bloemraad, I. 142
Boshier, R. 23
Bourdieu, Pierre 80, 85, 119
Brah, Avtar 94
Brandi, M.C. 17
British Columbia Teacher's Federation 107
Brodie, J. 38
Bruff, I.: three waves analysis 9
Butler, K.D. 14
Buzdugan, R.: and Halli, S.S. 60

Campbell, C.: and McLean, C. 84
Canada: business immigrants 10; census data (2001 and 2006) 16; foreign education and credentials (non-recognition) 31; global knowledge economy 50; ideological practice (Smith) 25; immigrant admission categories 10; immigrant service organizations (ISOs) 39, 40; immigration policy 26; investment in immigrant training and education 23; labour force survey (2006) 26; Ministry of Human Resources and Skills Development 42; points system 26, 42; skilled immigrants 26
Canada (Chinese immigrant women) 22–37; age and gendered familial relations 33–4; Canadianise their education and training 29; competition with white Canadians 32; computer network engineer 30; credentialism 29–31; employment trajectories 33; gendered and racialised construction 31–3; institutional ethnography (IE) approach 27; interviewees 27; jobs for the Chinese 32; language barriers 33; nursing as career choice 32; occupation-specific training program 28; occupational trajectories 28–9; recertification 29; senior doctor 29; settlement services 32; study context 26–8; training (financial considerations) 34; university teacher 30–1
Canada (informal learning of immigrant parents) 4, 106–23; active and skilled agents 117–18; advocacy and capacity building (immigrant students) 115–16; Aneeka (parent) 115; Canadian curricula from Internet 4, 106, 112–13; Chinese identity 114; Coalition for Equal Access to Education in Calgary 110; demographic information 110; discourses on immigrant parents 107–8; ESL parents 112; first-language knowledge by informal teaching 113–14; implications for practice 119–20; instilling hybridity by informal teaching 114–15; interacting with and observing other parents 111–12; Internet and child education 118; knowledge construction 108–9; Li, Fangfang (parent) 113; Li, Mary (parent) 114; Liang, Nicole (parent) 111–12, 117; Muslim stereotypes and misconceptions 115; parental knowledge 109; parents' school participation and prior knowledge 116–17; Parveen (parent) 115; racism and anti-immigrant sentiments 115; racism (combating) 118; Ma, Shaoli (Chinese immigrant) 111; Shin (parent) 115; significance of 118–19; study finding 110–11; study methodology 110; Tyrone (Sudanese parent) 111; Wang, Liming (parent) 112–13; Write Off Racism Poetry Contest 115–16; Xing, Fangfang (parent) 114, *see also* schools (Canada)

INDEX

Canada (knowledge economy and lifelong learning) 38–53; credentialed knowledge 47; education (immigrants') non-recognition 49; employment readiness class 48; feminist postcolonial theories 41; immigrant unemployment and underemployment 45; informal education issues 41; interviewee (Nadia) 44–5; interviewee (Xin) 44, 45–7; migration in the new economy 42–3; original research questions 40–1; racialized Others 45; recognition and justice 43–4; recognition and participatory parity 44–5; recognitional justice and the new economy 48–50; study background and methods 40–1; symbolic injustice 46, *see also* knowledge economy
Canadian government: *Knowledge Matters* 22
Canadian identity 50
Canadian labour market 2, 28
Caribbean Life in New York City (Sutton and Chaney) 84
Castells, M. 8
Castles, S.: and Miller, M. 10, 11
Cayn, T.: and Renaud, J. 60
Chan-Tiberghien, J. 9–10
Chaney, E.: and Sutton, C. 84
China: professional immigrant women from 22, *see also* Canada (Chinese immigrant women)
citizenship: inclusive and recognitive justice 142–5; pluralist 142
Cline, Z.: and Necochea, J. 108
Coalition for Equal Access to Education in Calgary 110
Coffield, Frank 98–9
Cohen, R. 14, 15
Coleman, H.L.: Gerton, J. and LaFromboise, T. 76, 77
Coleman, J.S. 80
community education: Tett on 100
Contu, A.: and Willmott, H. 57
Cray, E.: and Haque, E. 48
credential and certificate regime 29
credentialism 29–31
Creole: as antagonistic force (Portuguese) 97
Crowther, J. 39
cultural diversity: knowledge and awareness (South Korea) 136–7

deficit model 142
Delors, J.: learning dimensions 15
democratic racism 16
diaspora (prototypical): Jews as the 14
diasporas: common features 14
distributive justice 142
Duffy, D.: and Barrett, A. 60
Düvell, F.: and Jordan, B. 10, 11, 130, 143, 144
Dyson, L. 107

earnings *see* wage rate
Economic and Social Research Council (UK) 90–1
Elsdon, K.T. 109
Employment Permit System (EPS): South Korea 125
employment rates: Sweden 59–60
employment readiness class: Canada 48
ethnoculturally diversity 6
Europe: employment situation 17
European Economic Area 11
European Union (EU) 24

Falk, I.: and Balatti, J. 86; and Kilpatrick, S. 82
Farrell, L. 42
Fejes, A.: and Andersson, P. 3, 54–71
Ferguson, P.: and Bitew, C. 107
Field, J. 80, 82, 85
Fraser, Nancy 39, 40, 41, 46, 48, 144; dichotomization of redistribution 49; recognitional injustice 51
Freire, Paulo 97
Fuller, A.: *et al* 57

Germany: unemployment rates 17
Gerton, J.: LaFromboise, T. and Coleman, H. L. 76, 77
Gibb, T.: and Hamdon, E. 3, 38–53
Glick Schiller, N. 77, 78
globalisation: current discourses 38; and migration 2;
Gorman, R.: and Mojab, S. 25
Guo, S. 1–5, 6–21, 142–5
Guo, Y. 106–23; and Mohan, B. 119

Hall, Stuart 94
Halli, S.S.: and Buzdugan, R. 60
Hamdon, E.: and Gibb, T. 3, 38–53
Hannerz, U. 117
Hans, H.J. 78
Haque, E.: and Cray, E. 48
health care sector 60
healthcare assistants (HCAs): prior learning recognition (Sweden) 69
Henry, F.: *et al* 16
Hernandez-Leon, R.: and Zuniga, V. 82, 83
Ho, E. 14
human capital resources 16

immigrant adaptation 15–18
immigrant parents *see* Canada (informal learning of immigrant parents)
immigrants: as transnational nomads 10, 80
immigration and migration (interchangeability of term) 10
individual up-skilling 23
individuals: responsibility for learning 23

INDEX

Industrial Trainee Program (ITP): South Korea 125
informal learning of immigrant parents *see* Canada (informal learning of immigrant parents)
information and communication technologies (ICT) 42
intercultural capability: South Korea 134–6
international governmental organisations (IGOs) 8
International Organisation for Migration 11
Italy: brain waste 17

Jackson, S. 4, 89–105
Jarvis, P. 6, 8, 15, 81
Jews as the prototypical diaspora 14
job-seeking activities 2
Jordan, B.: and Düvell, F. 10, 11, 130, 144
Jorgenson, S.: and Shultz, L. 38

Kearney, M. 77
Kennedy, M.M. 73
Kilpatrick, S.: and Falk, I. 82
Kim, J-H. 4–5, 124–41
Kivisto, P. 12, 13
knowledge: credentialed 47; mobility discussion (Sweden) 67–9; recognition and mobility 55–6; situated character 56; Western hegemony 42
knowledge economy 42; education and participation 43; gender stratification 42, *see also* Canada (knowledge economy and lifelong learning)
Knowledge Matters (Canadian government) 22
knowledge societies 98
knowledge workers 51
Kofman, E. 42
Korea *see* South Korea

labour force survey (Canada) 26
LaFromboise, T.: Coleman, H.L. and Gerton, J. 76, 77
Lareau, A. 108, 119
Lave, J.: and Wenger, E. 55, 56, 57
learning: informal 89; non-formal 89, 90; through work 16, *see also* Canada (informal learning of immigrant parents)
learning in communities (elements): Wenger on 102
learning through social spaces (London) 4, 89–105; Asian Women's Group 102; different spaces, different voices 95–8; English pronunciation problems 96; interview extract 92–4, 95–6, 97, 99, 100, 101; language as obstacle to participation 96; relational capital 103; social networks 102; social spaces 101; study research 90–1

Learning to Be (UNESCO) 23
Lewkowicz, P. 26
Li, G. 107
lifelong learning: current criticism 6; discourse 22–4; as a mechanism of neo-liberal control 24; policies and practices 2
Liu, L. 117
Livingstone, D.W. 109
London: city of migrants 91–5; as the post-colonial city *par excellence* 92, *see also* learning through social spaces (London); United Kingdom (UK)
Lopez, G.R. 117, 119
Lowe, G. 23

McDonaldisation 8
McGrew, A.: globalphobia and globalphilia 7
McLean, C.: and Campbell, C. 84
McLintock, A. 90
Marx's analysis of political economy 25
mass migration: as world disorder 6
Mezirow, J. 130
Migrant Workers' Centre Seoul 4
migration 1; and economic development 58
migration and immigration (interchangeability of term) 10
Miller, M.: and Castles, S. 10, 11
mobility 54–5; ascending vertical 57; individuals (good) 56; of refugees 56
Mohan, B.: and Guo, Y. 119
Mohanty, C.T. 95
Mojab, S. 38; and Gorman, R. 25
Monkman, K. 78, 79
monoculture 50
Morrice, L.: and Bellis, A. 96
multicultural learning: investigations South Korea 129; settings South Korea 128–9
multiculturalism: Canadian state policy 24

Nakhaie, M.R. 61
National Agency of Higher Education (Sweden) 63
National Board of Health and Welfare (Sweden) 63
national boundaries: barriers to efficiency 11
Necochea, J.: and Cline, Z. 108
Nee, V.: and Alba, R. 77, 78; Semau, S. and Sanders, J. 84
Ng, R.: ideological frame 24; and Shan, H. 2, 22–37
nomads (transnational): immigrants as 10, 80

OECD: annual report 11
OECD countries: transnational migration trends 1

Pedraza, S. 72, 77

INDEX

points system: Canada 26, 42
population growth 1
Portes, A. 13; *et al* 12–13; and Rumbaut, R.G. 75, 76
prior learning assessment and recognition (PLAR) 18, 55
professional occupations: lack of access 18
Putnam, R.D. 81

qualifications: role of 60

Ran, A. 107
Rawls, J. 142
recertification 29
recognition of prior learning (RPL) 55, 57, 60; as a sorting mechanism (Sweden) 65–6; Swedish policy 58, 61–3, 64, 65, 67, 68; Swedish policy (upper secondary level) 62
recognitional justice 143
recognitive justice and inclusive citizenship 142–5
refugees: admission to Sweden 55; mobility of 56
Reitz, J.G. 15, 42
Renaud, J.: and Cayn, T. 60
retributive justice 143
Ritzer, G. 8, 9
Robertson, R.: and White, K.E. 8, 9
Robertson, Susan 50
Rogers, A. 7
Rowbotham, Sheila 97
Rumbaut, R.G.: and Portes, A. 75, 76

Sanders, J.: Nee, V. and Semau, S. 84
Sargent, Naomi 99
Satzewick, V.: and Liodakis, N. 14–15
schools (Canada): doublespeak of parental involvement 117; parents' active involvement 107
Schugurensky, D. 43
Scott, K. 50
Semau, S.: Sanders, J. and Nee, V. 84
Shan, A. 29
Shan, H.: and Ng, R. 2, 22–37
Shultz, L.: and Jorgenson, S. 38
Silvey, Rachel 95
situated learning 57
skilled immigrants: Canada 26
Smith, Dorothy: abstract ideas and concepts 25; Canadian ideological practice 25; IE approach 27
social capital 81; conduit for lifelong learning 81–2; geographic implications 83
social capital and lifelong learning (USA) 72–88; forces of migration 75–6; literature review 73
social capital theory 82

social justice 142
social mobility: downward 18
social services: barriers 16
South Korea (social configuration) 4, 124–41; altered social conditions 125; collective discussion 139; cultural diversity (knowledge and awareness of) 136–7; democratic attitude and civic virtue 138–9; Employment Permit System (EPS) 125; global village and social practice 127; Industrial Trainee Program (ITP) 125; intercultural capability 134–6; intercultural capability and social activities 135–6; Korean volunteers interviews 135; Korean's pride in their nation's ethnic homogeneity 136–7; learning engaging in migration 127–9; long-term perspectives and systemic readiness 140; migrant worker numbers (2005–2006) *126*; migration and learning conceptual framework 127; multicultural Korea 126; multicultural learning (investigations) 129; multicultural learning settings 128–9; multicultural practice and changed social landscape 125–7; self efficiency and self esteem 133; study discussion and conclusion 139–40; study findings 132–9; study method 131–2; transformative learning theory 130–1; world culture class 134, 137, *see also* Sung-Dong District Workers' Centre (Seoul)
Sparks, B. 75
Sung-Dong District Workers' Centre (Seoul) 131, 133; cultural diversity 138; world culture class 134, 137
Sutton, C.: and Chaney, E. 84
Sweden 3, 54; admission of refugees 55; asylum seekers and refugees 59; employment rates 59–60; healthcare assistants (HCAs) 69; as immigrant country (contextualisation) 58–61; immigrants from Nordic countries 61; knowledge mobility discussion 67–9; knowledge transfer one context to another 66–7; mono-cultural country 58; National Agency of Higher Education 63; National Board of Health and Welfare 63; post-industrial economy 59; RPL policy 58, 61–3, 64, 65, 67, 68; RPL policy (university level) 62–3; RPL policy (upper secondary level) 62; RPL as a sorting mechanism 65–6; unemployment rates 17; vocational curriculum 67; vocational knowledge 67; vocational knowledge (challenges recognising) 63–7; vocational language skills 63–4; wage rate 60–1
Swedish labour market 64, 65
Swedish upper secondary diploma 62
Swedish urban validation centres 65

INDEX

Terrazas, A.: and Batalova, J. 73
Tett, Lyn: community education 100; *et al* 96
Thomas, G. 8
transformative learning theory: South Korea 130–1
transnational migration: mapping 10–12
transnationalism: diaspora and migration 12–15; from above and from below 13
trends (emerging) and challenges 6–21
Trudeau, Prime Minister Pierre 24
Turkish immigrants: Europe 17

UNESCO: intercultural learning competency 136; *Learning to Be* 23; migrant (definition) 92; recent publications 23
United Kingdom (UK): Economic and Social Research Council 90–1; Home Office 92, *see also* London
United States of America (USA): African Caribbean immigrants 83–4; assimilation model 76; civil rights protests 1960s 76; European immigrants (early) 76; immigrants transnational orientation 76–80; immigration 72; immigration population profile 73–5; as land of opportunity 75–6; Latin American immigrants 74; population diversity and racioethnic makeup 73, *see also* social capital and lifelong learning (USA)
US Bureau of the Census Report (2003) 74

validation (of prior education) 55, 61, 62

Van Hear, N. 14
Venn, Couze 90
vocational knowledge: challenges recognising (Sweden) 63–7; Sweden 67
vocational language skills (Sweden) 63–4

wage rate: less than native-born 11; Sweden 60–1
Wan, Y. 107; study of Chinese immigrant parents in USA 111
Welch, A.R. 9
Wenger, E. 55; community of practice 57; and Lave, J. 55, 56, 57; learning in communities (elements) 102
Westin, C. 17
White, K.E.: and Robertson, R. 8, 9
Willmott, H.: and Contu, A. 57
Woolcock, M.: and Narayan, D. 81–2
world economy: integration 10
Write Off Racism Poetry Contest 115–16

Yang, Daniel 111
Yao, E. 108
Young, I. 144

Zuniga, V.: and Hernandez-Leon, R. 82, 83